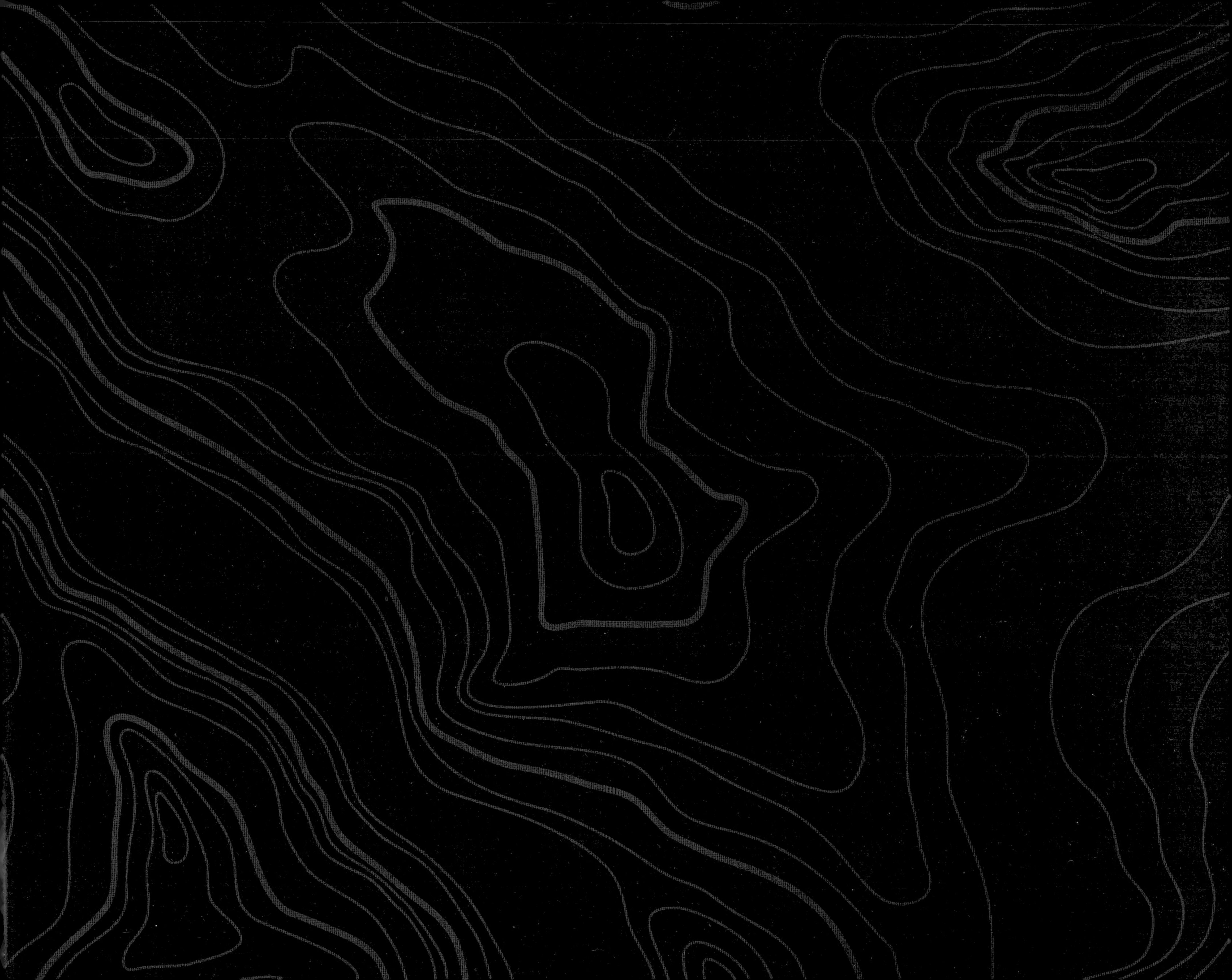

El Paso 120

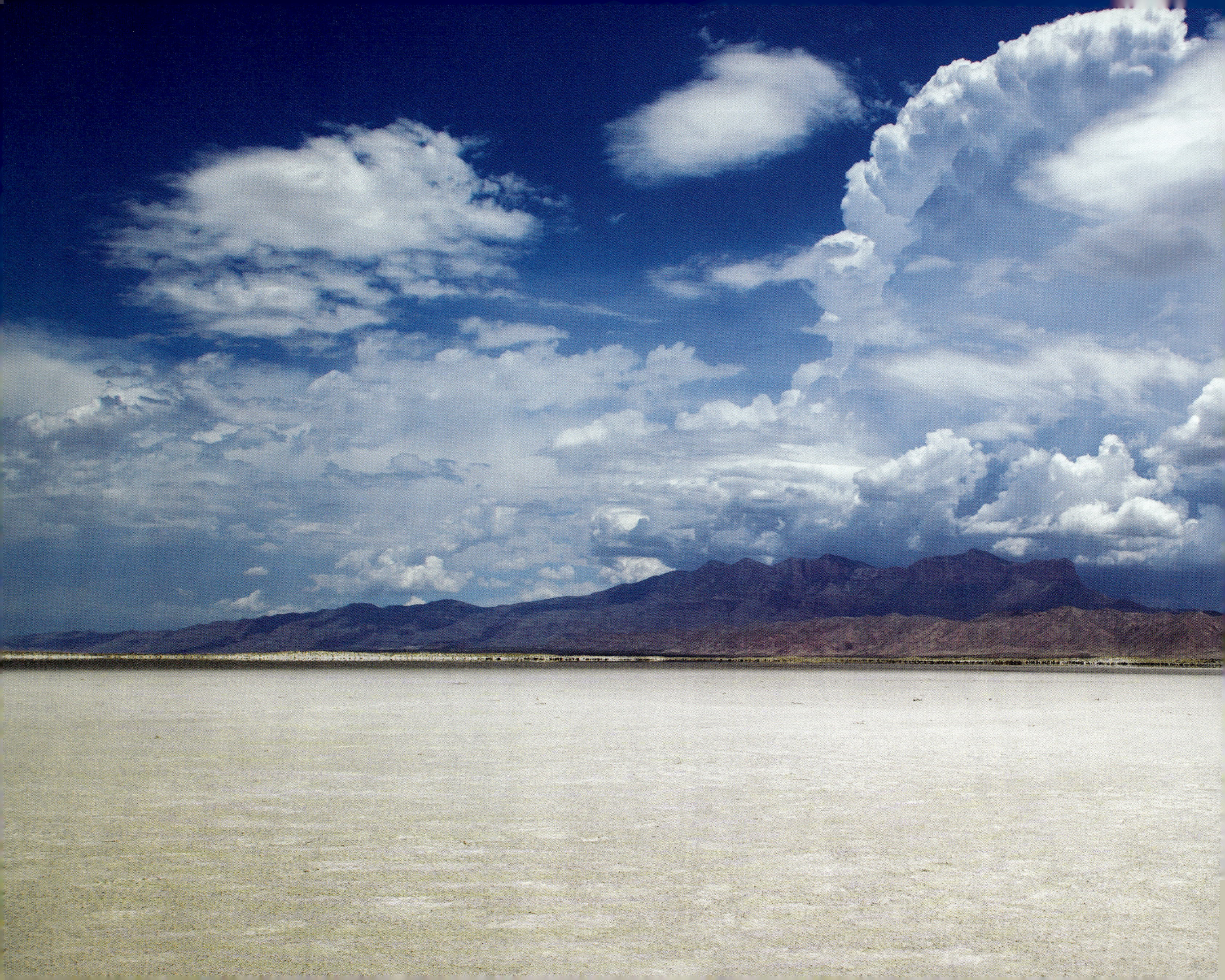

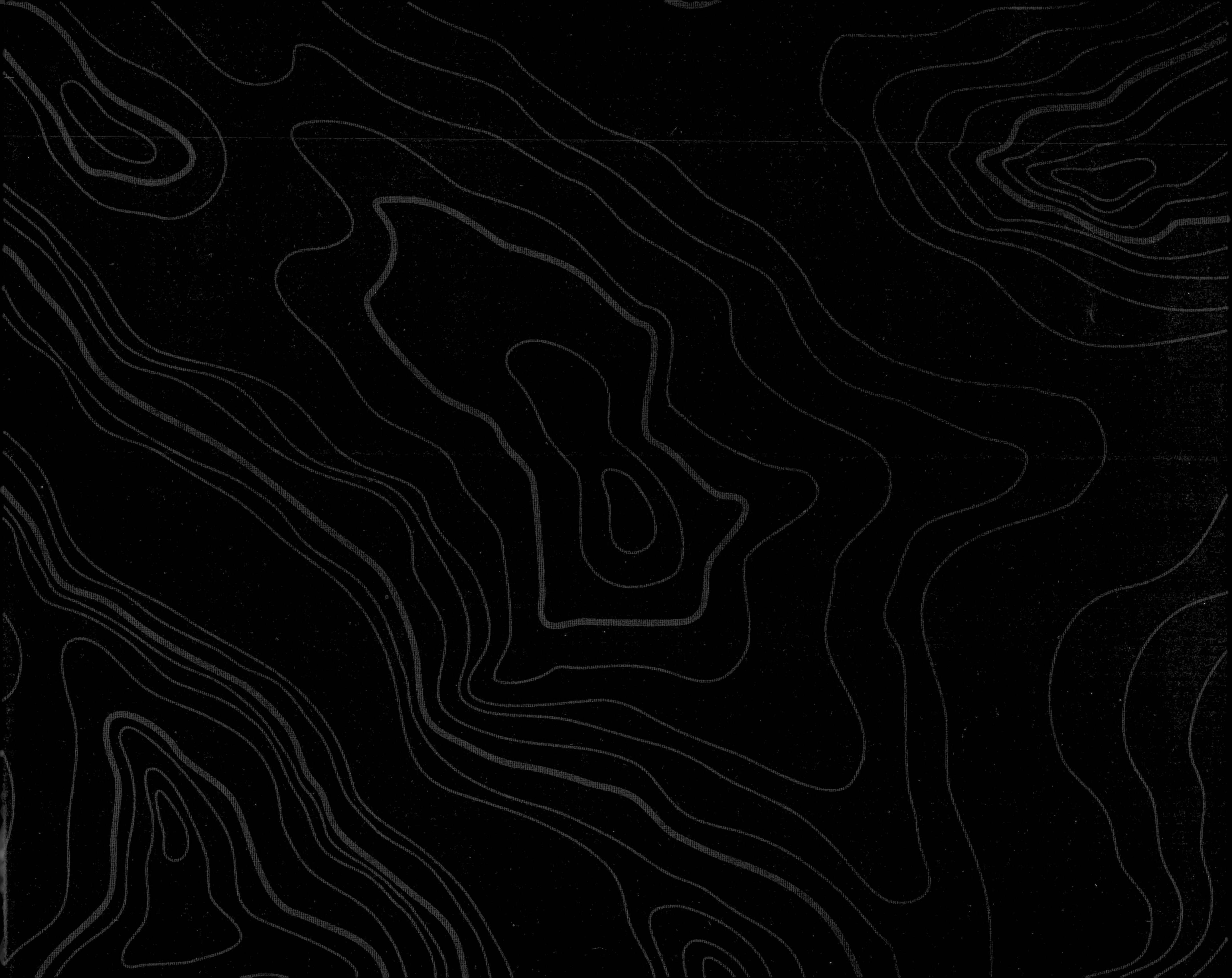

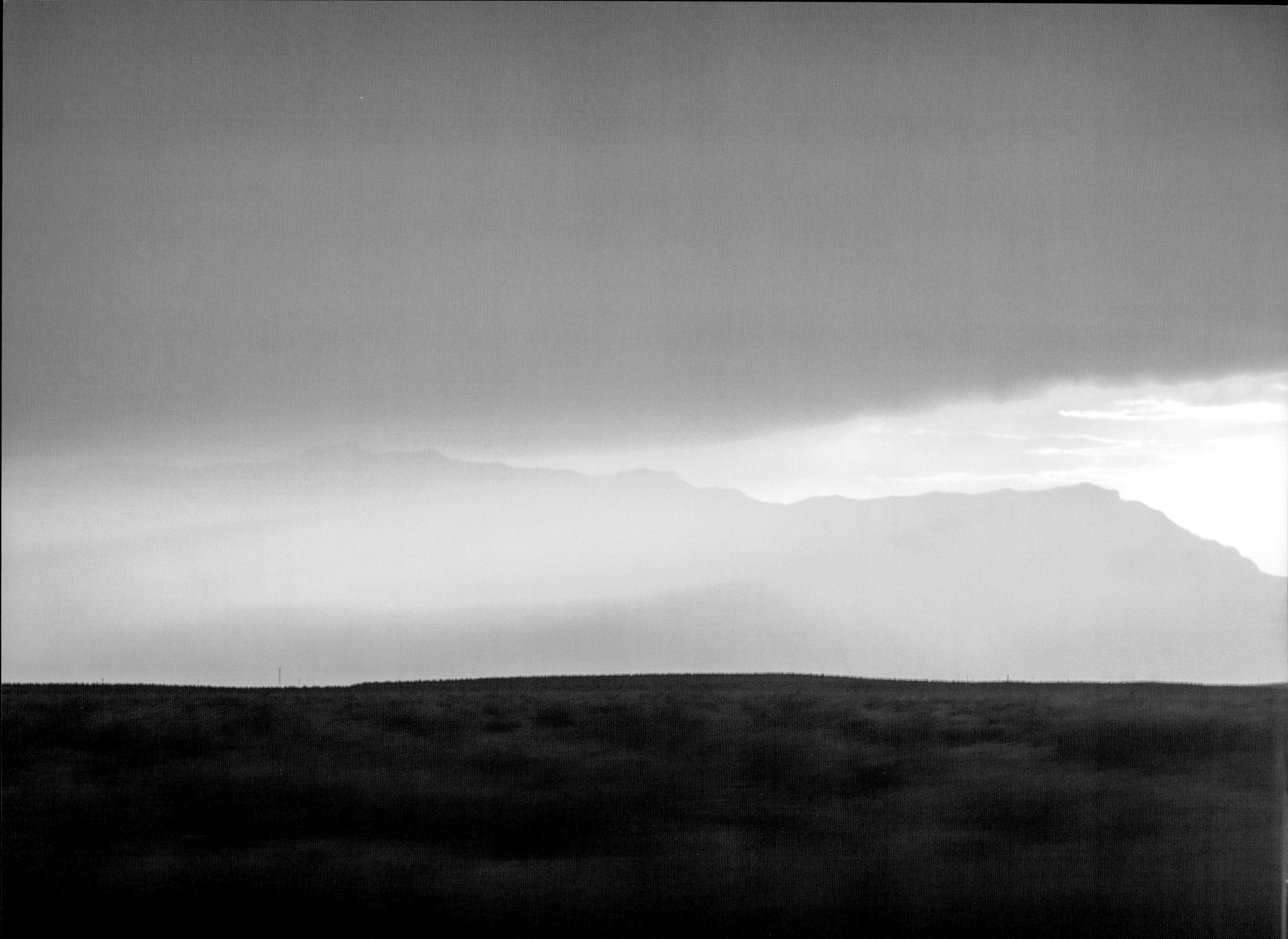

El Paso 120

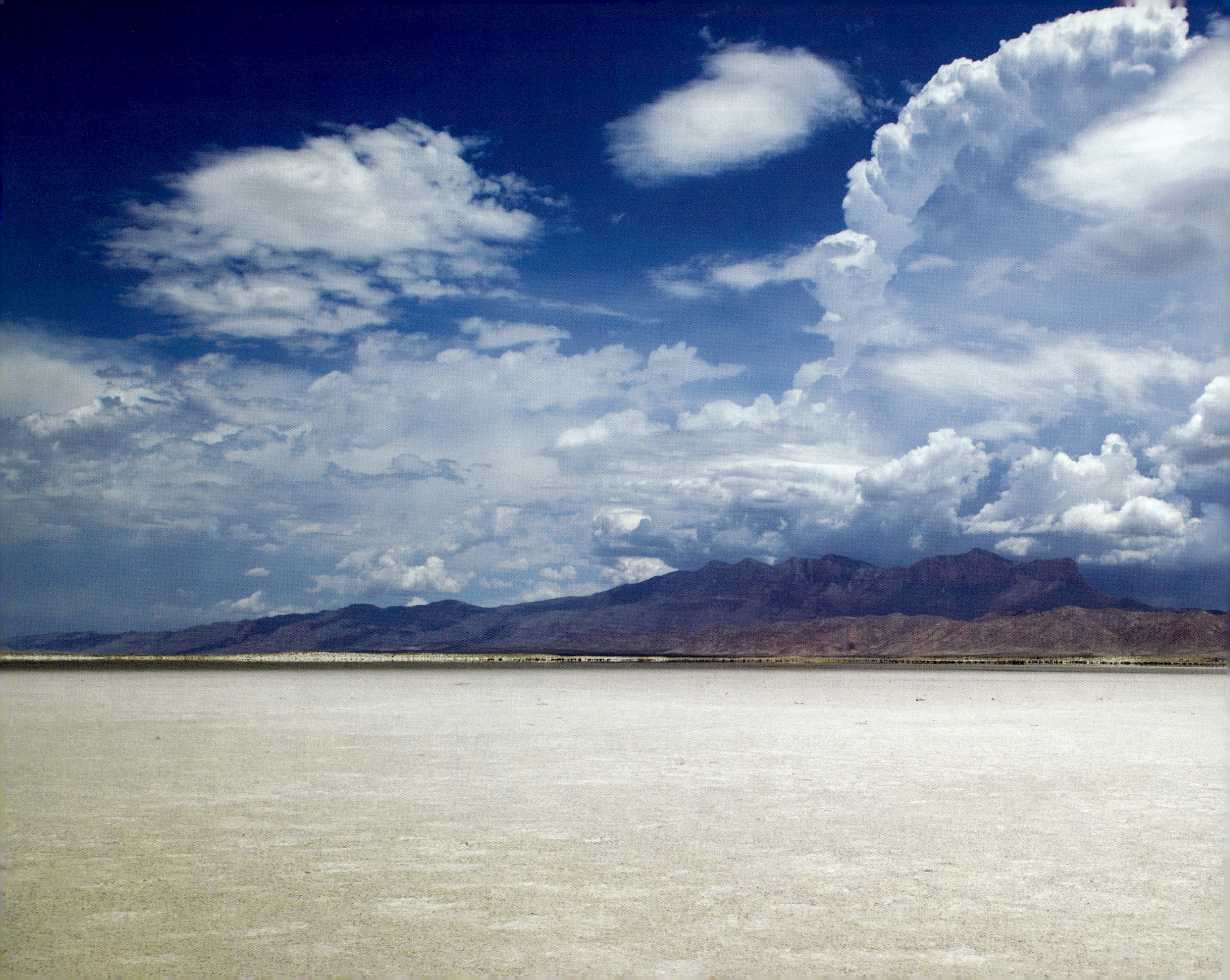

El Paso 120

EDGE OF THE SOUTHWEST

MARK A. PAULDA

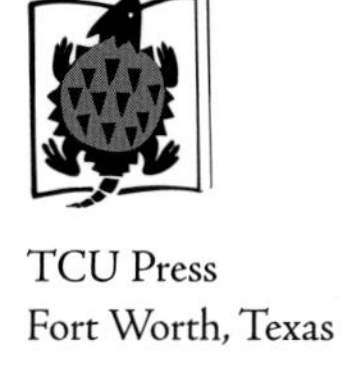

TCU Press
Fort Worth, Texas

Library of Congress Cataloging-in-Publication Data

Paulda, Mark, photographer.
El Paso 120 : edge of the Southwest / Mark A. Paulda.
pages cm
ISBN 978-0-87565-602-1 (cloth : alk. paper)
1. El Paso (Tex.)--Pictorial works. 2. Texas, West--Pictorial works. 3. New Mexico--Pictorial works. 4. Landscape photography--Texas. 5. Landscape photography--New Mexico. I. Title.
F394.E4P39 2014
976.4'96--dc23
2014011861

TCU Press
P.O. Box 298300
Fort Worth, Texas 76129
817.257.7822
www.prs.tcu.edu

To order books: 1.800.826.8911

Designed by Bill Brammer
www.fusion29.com

"The images of El Paso and 120 miles around conjure so vividly something of the character of the wonderful Southwest. Under a sky that seems limitless, the roads invite one to travel, to explore, to become a pioneer. When I see these great unending routes piercing the vastness of the territory, they trigger in me the beginnings of an understanding of the importance to the American people of the concepts of freedom and opportunity."

DARAGH MCDONALD
LONDON, ENGLAND

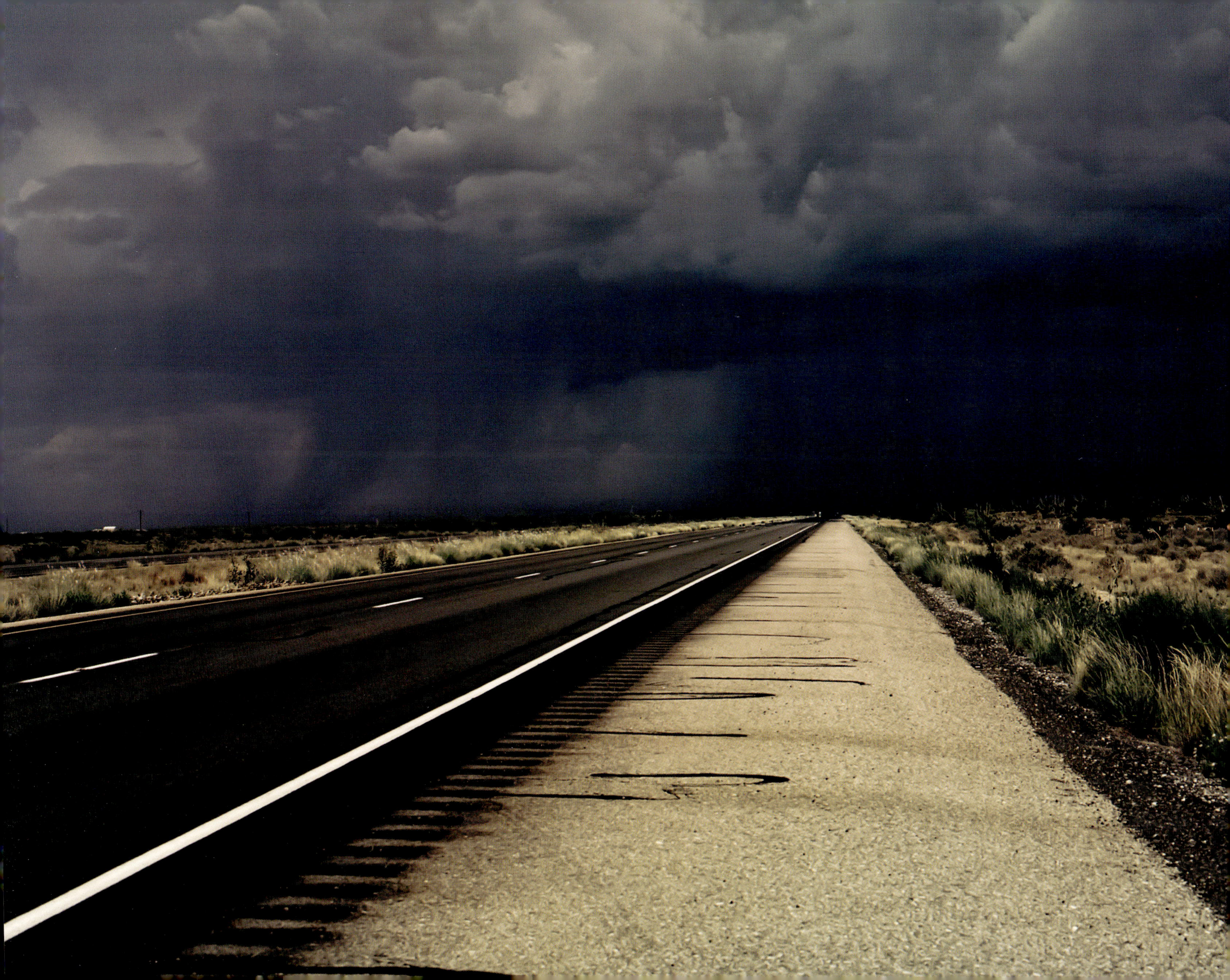

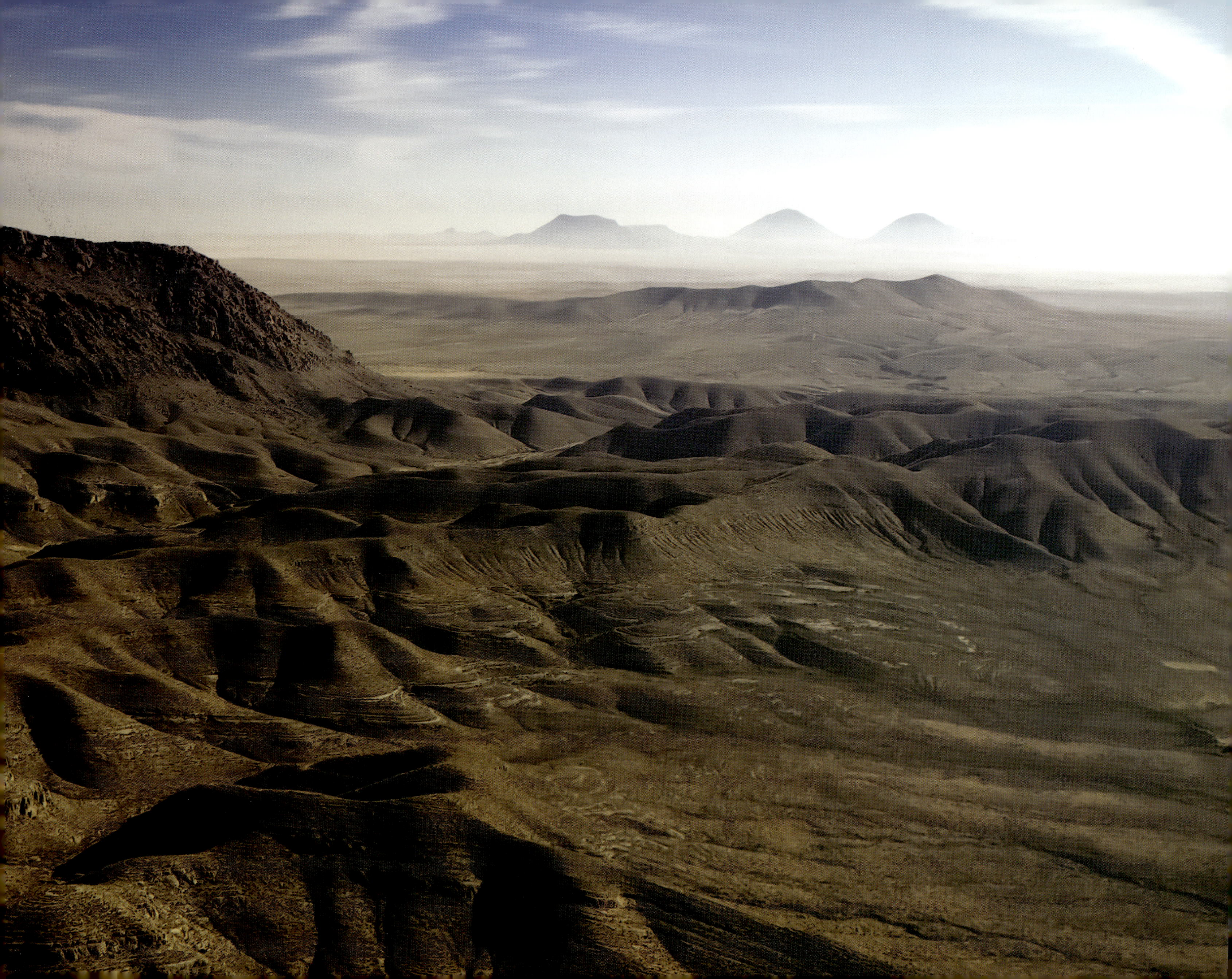

Foreword

El Paso 120: I am told that this title defines a place, so exactly where are we? Thanks to Mark Paulda's award-winning photographic artistry, we are embedded in a southwestern landscape of myth and legend. This is the Texas that we thought we knew, here within the roughly 120-mile radius surrounding El Paso. People quickly become very small in these wide-open vistas. The scale of the region is not easily conveyed, and most artists fail in their attempts. The photographer here has worked with the southwestern light and shadows to create images as memorable as the landforms.

These are the mountains—the Huecos, Diablos, Franklins, Guadalupes, and other ranges—that continue to challenge travelers. We hike them today only at some risk, as they've not yet been "civilized." Looking at the city of El Paso below, from the knife-edged peak of the Franklin Mountains, novice hikers routinely call for help in getting down. However, the physical challenges presented only entice the extreme sports enthusiasts and, in this instance, our guide and photographer. From these ranges down to the intermontane basins, we find the northern extent of the great Chihuahuan Desert. With less than eight inches of annual precipitation as the norm, life struggles here to exist. But exist it does, with impressive tenacity and variety. The beautiful golden poppies shown among Mark's photos bloom across the "bajada"—the lower flanks of the Franklin Mountains—often only after an absence of several years.

Ranging through far West Texas and adjoining portions of southern New Mexico, the artist presents these timeless landscapes to us through his lens. As we see in his work here, there is a great beauty to the mountains and desert floor. The gypsum dunes of the White Sands National Monument provide a constantly changing foreground to the dark and distant mountains. Only in the highest mountains, such as the Sacramentos, is there a natural vegetative cover sufficient to conceal the bedrock. The exposed geology is often the prime agent of variations in the colors, textures, and tones. The Rio Grande flows along an ancient rift valley pocked by volcanic craters and lava flows such as those shown here at the Kilbourne Hole. Mark presents these amazing vistas but mostly leaves any interpretation to the viewer.

Claiming El Paso, Texas, for his hometown, Mark Paulda has not lost the sense of awe for the local landscape and tries to share that both with the natives and with those who have never ventured into this corner of the world. I learned from people who grew up in these open spaces that the rest of the world just seems too claustrophobic and shut in to them. We can appreciate some of that sense of place through the scenery captured in the pages that follow.

JOHN MOSES
General Superintendent
TEXAS STATE PARKS, EL PASO

Introduction

All too often the El Paso area is an afterthought in any publication chronicling West Texas or the Southwest. When I view photography books illustrating this vast area or read magazine articles, the message I receive is always the same: "Oh, by the way, there is a dusty place in far West Texas called El Paso; it is stuck out in the middle of nowhere." This corner of Texas is a footnote, if you will. No doubt this area is overlooked due to El Paso's distance from other civilization. I say this lightly, though there is some truth to the thought. After all, El Paso seems to be a never-ending drive from other cities: twelve hours from Dallas, nine hours from San Antonio, four hours from Albuquerque, five hours from Midland-Odessa, and seven hours from Phoenix. So yes, I do understand why this area is considered "the edge" and off the radar for most. It seems perfectly natural, if one mainly travels along Interstate 10 through West Texas and southern New Mexico, for a traveler not to give El Paso much thought. As one looks out the window of a moving car, the easy conclusion would be that there is not much more to see than a plethora of tumbleweeds, desert brush, a few mountains, and a sea of wide-open space. Quite frankly, the roads one usually navigates move directly through the least interesting parts of the landscape.

Admittedly, the shape of this project didn't immediately occur to me. I, too, based my judgment of the area on Interstate 10, not really piecing all the bits together, despite the fact that I am based here. The adventurer in me would visit the areas covered in this book independently; each a day trip and roughly a two-hour drive, or 120 miles, from El Paso. White Sands National Monument in southern New Mexico and the Guadalupe Mountains-Salt Flat area are two of my favorite destinations, though the landscape found in the Lincoln National Forest at Cloudcroft has always offered an interesting contrast to the desert plains—and the cooler climate of Cloudcroft can be a refreshing change from the heat of the Chihuahuan Desert. My visits to Hueco Tanks State Park and Historic Site directly east of El Paso have been sporadic, although I enjoy my amateurish attempts at rock climbing, and City of Rocks, between Deming and Silver City, New Mexico, allows my imagination to run wild, thinking I am visiting the Flintstones' Bedrock. Van Horn? Indeed, the Van Horn area—the "Gateway to Big Bend Country"—offers some of the most rugged and inspiring landscape in far West Texas. Seeing the sunrise over the Sierra Vieja mountains at the Coal Mine Ranch will be forever etched in my memory, and the largest collection of Precambrian rock formations in the world at the Red Rock Ranch is a delight.

Most notable for me, however, is El Paso, as this is home. The Franklin Mountain range runs directly through the city and is the largest urban state park in the United States. For me, the Franklins are old friends that I miss when I travel around the world. In fact, this range is literally just outside my back door, and my friend Eric and I hike its slopes almost weekly. Each of the aforementioned destinations is "just around the corner" in local terms, since driving times to other areas are four hours or more. While each of the areas photographed for this book have captivated me, I find the roads to and from equally fascinating. I believe the wide-

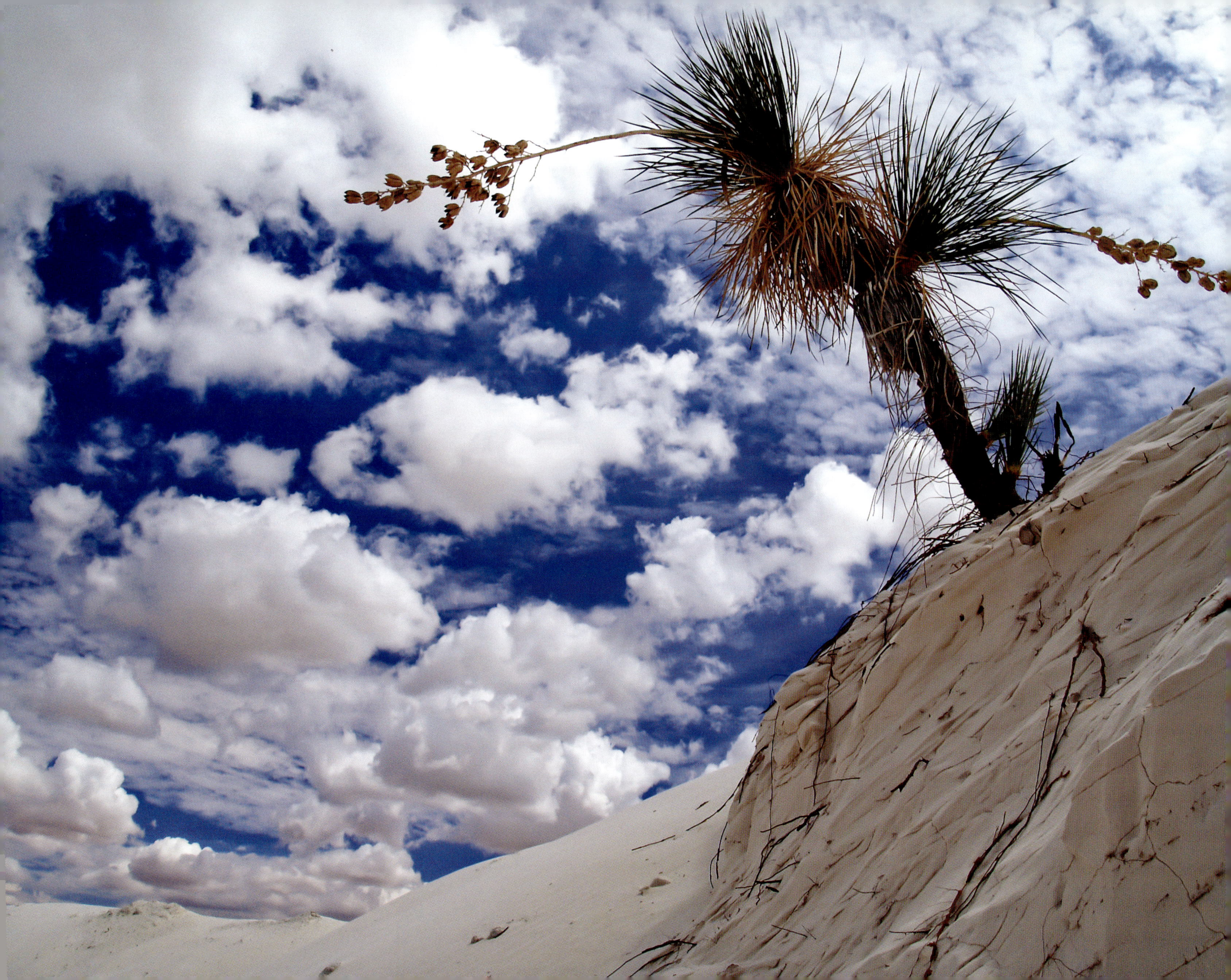

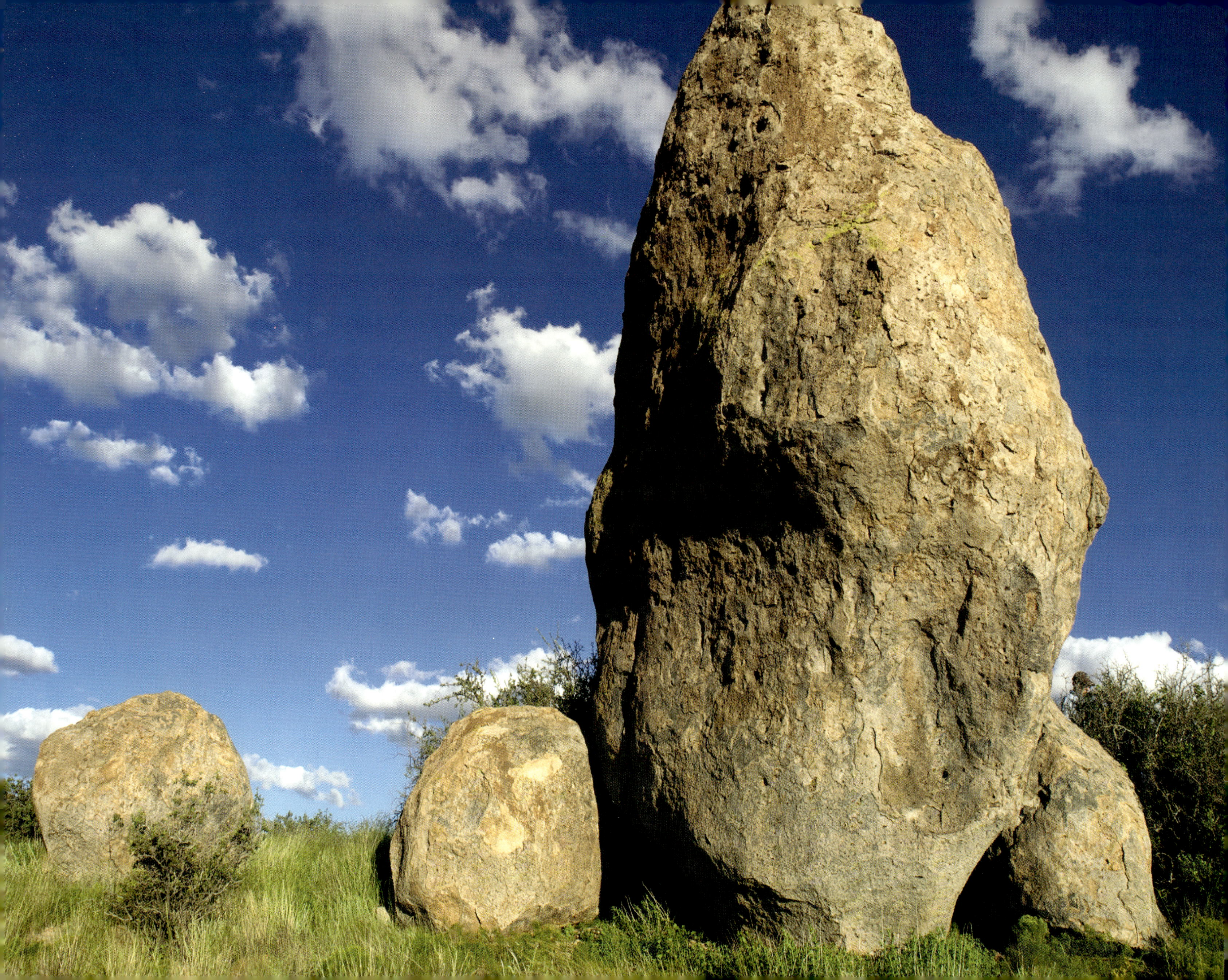

open spaces that unfurl along these long, unobstructed roads epitomize the spirit of freedom many of us in the West feel. While I travel quite often throughout the world, each time behind the lens of my camera, I can safely say the landscapes of West Texas and southern New Mexico touch my soul more deeply than any other place. A spirit of freedom that is second to none wells up in me when I stand upon a high desert ridge: the sky above me opens up its cobalt tent, and the land below it stretches toward a horizon that seems to recede into infinity. Not only do deep fresh breaths fill me, but I can actually hear my breathing because the sounds of the cosmopolitan world are nowhere nearby. The weight of the world swiftly lifts off my shoulders—I begin to connect with that which is around me, begin to move back toward my own center. In a way, this great landscape offers me the freedom to feel whole again. No competing demands tug at me from different directions. There is silence. Time is once again my friend.

The roads pictured in this book were the avenues I traveled for the most part, but it was in the air where *El Paso 120* came together. As I flew around the area in a twin-engine plane with Suzie Azar, my pilot and the former mayor of El Paso, I realized El Paso is not at the edge but right in the middle of an amazing landscape. And it is a landscape that is quite significant to the rest of the world, as you will soon discover.

One might think I deliberately used a mathematical compass on a map to draw out what would be included in this book, but this is not the case. Flying above it, as a bird would, allowed me the opportunity to pull together what I had already explored on the ground. Surveying the land from atop El Paso's Franklin Mountains, I can glimpse each of the areas portrayed in *El Paso 120*. A number of these destinations, all within striking distance of the city, are significant icons in the natural world. Guadalupe Peak is the highest point in Texas, at 8,749 feet. El Capitan, a massive limestone formation, is the Guadalupe Mountains' most recognizable feature. The remarkable City of Rocks is a fantasyland of wind- and water-sculpted volcanic rock. Only six other places in the world have anything like them. Near Kilbourne Hole, New Mexico, a lava tube (cave) at Aden Crater yielded up the skeleton of one of the last giant ground sloths in North America. The nine-foot-long skeleton, with much of its skin and hair still preserved, is now at the Yale Peabody Museum of Natural History. At White Sands there is the world's largest gypsum dune field, where great waves of gypsum lap nearly three hundred square miles of desert. White Sands National Monument preserves a major portion of it. Then there are the Hueco Tanks, known in the nineteenth century as the last source of water between the Pecos River and El Paso. The site is now one of the most popular destinations in the world for rock climbers.

Not only have I had the luxury of discovering the El Paso area, but each trek has helped me find my balance. I can think clear thoughts. Any and all stress goes away. I have traveled these roads from El Paso countless times to escape the pressure of cosmopolitan life. I get lost behind my camera. My mind wanders with each trek, wondering what the area was like underwater millions of years ago, or what the Spanish explorers thought when they came upon this terrain, making their way northward. Can you imagine what they must have thought when out of the brown desert arose the largest white gypsum sand dunes in the world? The idea of this fascinates me and in turn inspires me to venture further.

As you view my photographic exploration, I hope you, too, discover that El Paso is not at the edge but instead at the very center of some remarkably amazing landscapes. One may think 120 miles is a long way to get anywhere. But within these wide-open spaces, it's only just down the road and around the corner. With good fortune during my next journey, I shall find you discovering firsthand El Paso and the wonders radiating 120 miles in all directions from the city. Make sure to say "Hello," when we meet.

MARK A. PAULDA
Wandering Wayfarer and Photographer

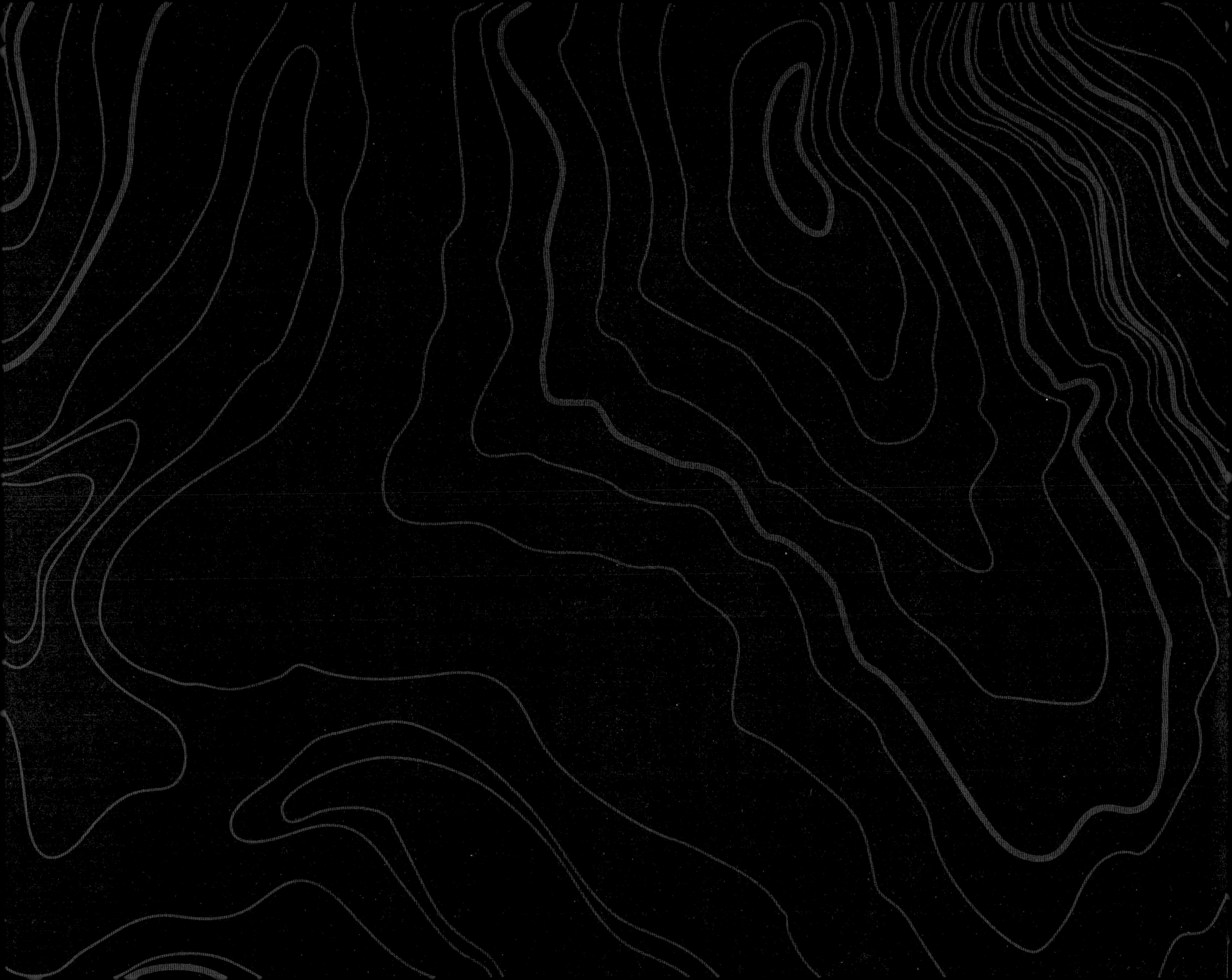

Coal Mine Ranch

Coal Mine Ranch

DISTANCE FROM EL PASO
120 miles east

LATITUDE
30˚4’33” N

LONGITUDE
-104˚73’64” W

ELEVATION
3,750 feet (1,143 meters)

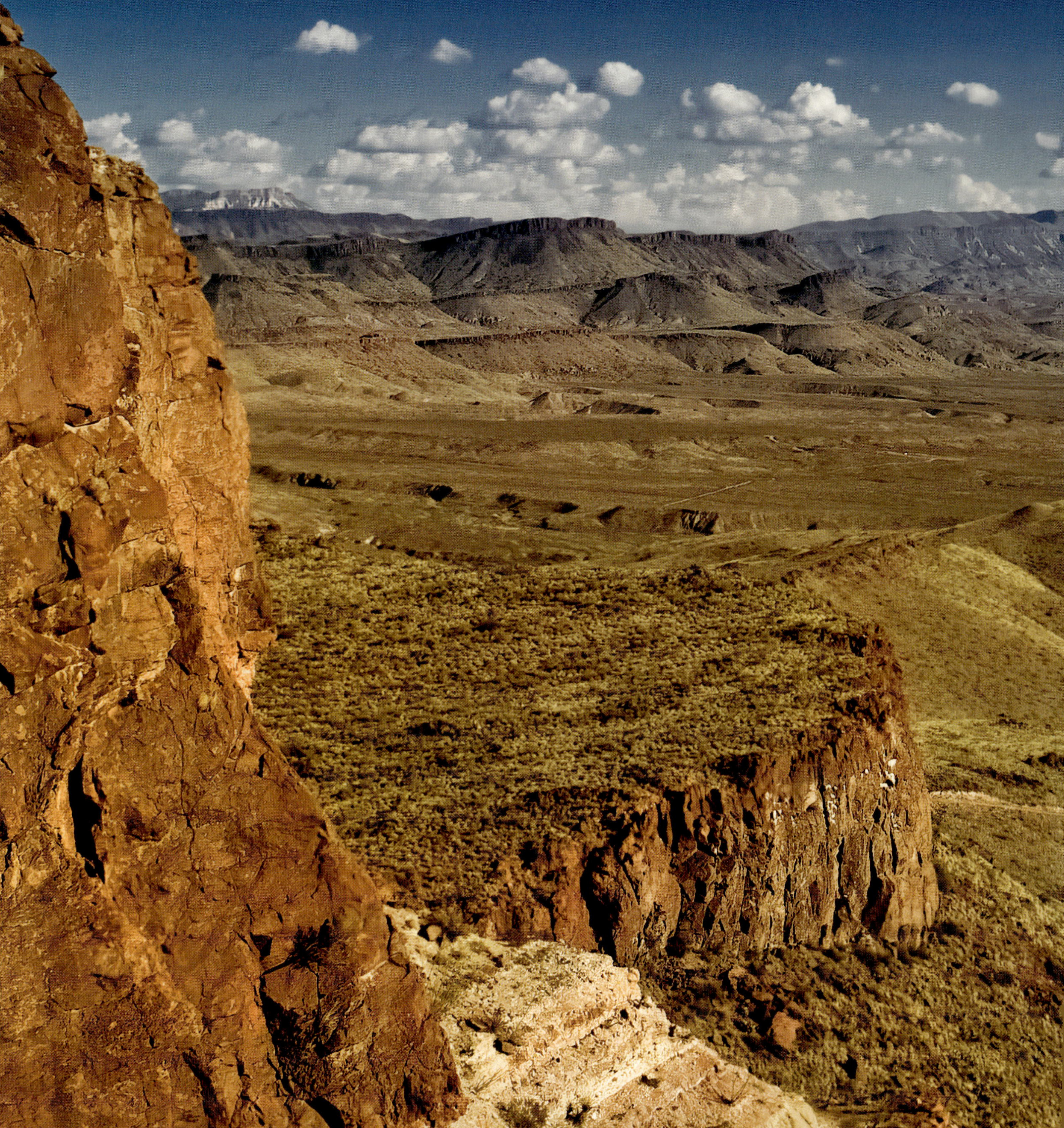

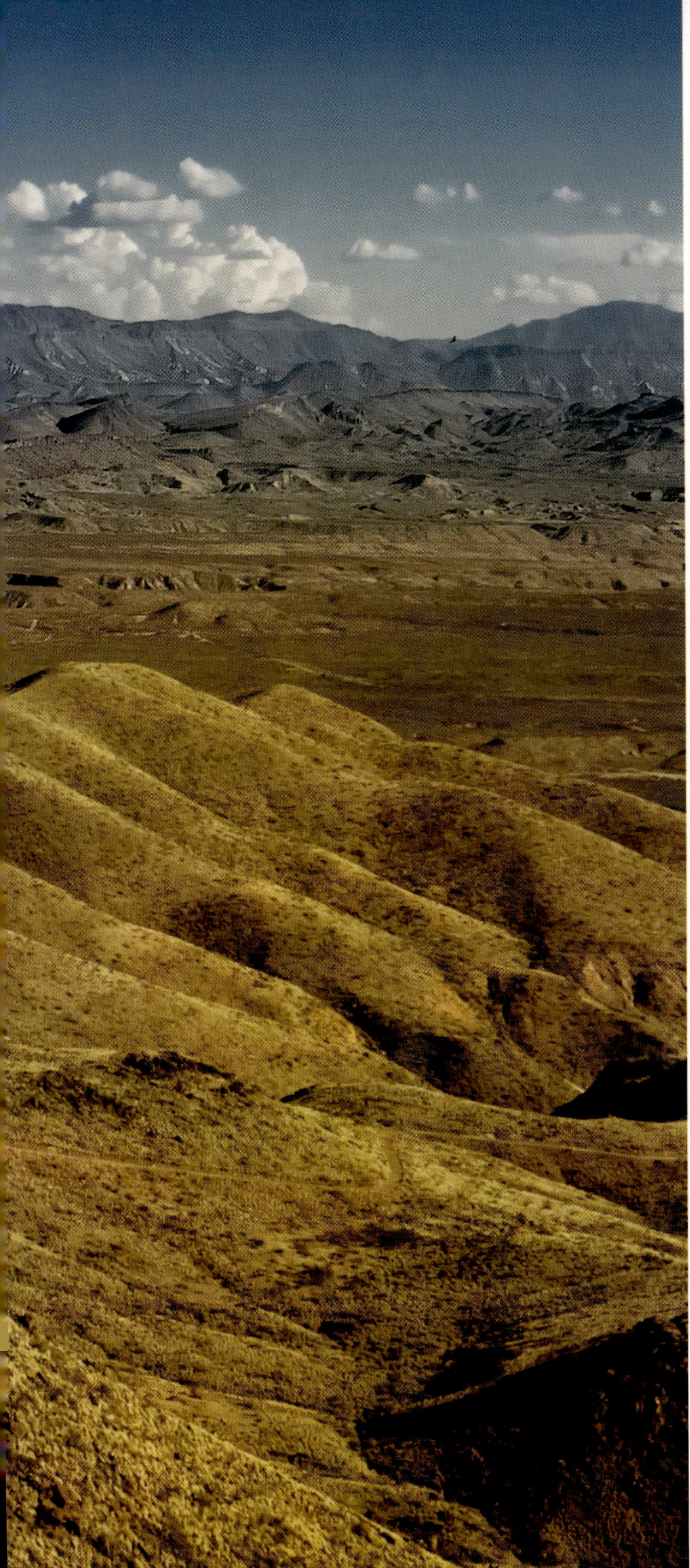

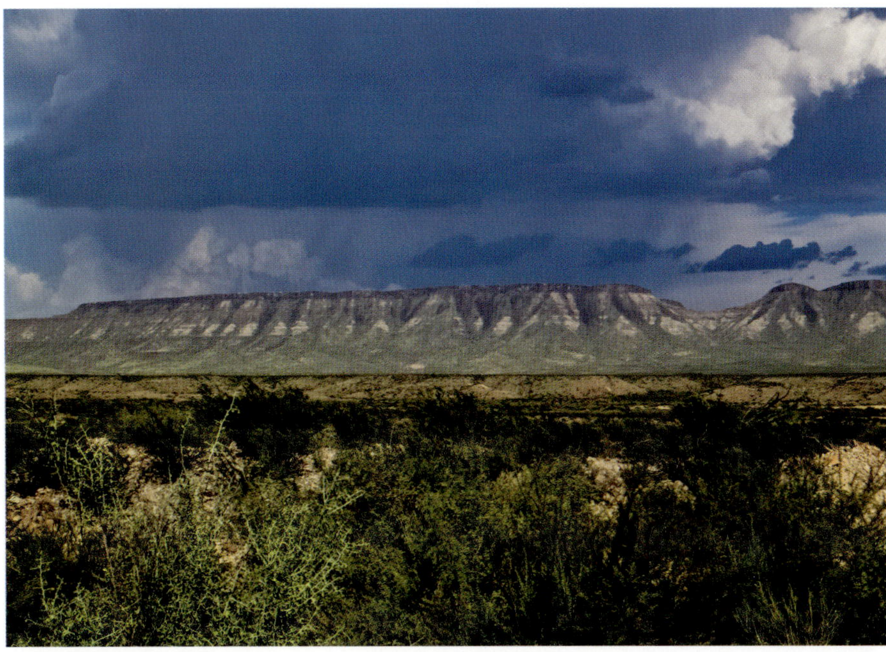

The 27,500-acre Coal Mine Ranch is a privately owned investment and playground for a group of businessmen who have owned the ranch for more than twenty years. It lies on the rear side of the Sierra Vieja mountains, a world away from the flat, grassy desert plains of Highway 90. From the end of the pavement on Chispa Road, thirty miles of rough dirt road winding through steep arroyos lead to the Coal Mine Ranch. This road features its own tunnel, twenty feet high and fifty yards deep, blasted from solid rock.

Eighty-five-million-year-old fossils of clams, turtle shells, coral, and snails can be found below the sandstone bluffs where once a river delta said to be six hundred miles wide—bigger than the Amazon—fanned out as it approached the sea. Deeply nestled in West Texas, the ranch is about solitude, introspection, and the crackling of the campfire.

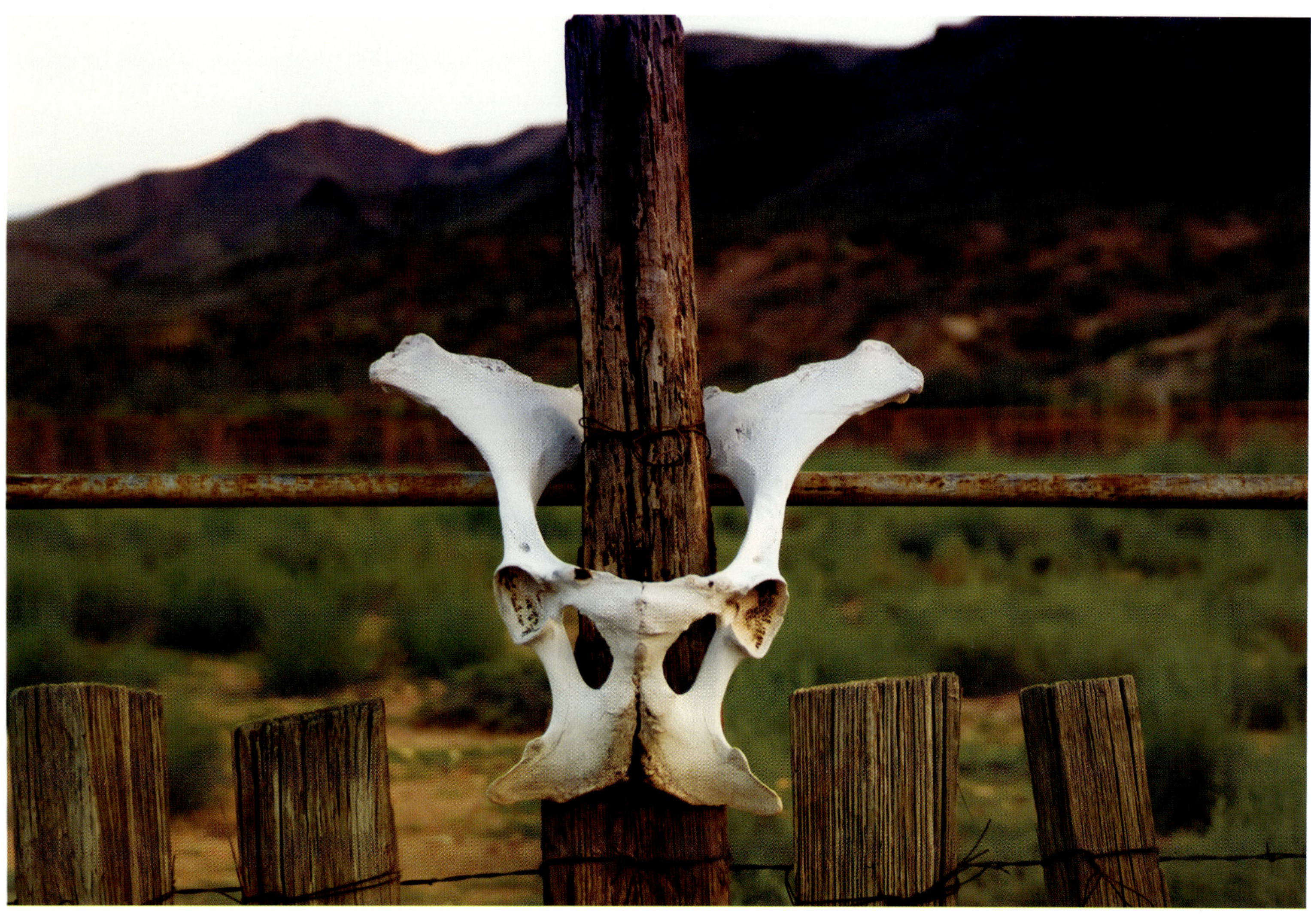

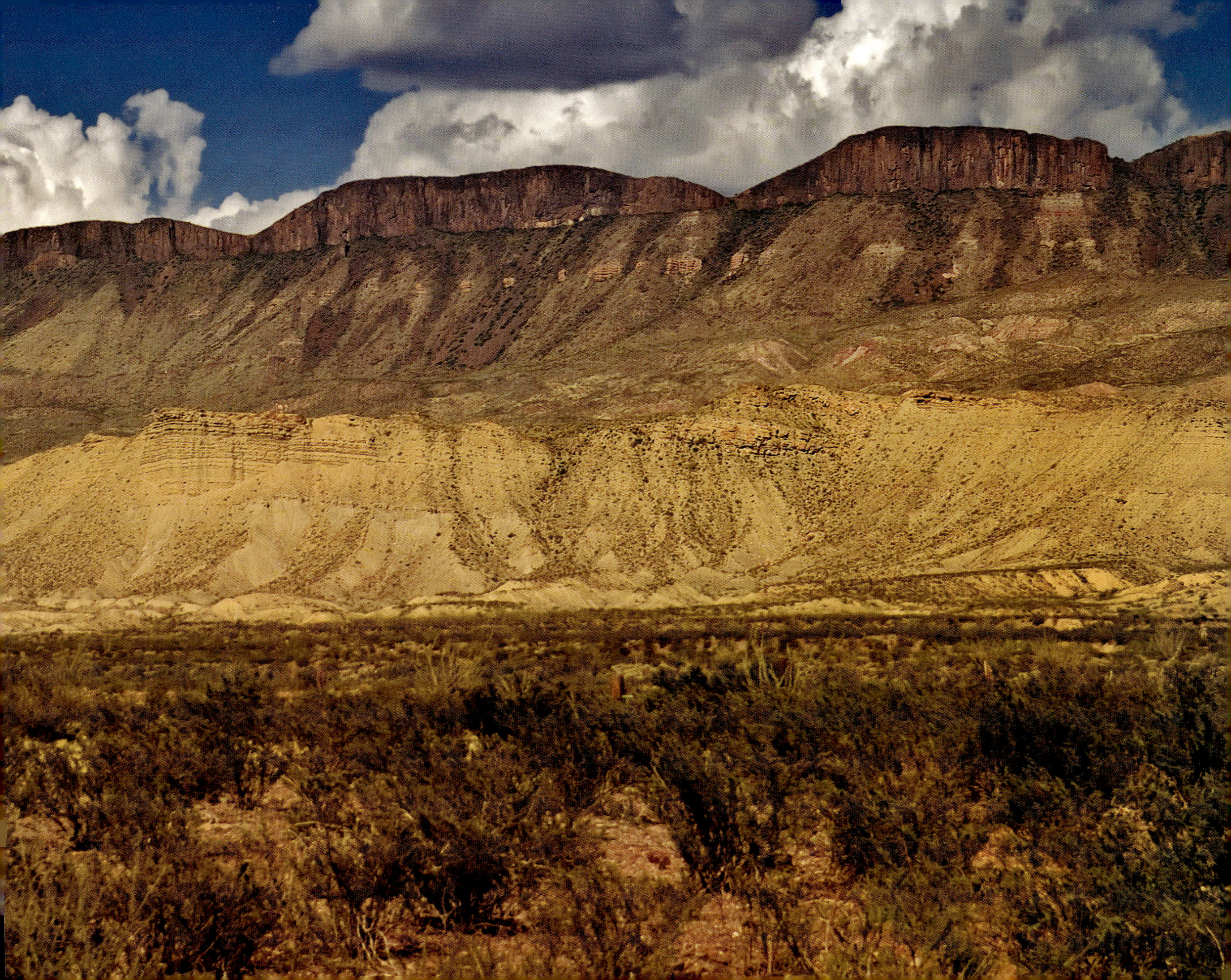

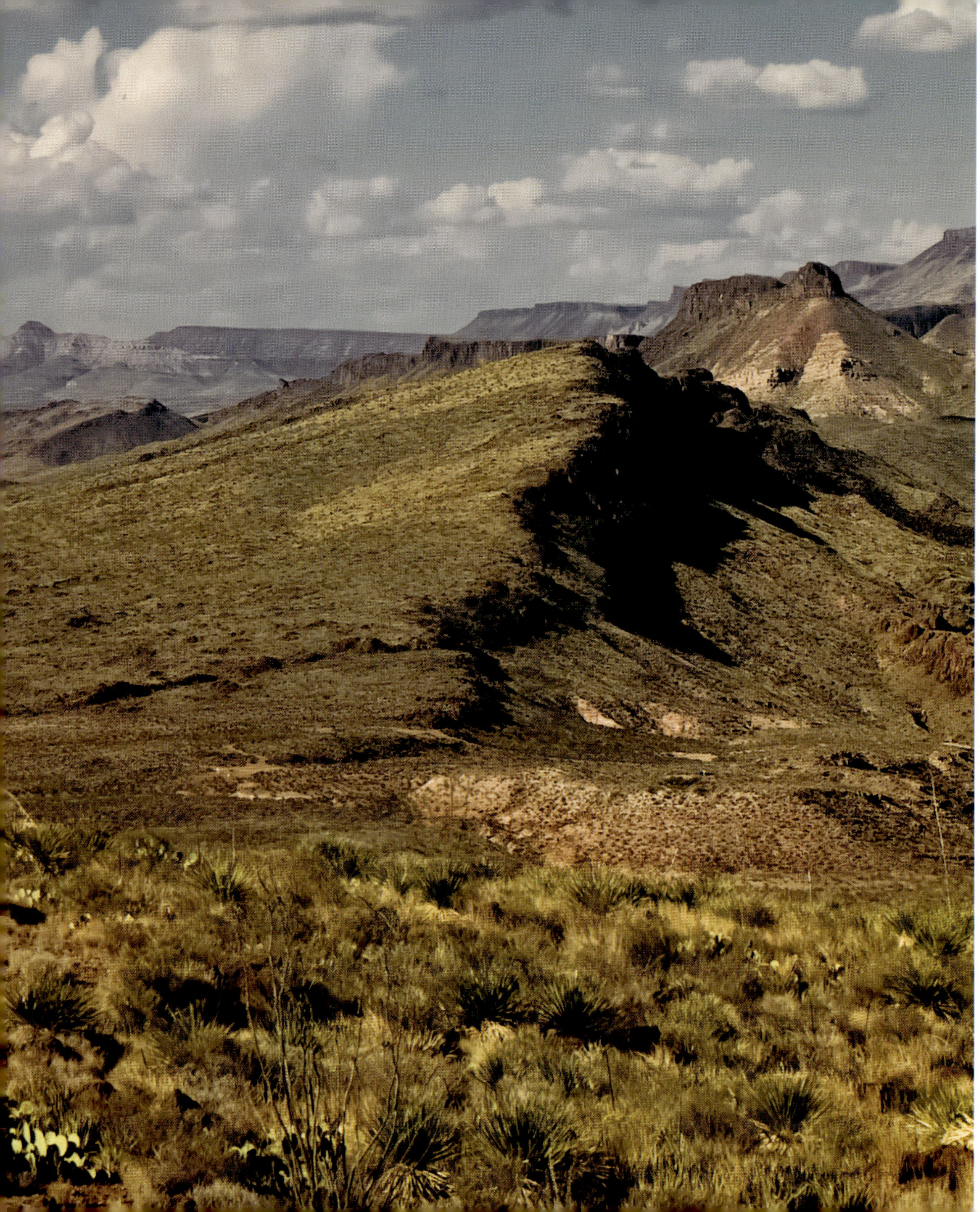

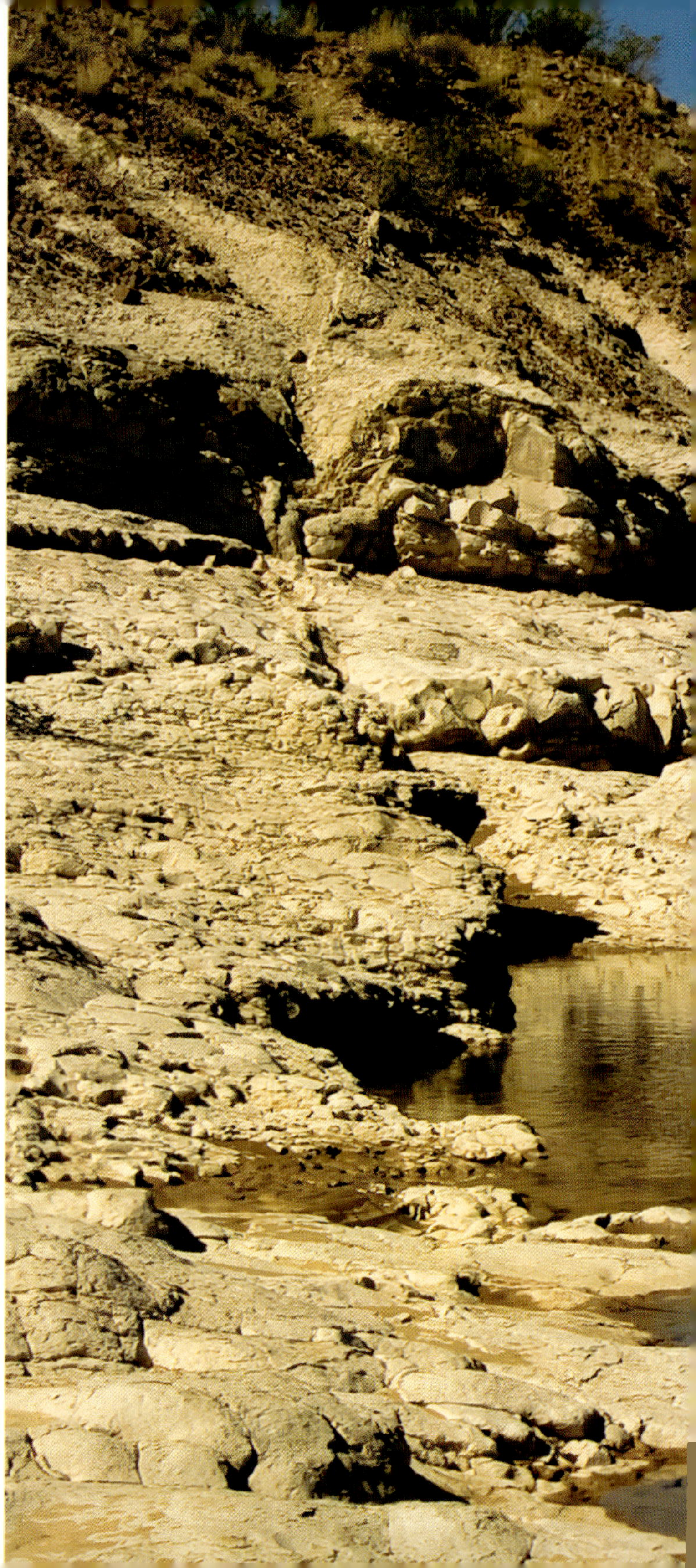

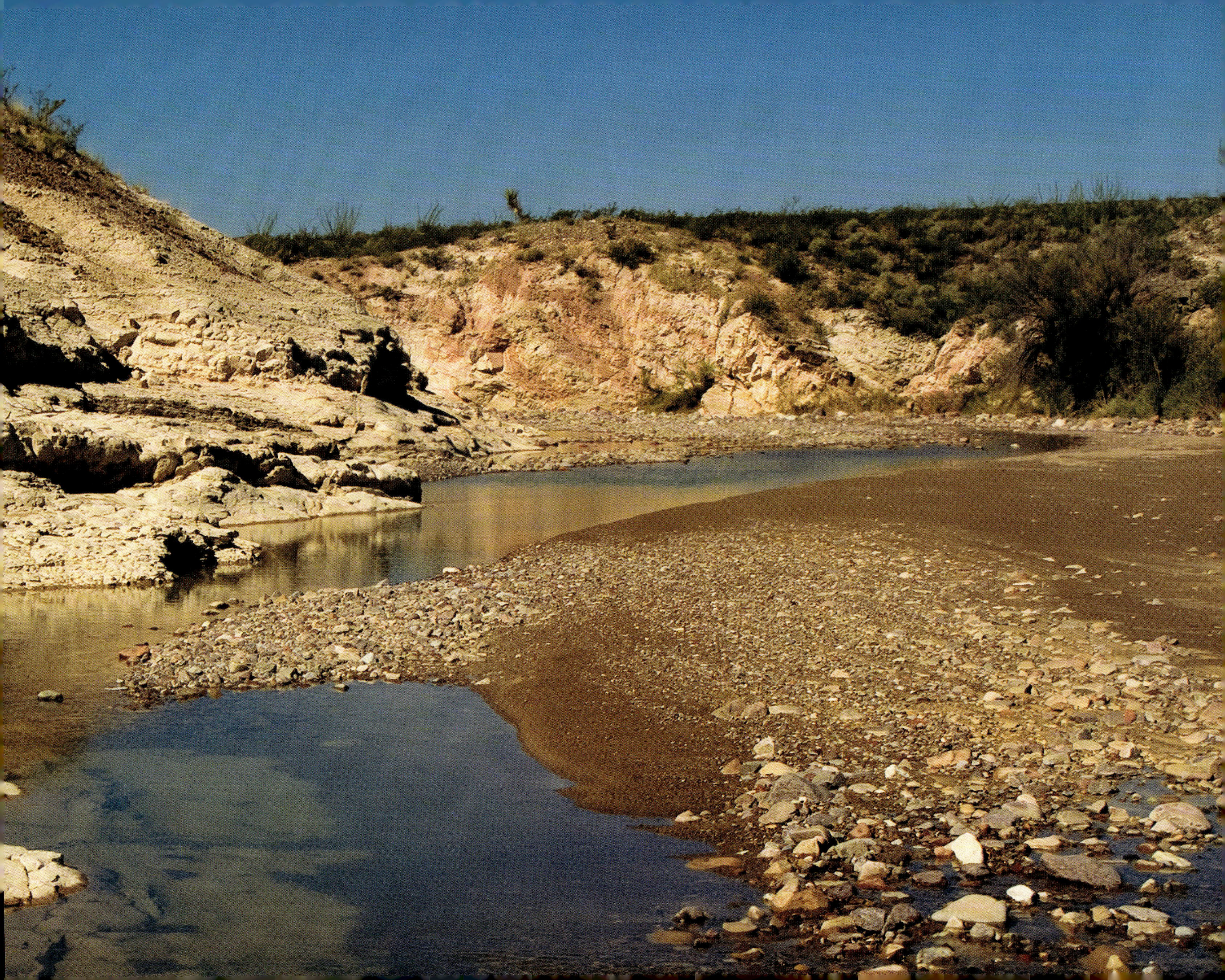

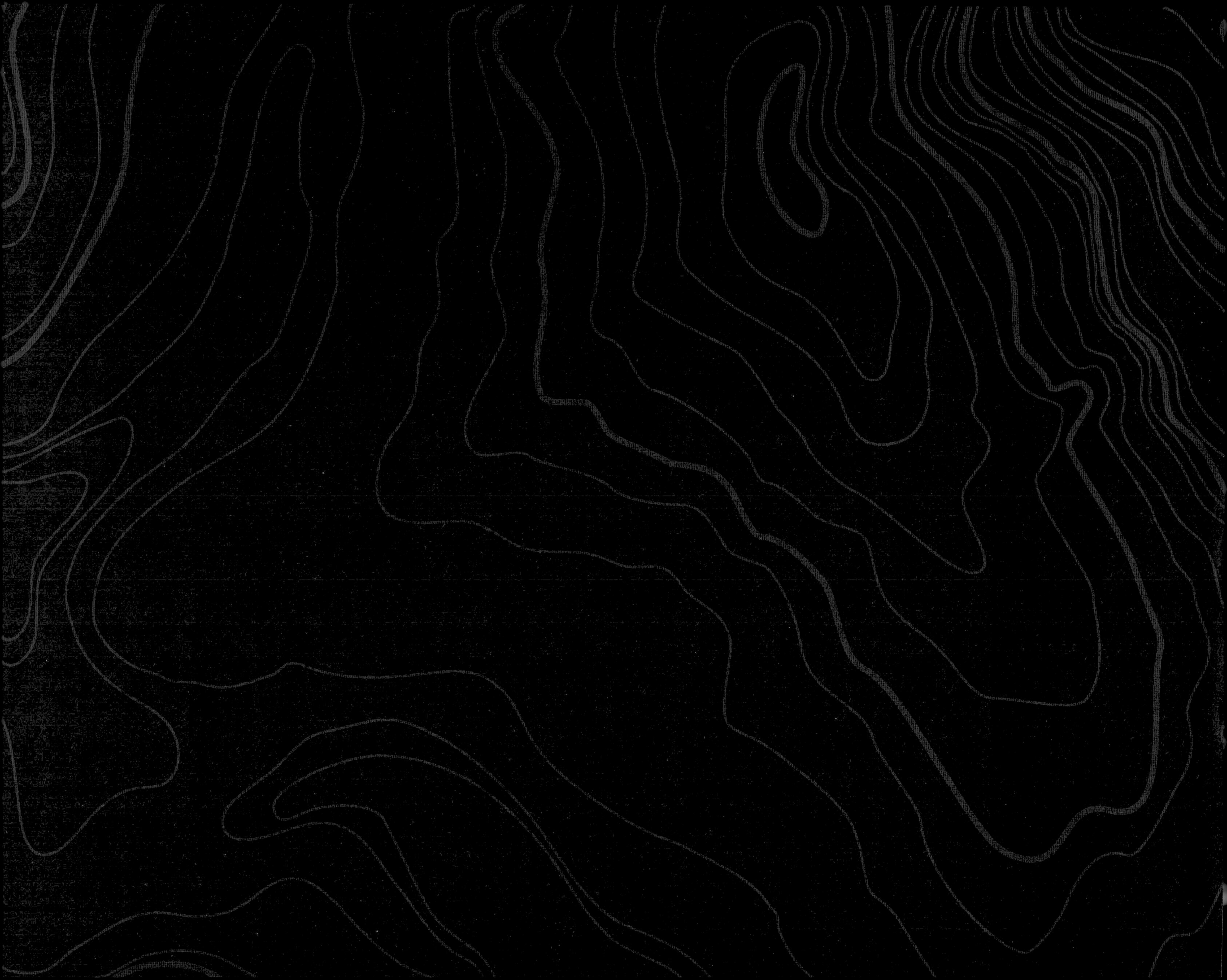

Red Rock Ranch

Red Rock Ranch

DISTANCE FROM EL PASO
120 miles southeast

LATITUDE
31°2'33"

LONGITUDE
-104°49'50" W

ELEVATION
4,047 feet (1,233 meters)

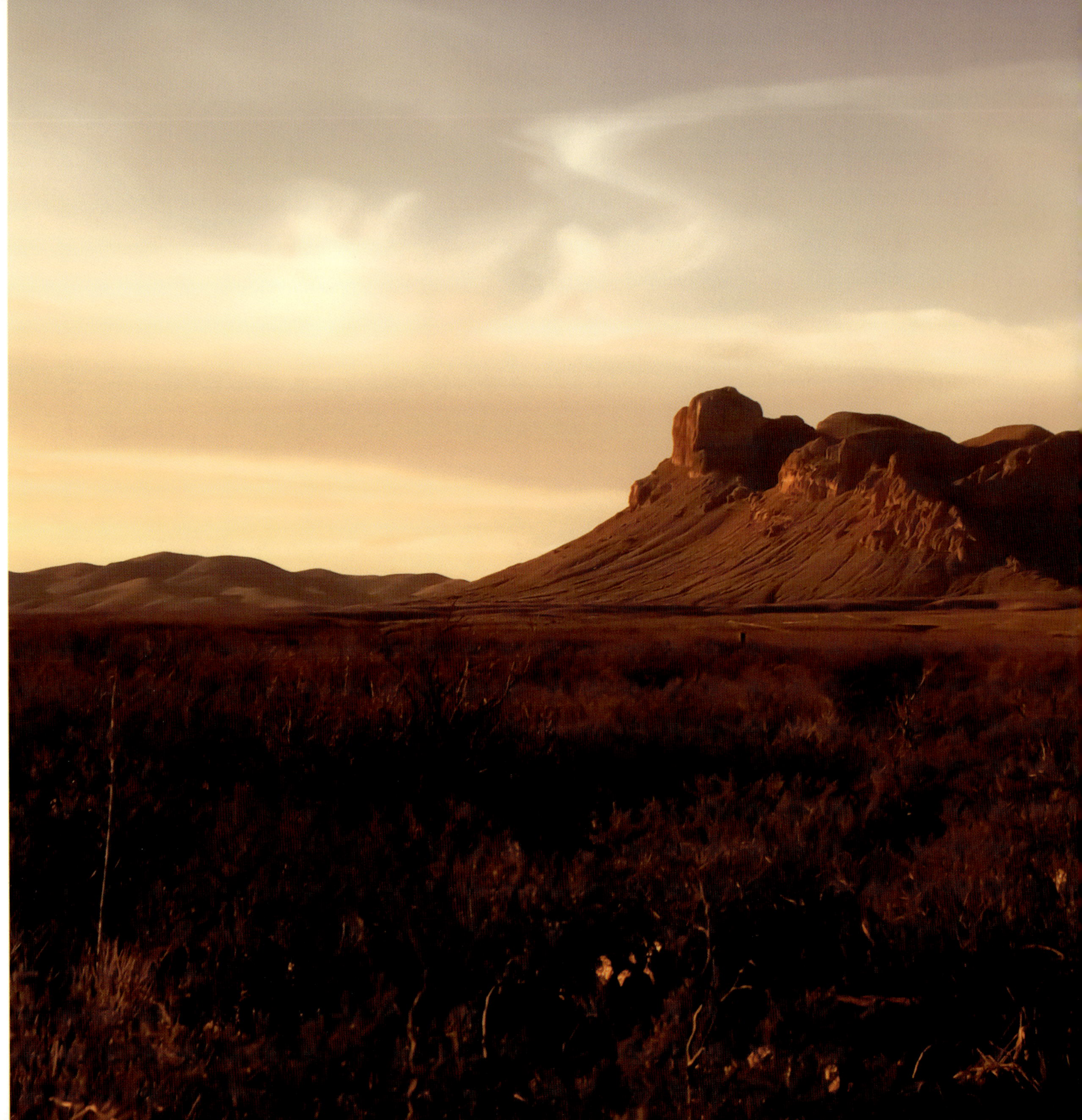

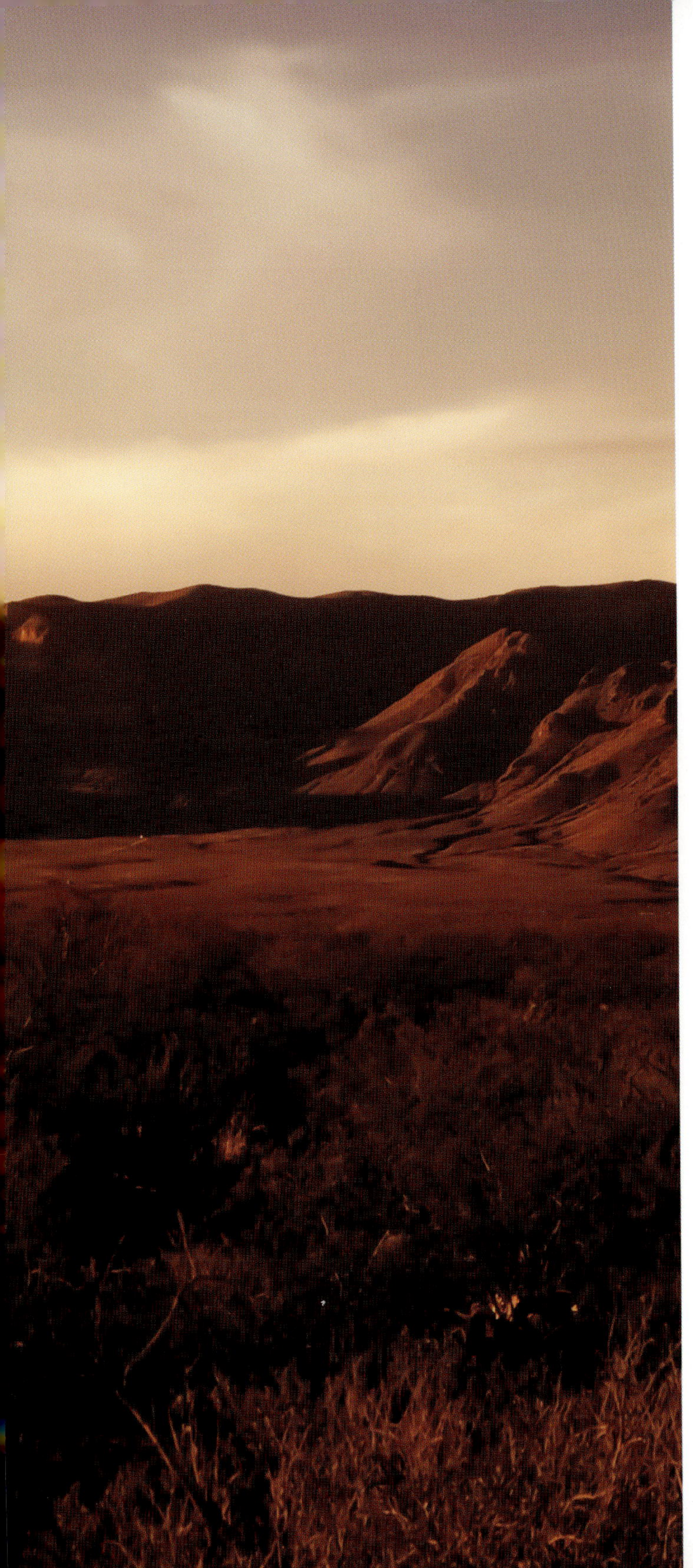

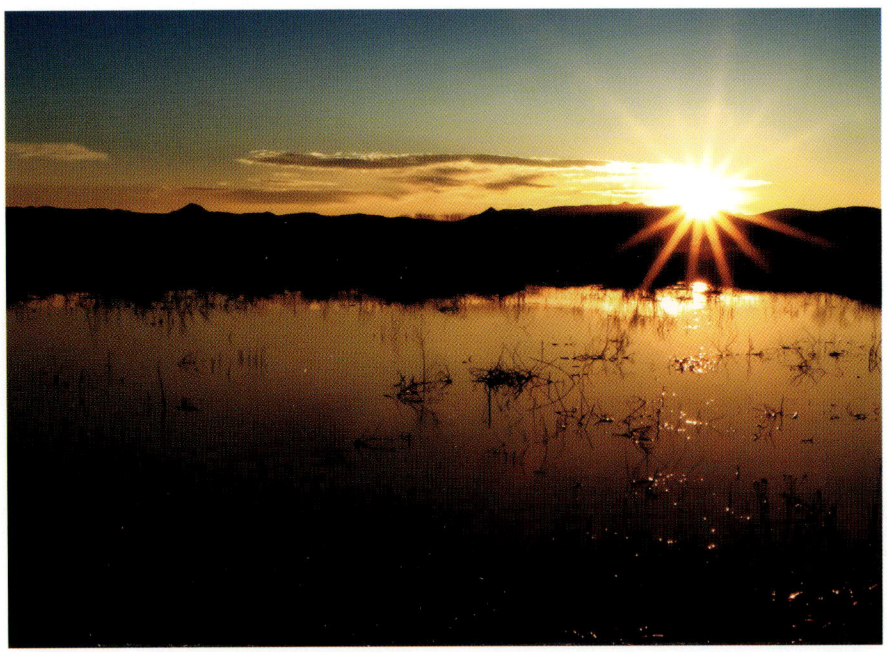

The Red Rock Ranch in the Beach Mountains, two miles north of Van Horn, is one of the only public tours offered on private land in West Texas. Some of the rocks on the ranch are more than a billion years old, among the oldest in Texas. The Precambrian sandstone outcropping found at Red Rock is one of only four natural Precambrian sandstone exposures in the Western Hemisphere. "Imagination can be as creative as one wishes," according to ranch owner Darice McVay. "E. T. under a camel's chin, Donald Duck or Puff the Magic Dragon, an Indian satellite dish, and Red Rock Ranch's very own Easter Island rock" are all rock formations created by wind erosion over millions of years. Many of these formations are naturally balanced, as if a sculptor has worked magic.

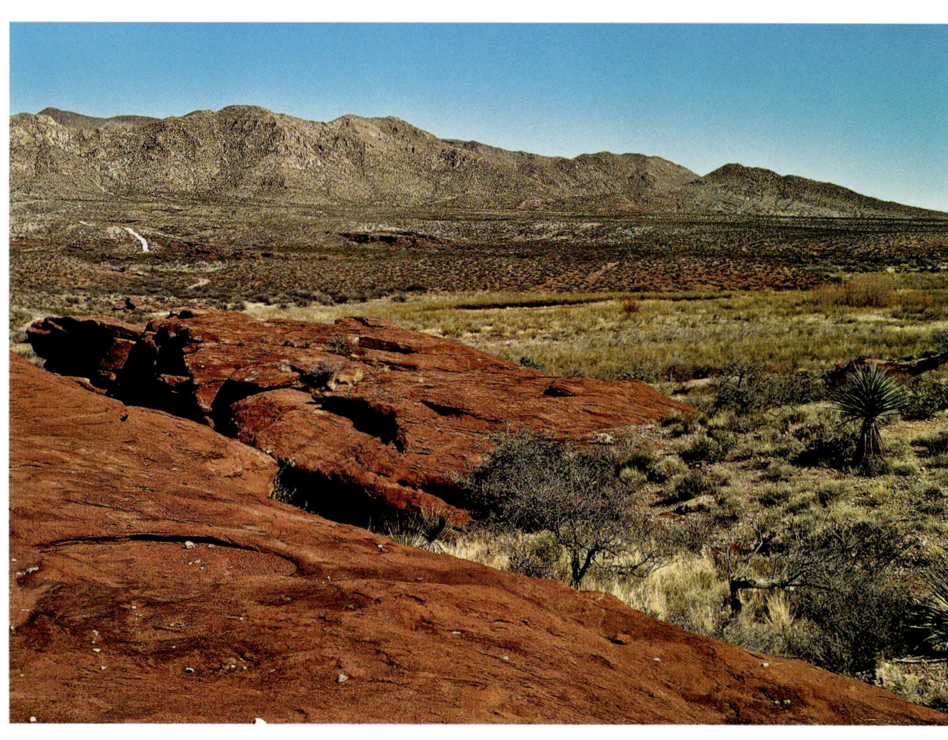

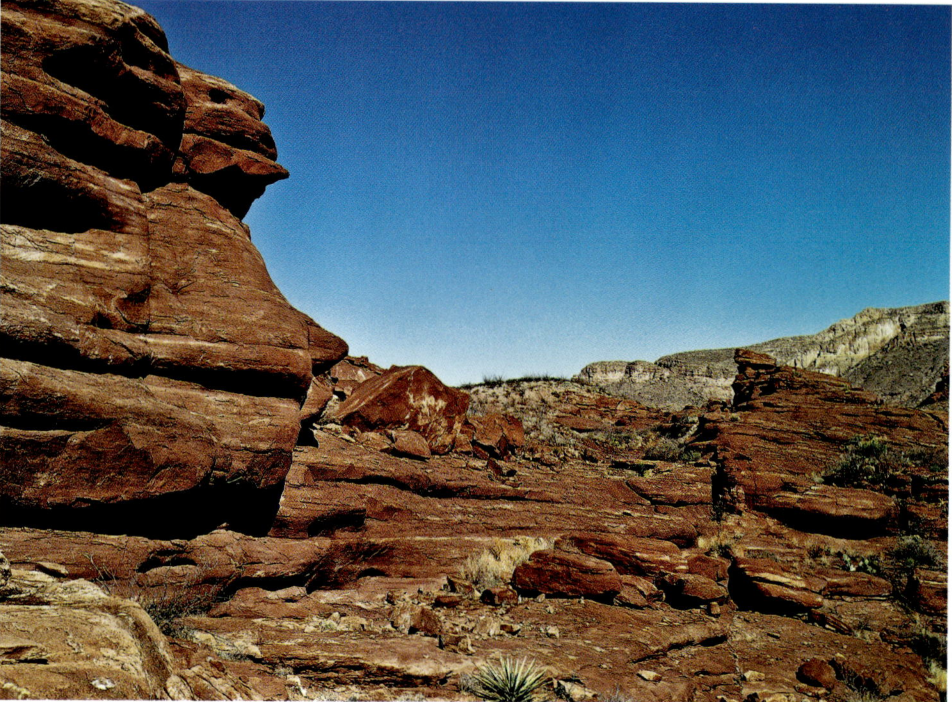

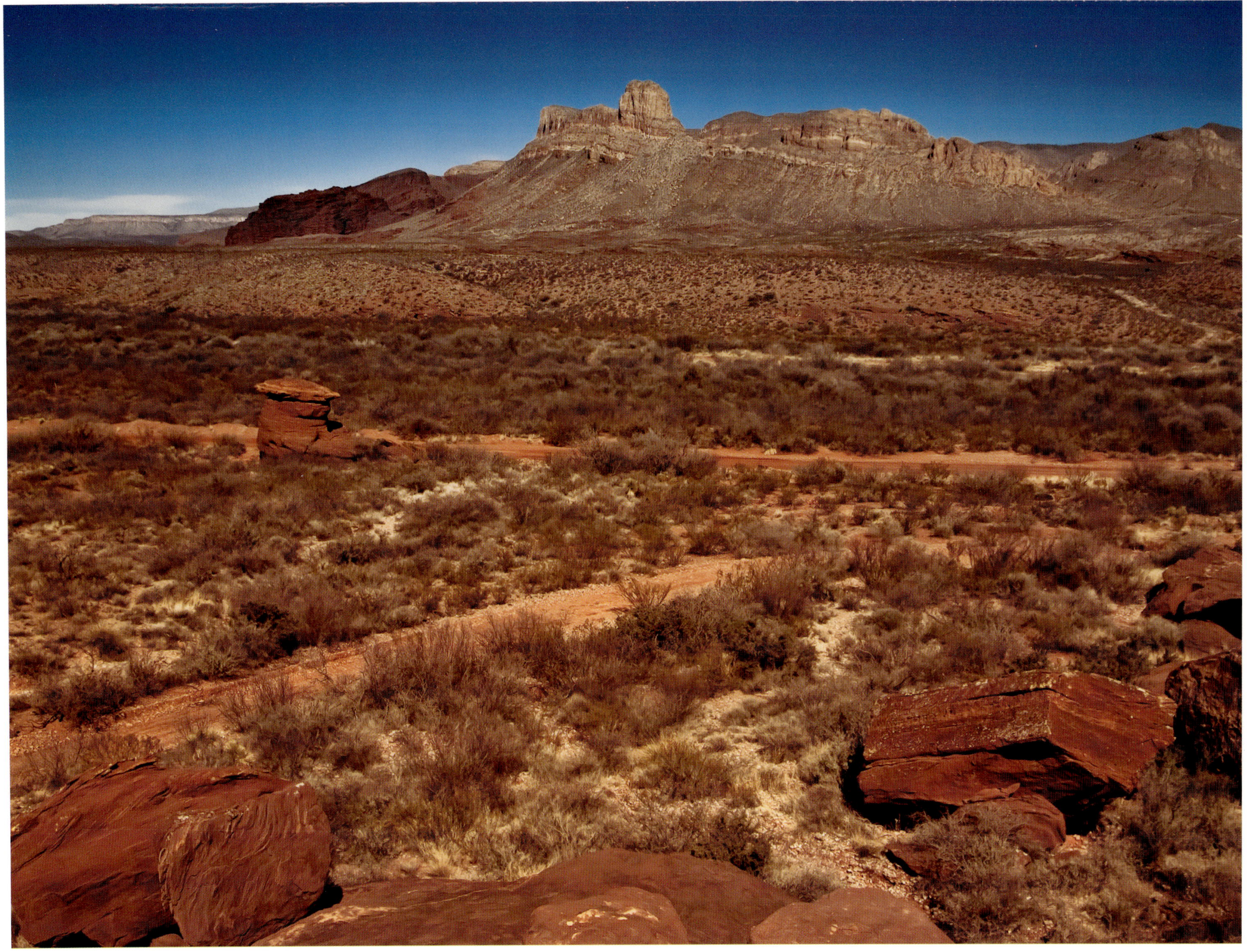

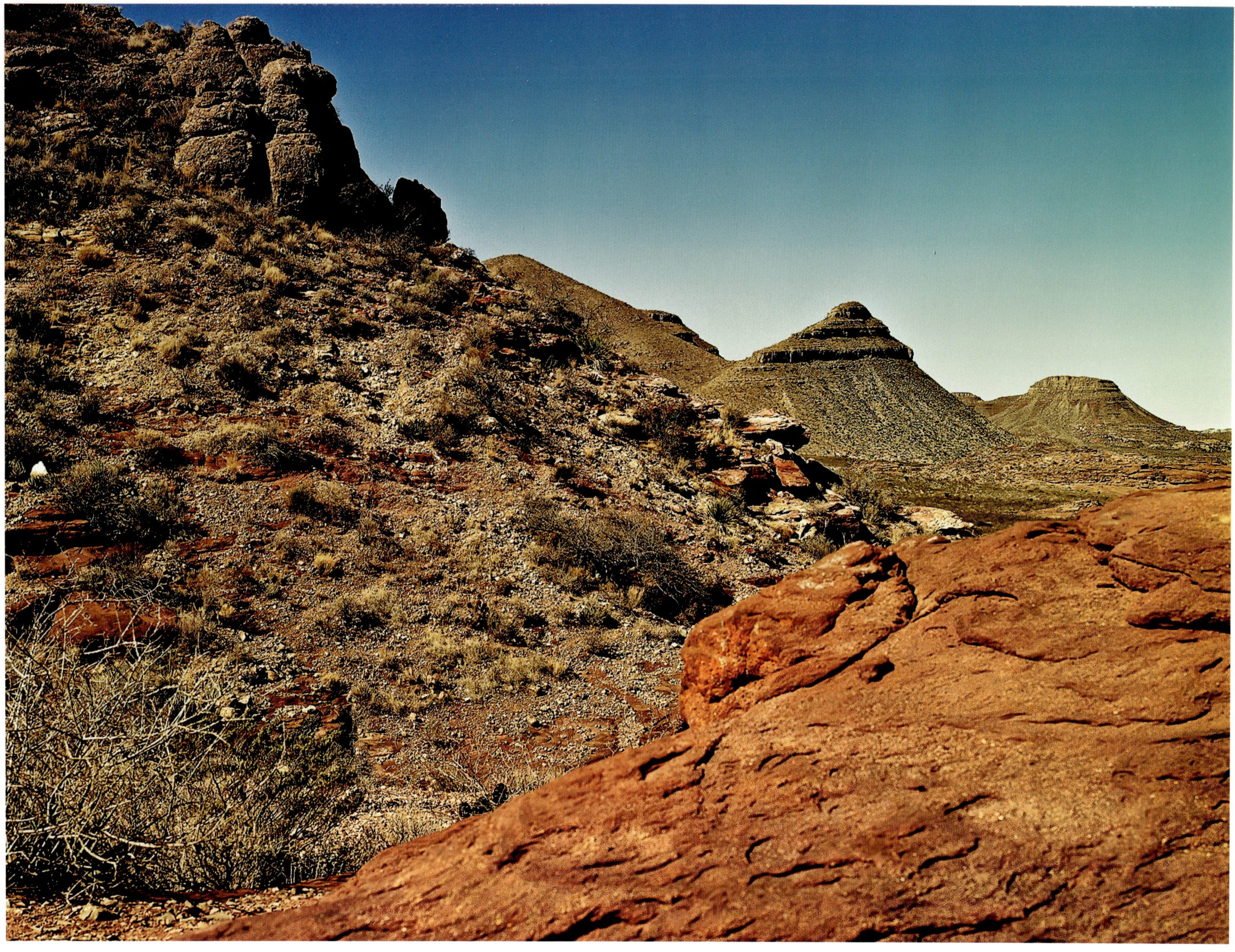

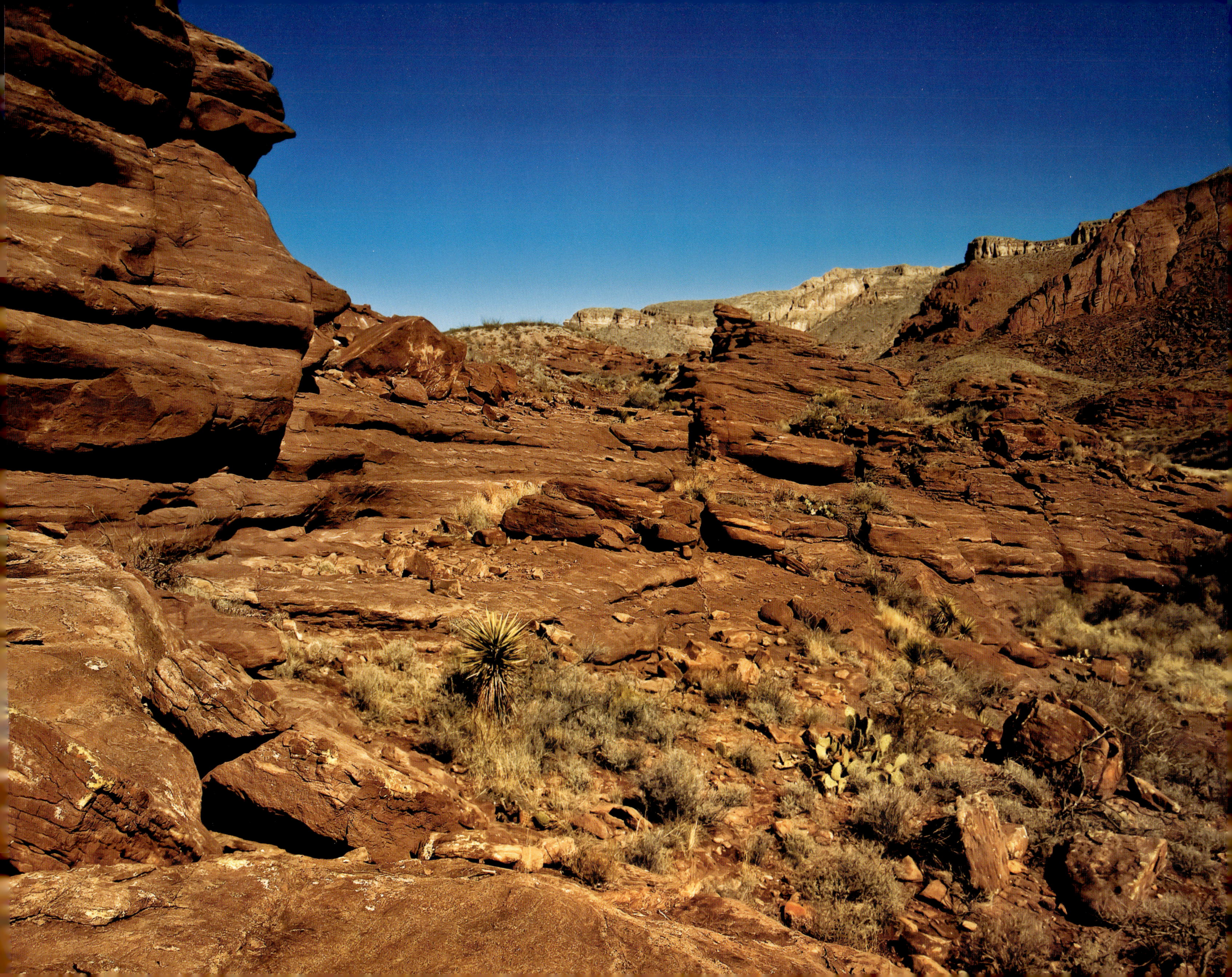

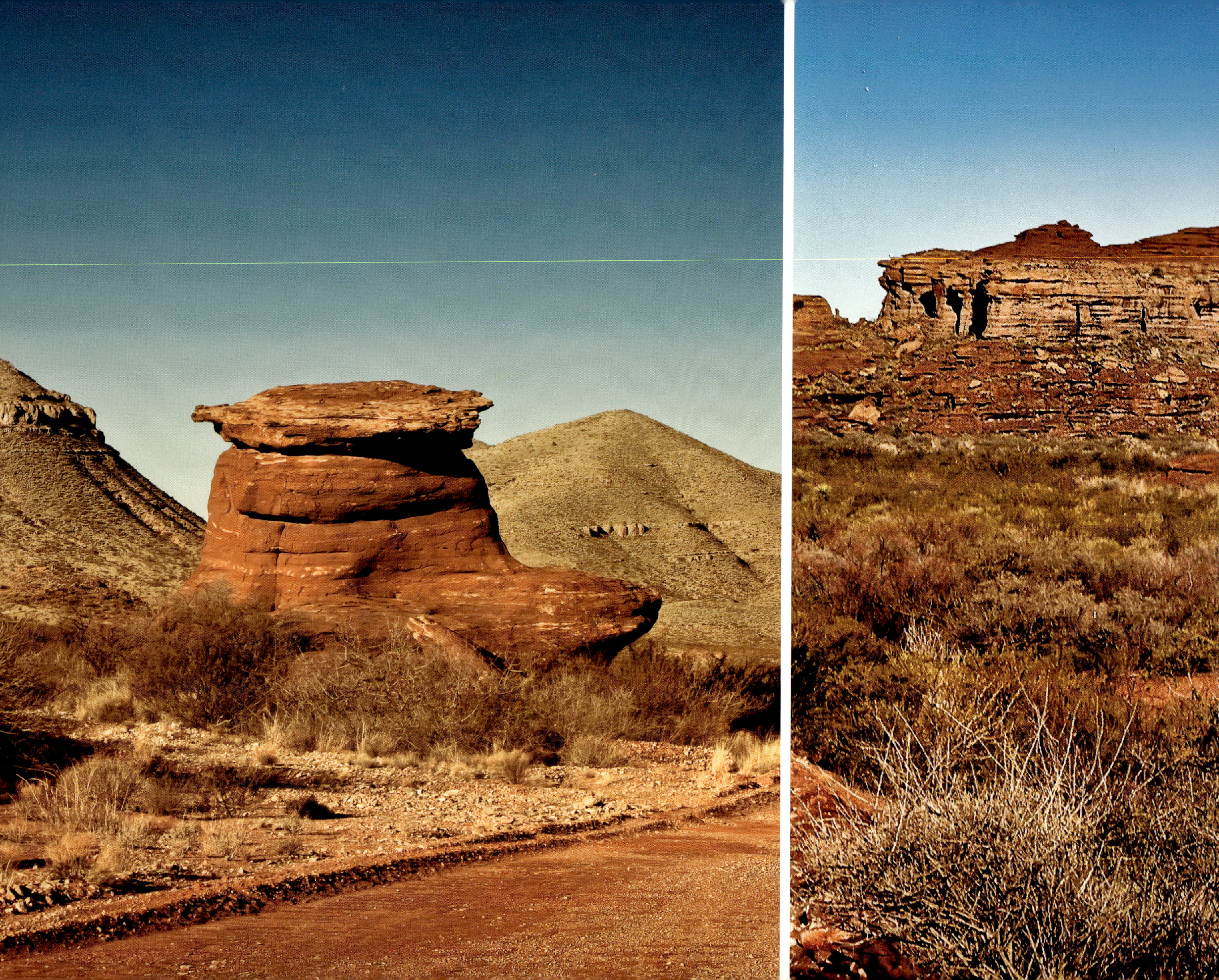

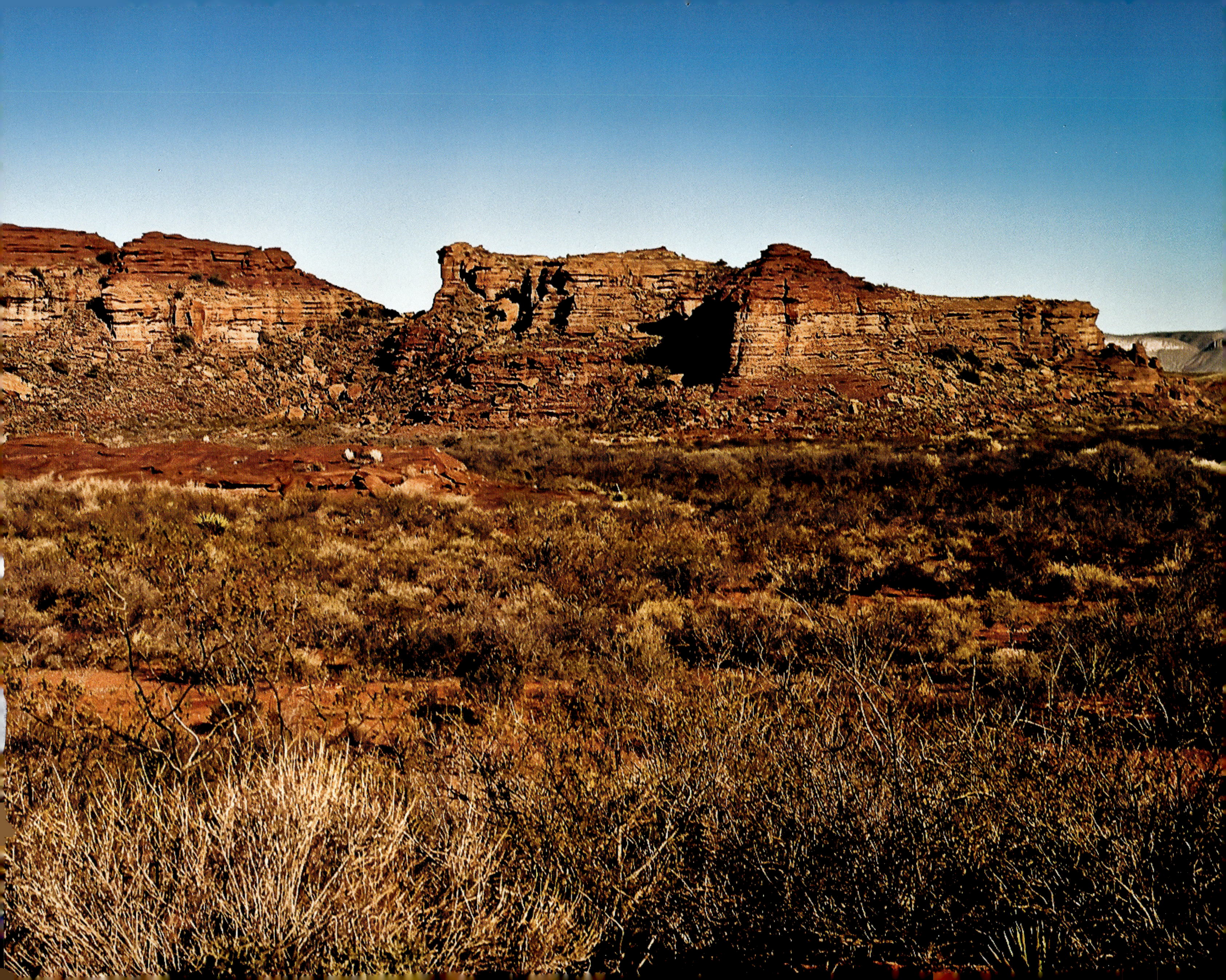

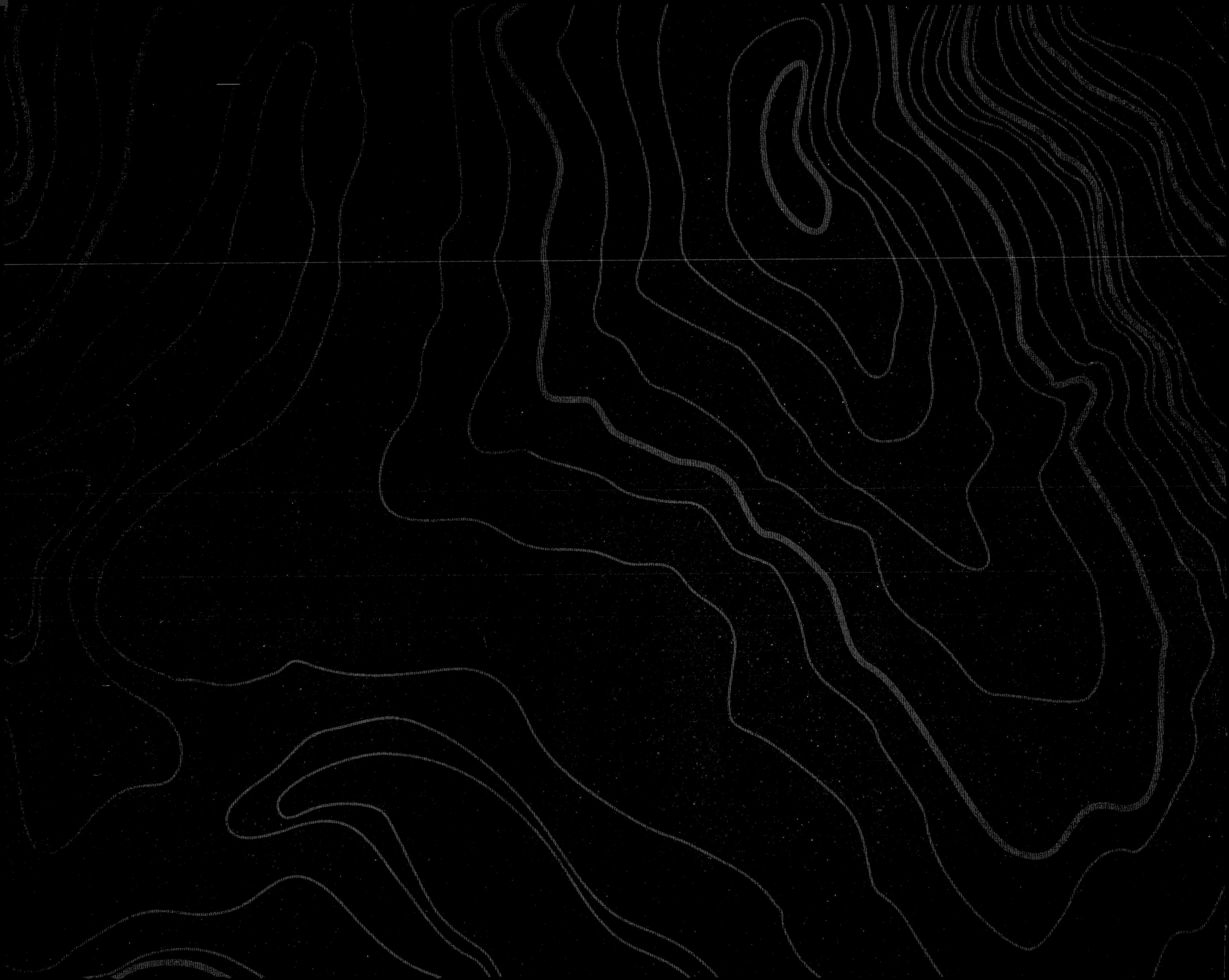

Guadalupe Mountains and Salt Flat

Guadalupe Mountains and Salt Flat

DISTANCE FROM EL PASO
120 miles northeast

LATITUDE
31°55'0" N

LONGITUDE
-104°52'0" W

ELEVATION
8,749 feet (2,667 meters)

AREA
135 square miles
(350 square kilometers)

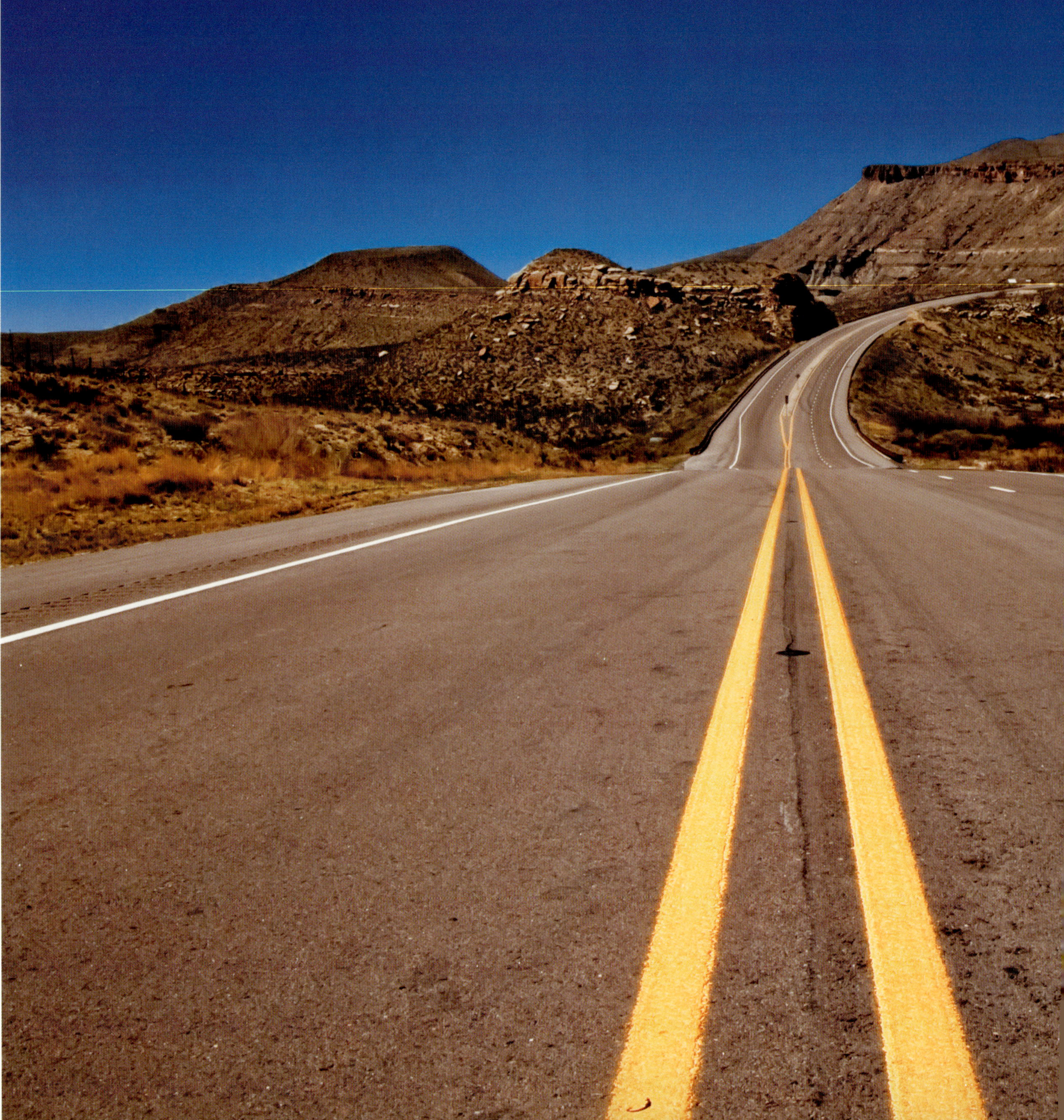

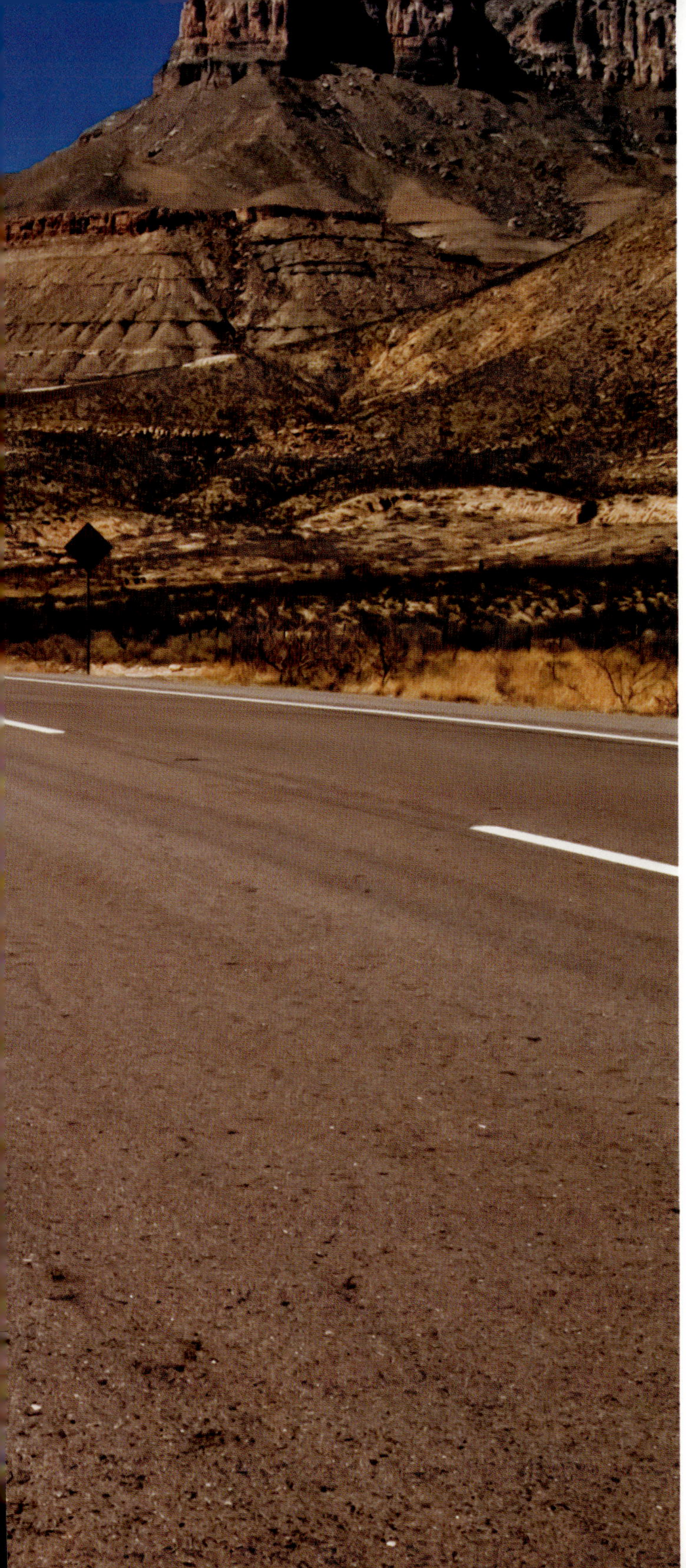

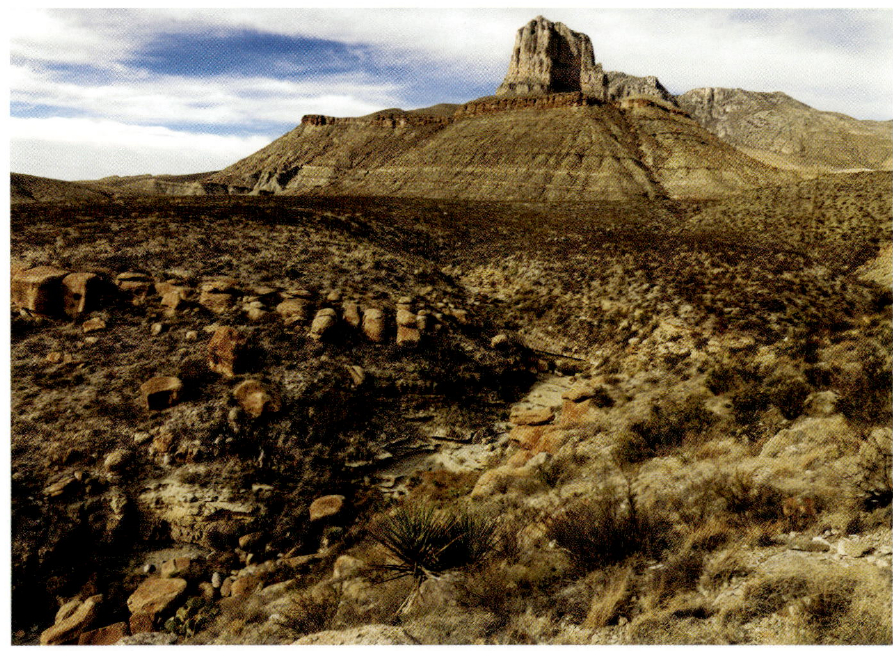

El Capitan, projecting from Texas's highest mountain range, watches over me as I wander the barren salt flat at its base. A pulsating wind whips down from the Guadalupe Mountain range as I survey the area for the ideal spot to set up my camera gear. Each of my steps disrupts the slightly soft, cracked surface, leaving an unmistakable trail behind. I stop, making sure my prints are out of the image frame, when all of a sudden a blast of wind rips off my hat, sending it in a rapid tumble across the dry lakebed. I lurch for it, my hand grabbing empty air, then stand still and watch the hat disappear into the desert brush half a mile away. Strangely, there was an odd delight watching this, and I must wonder if El Capitan let out a slight chuckle at nature's power over me. Perhaps one day I will venture back in search of the lost hat, though I would be more inclined to search for new ways to capture these scenes in my lens.

The Guadalupe Mountains encompass parts of the most extensive Permian limestone fossil reef in the world. Over two hundred fifty million years ago, a four-hundred-mile-long limestone reef formed along a shelf

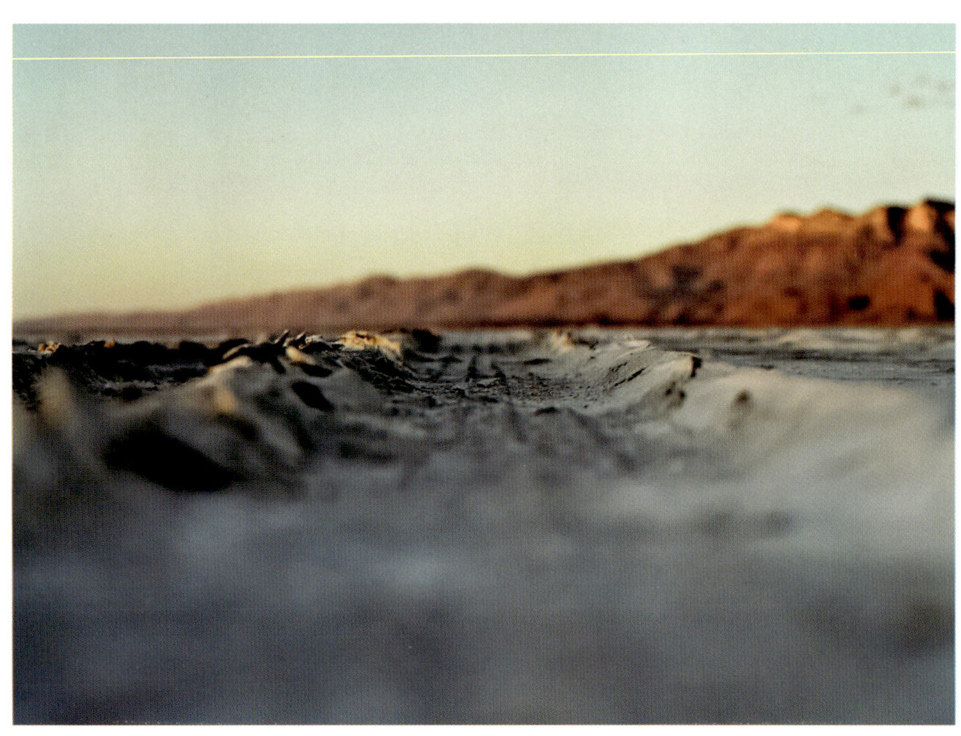

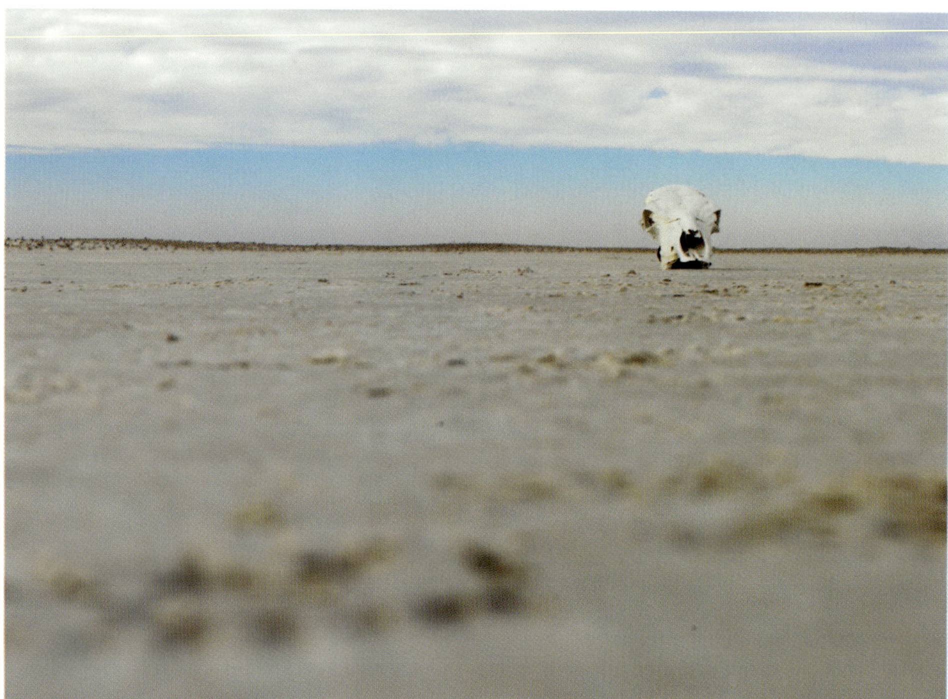

in the Permian Sea. These mountains are part of the reef's remains, shaped by thousands of years of weathering. Guadalupe Peak is the highest peak and highest point in Texas, standing at 8,749 feet. In 1972 the Guadalupe Mountains were designated a national park.

The meandering Salt Flat seen today at the base of the range is what remains of a series of shallow seas that covered much of the area two million years ago. Sediments washed into the seas from the mountain slopes. The water evaporated, leaving behind a thick layer of minerals, primarily table salt or gypsum.

Throughout West Texas and southern New Mexico, two-lane desert highways stretch to vanishing points on horizons that seem to reach infinity under a limitless dome of sky.

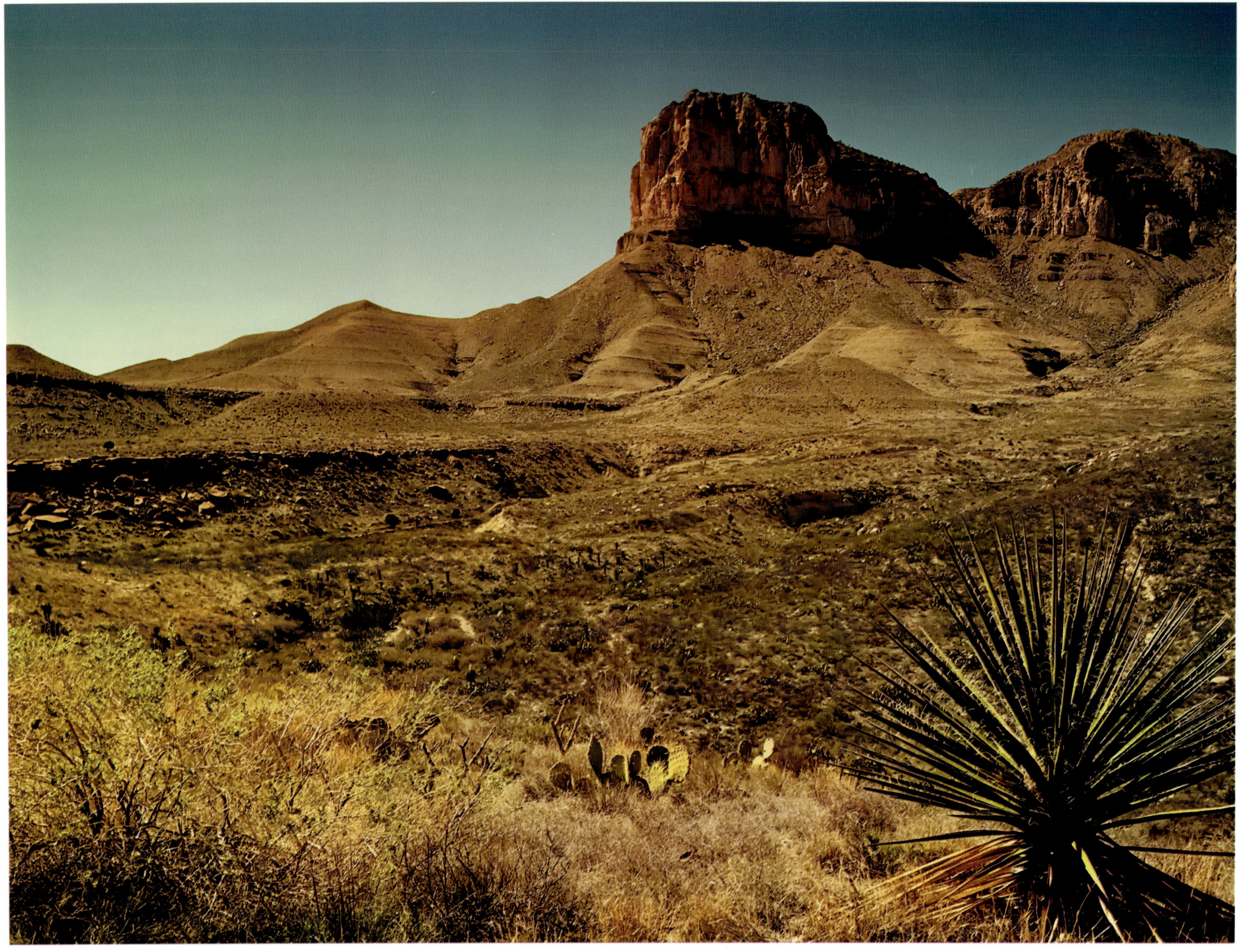

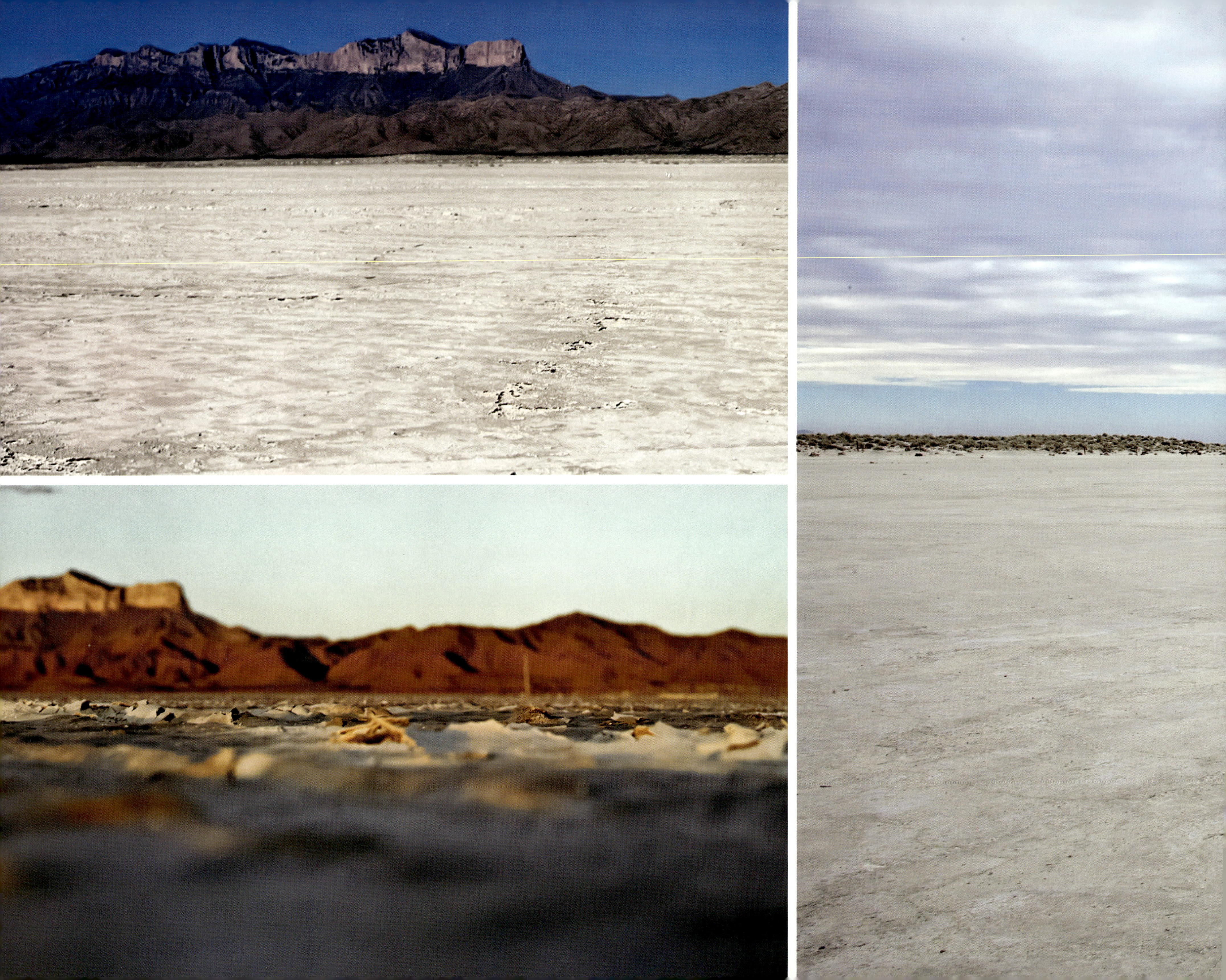

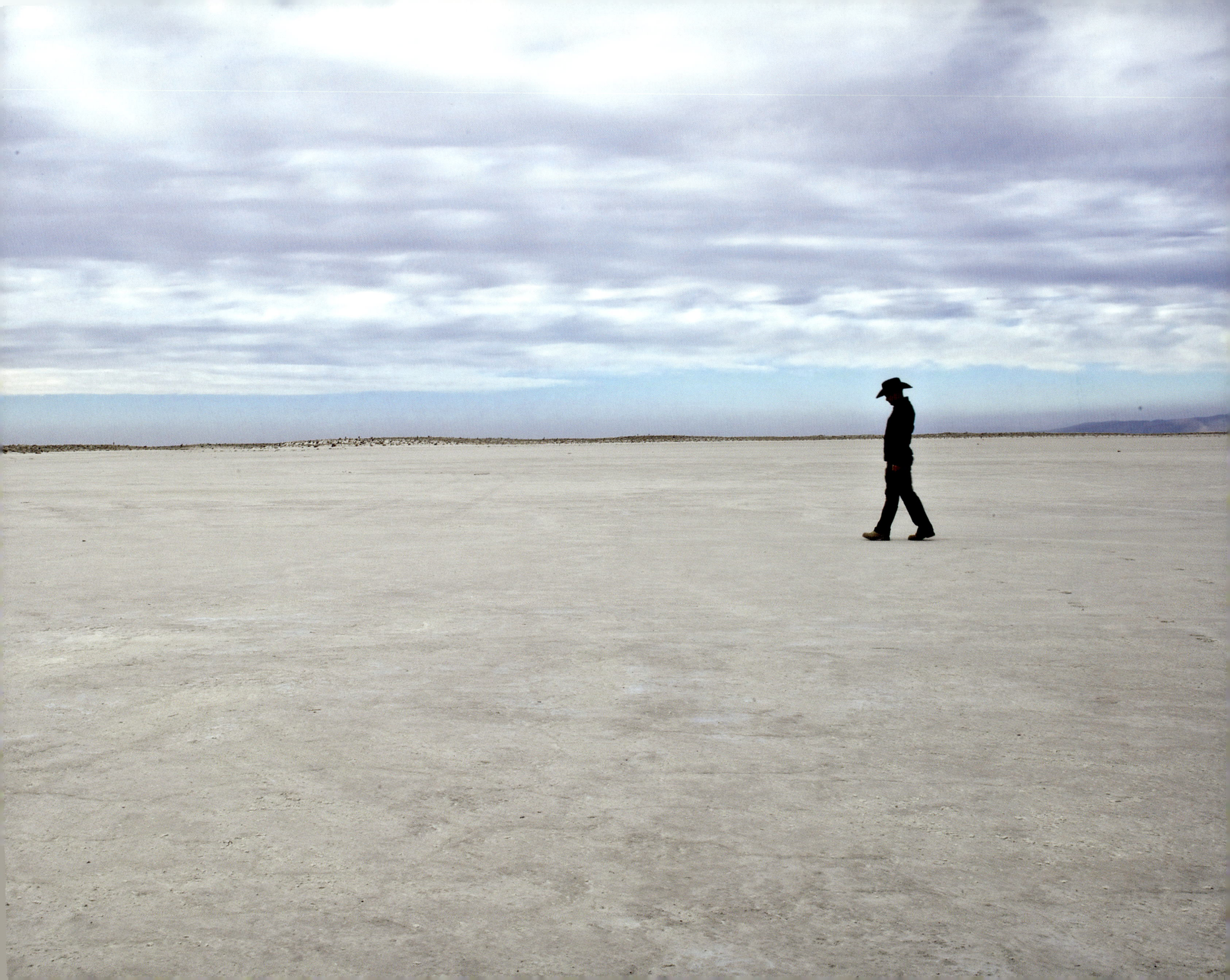

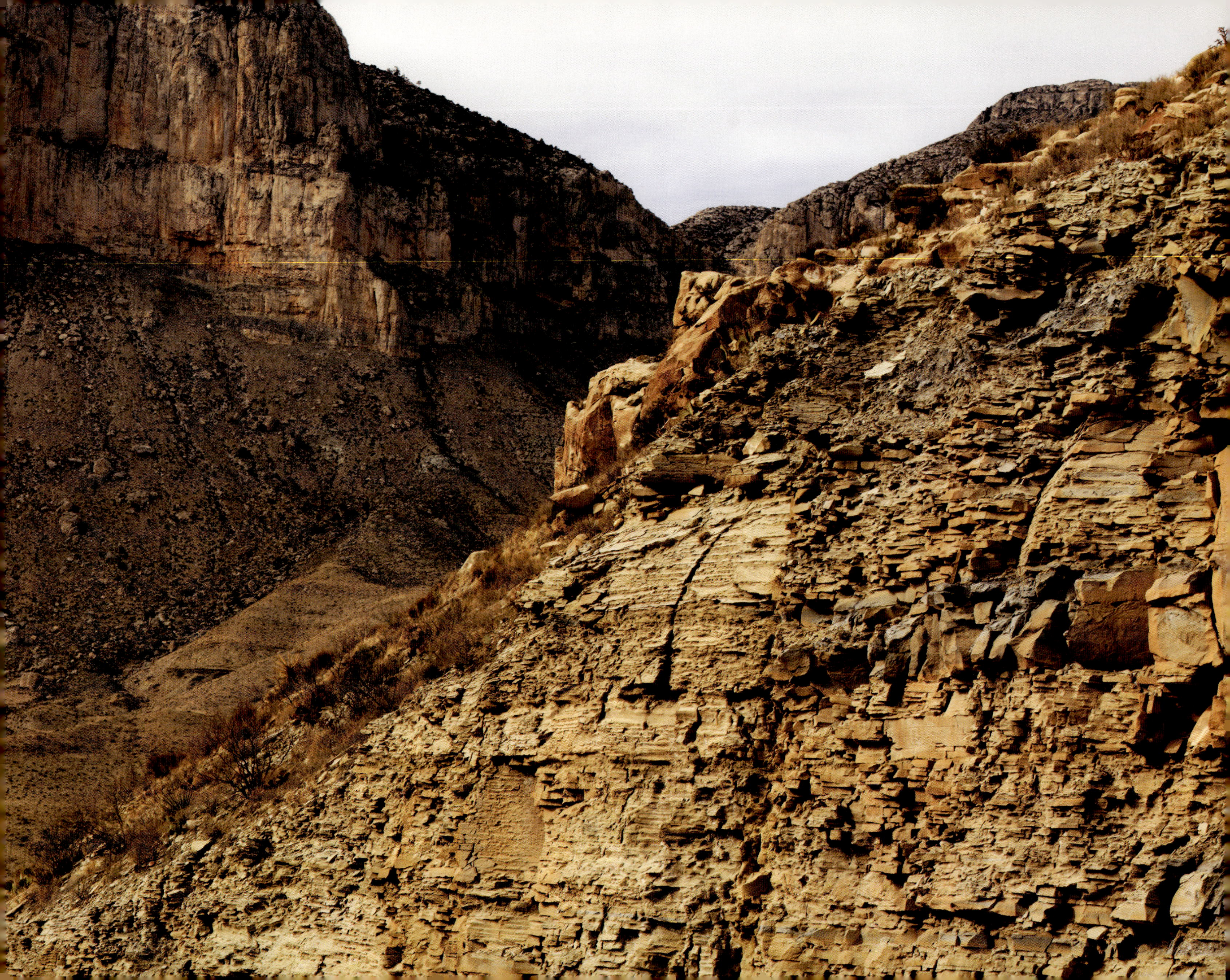

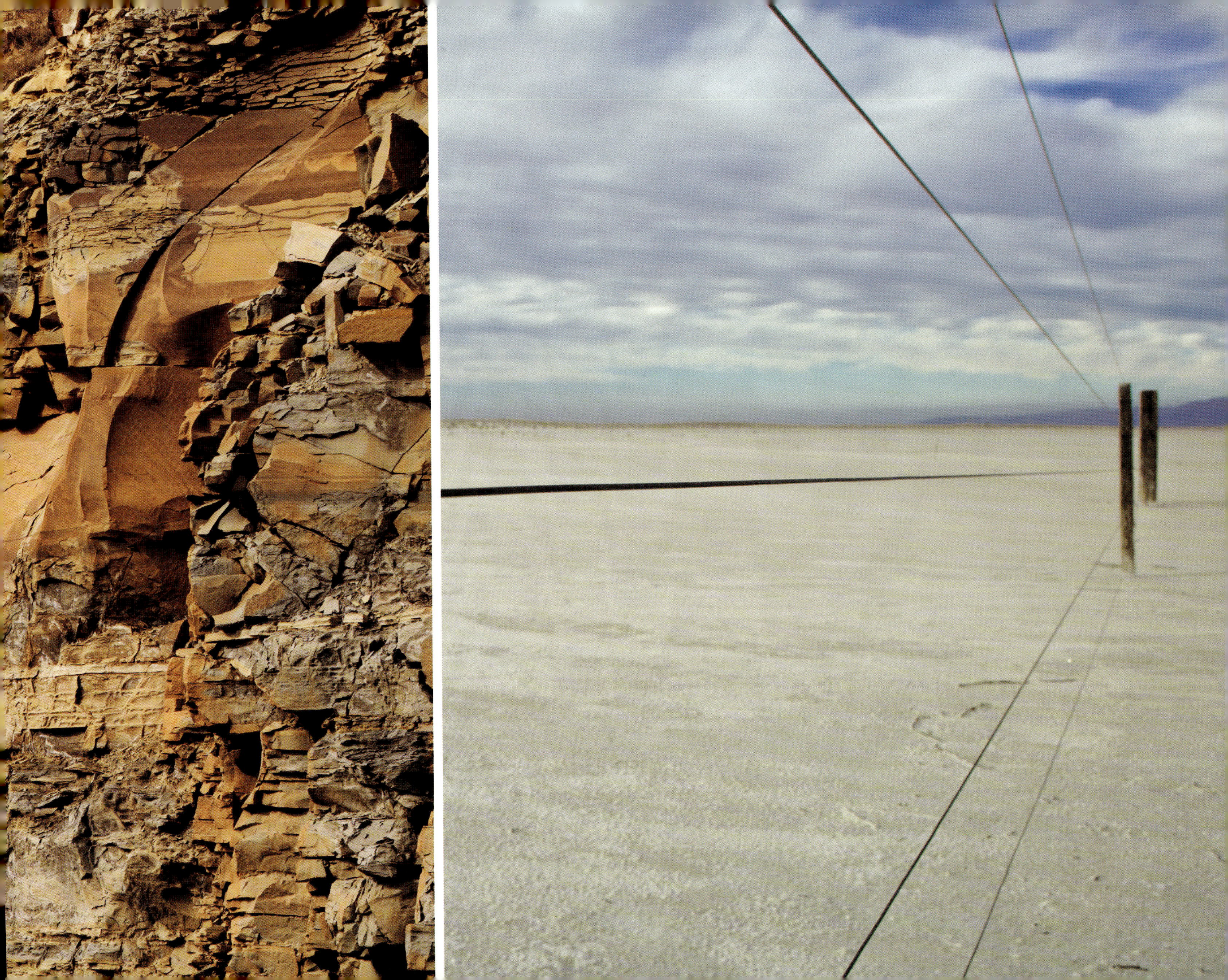

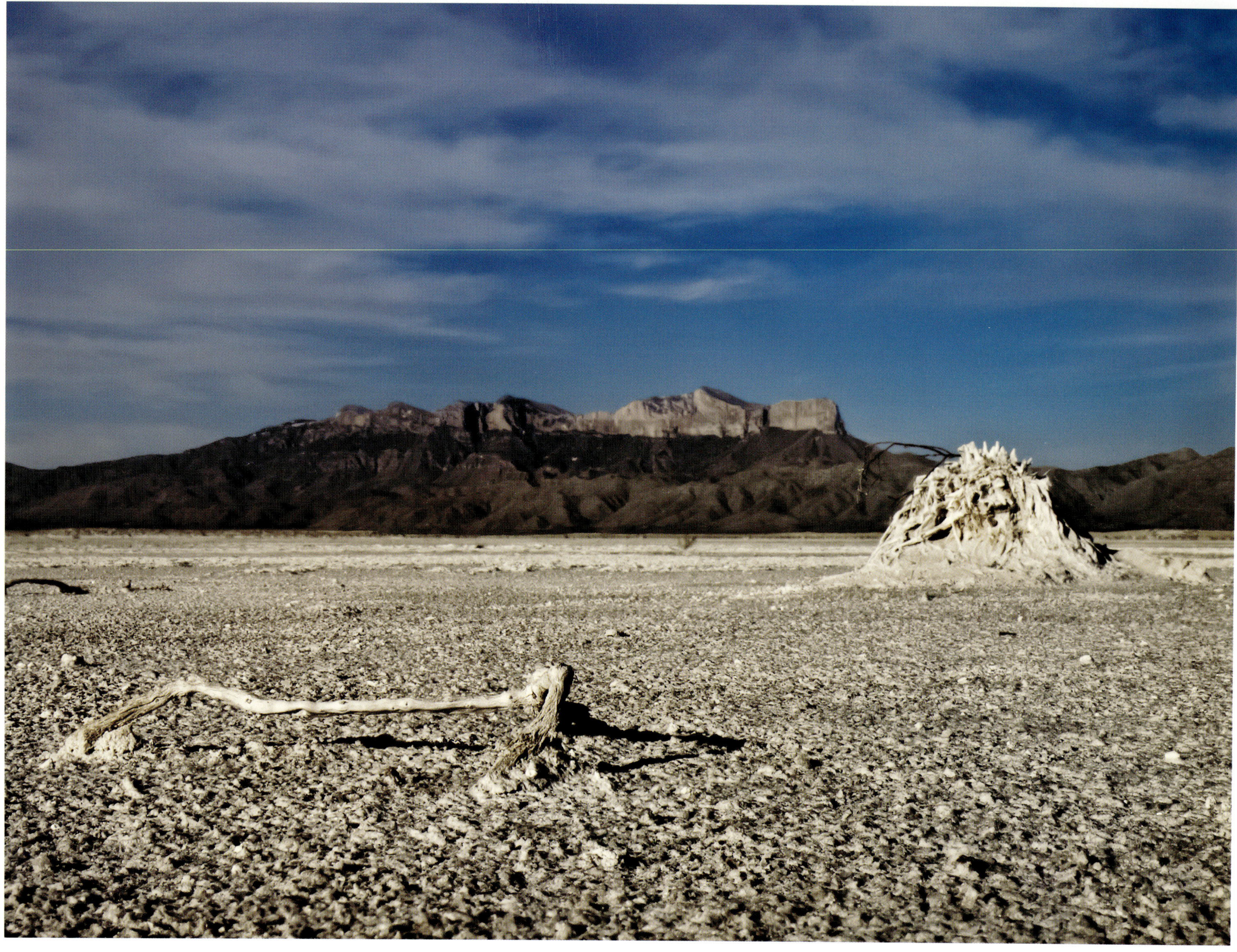

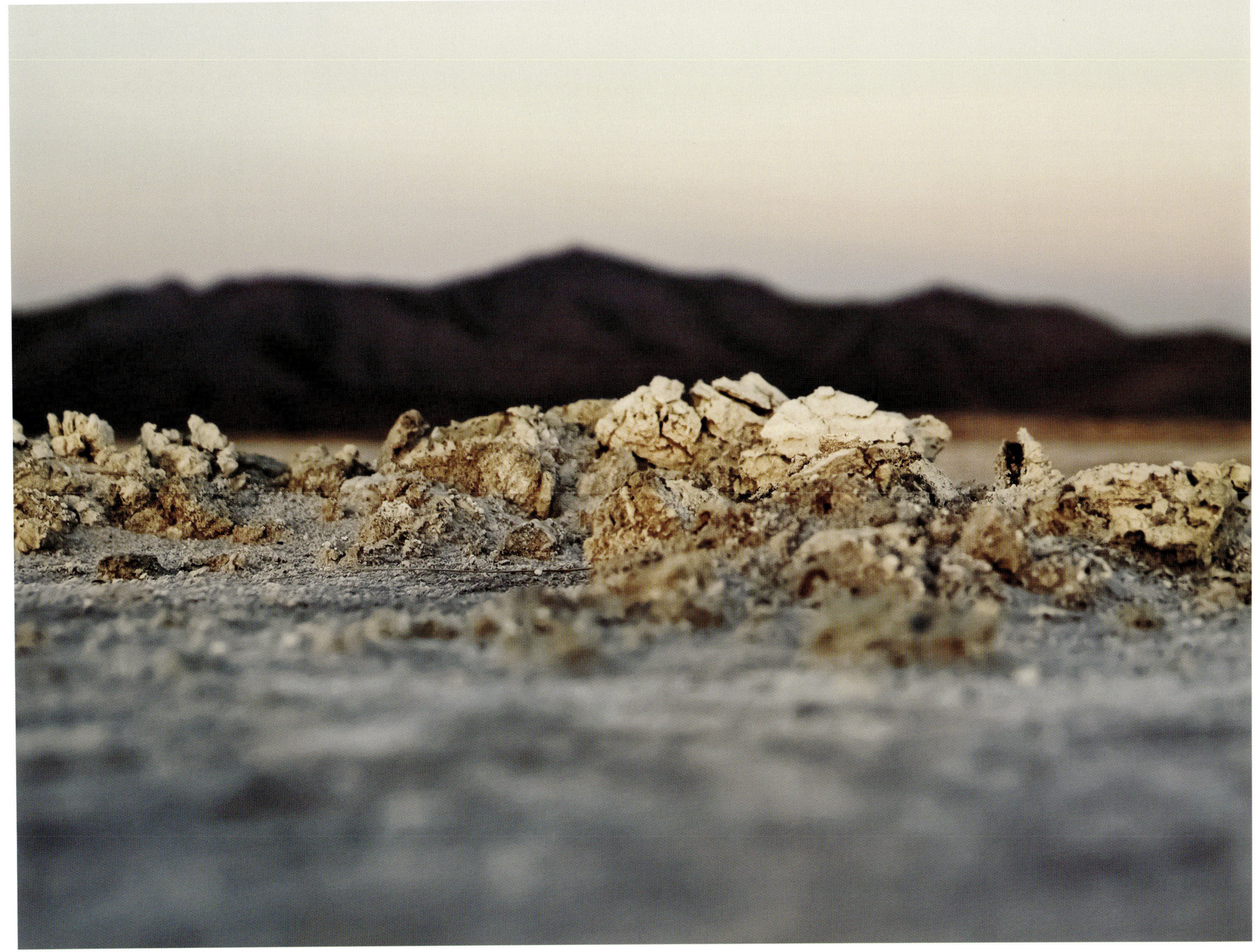

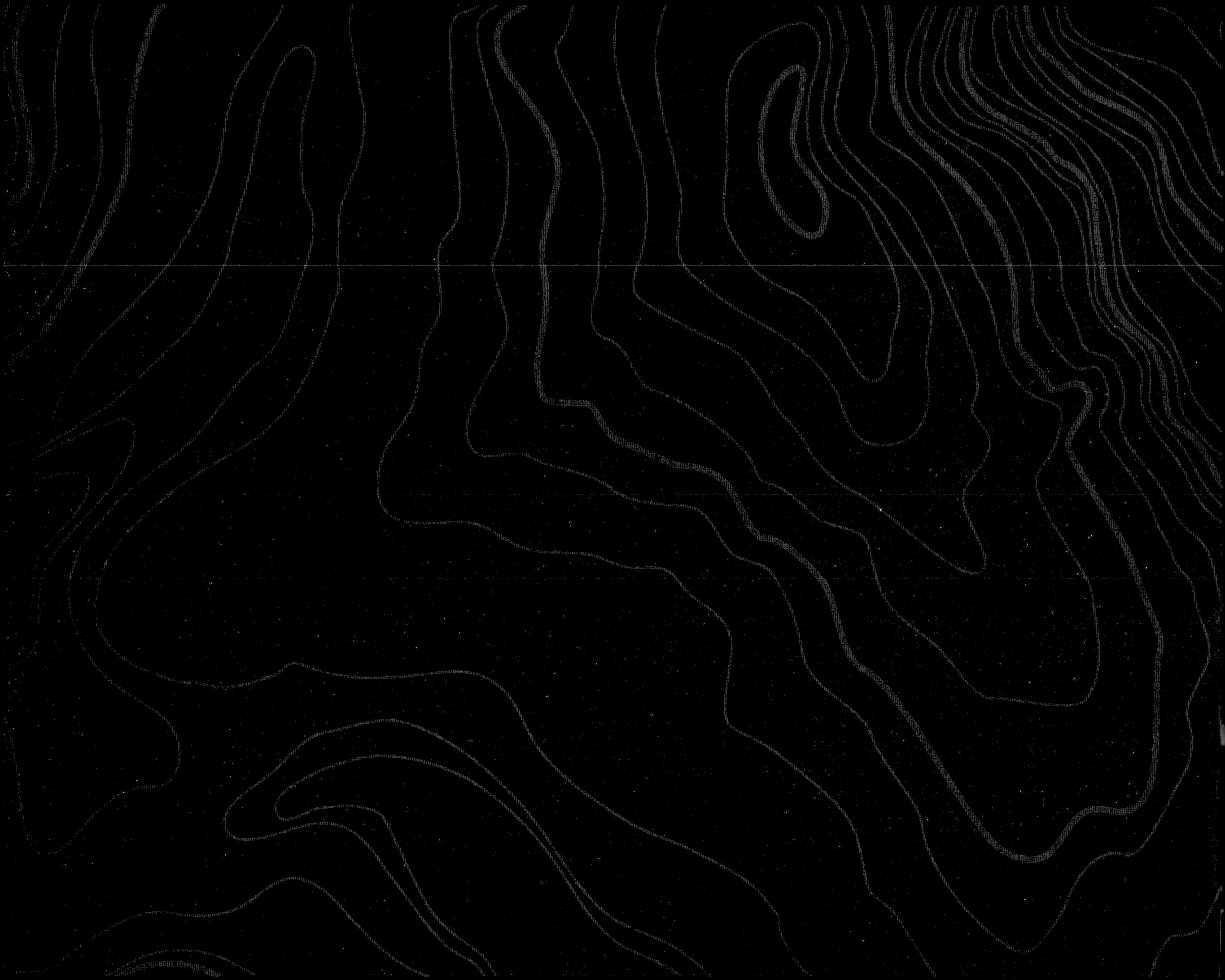

Hueco Tanks and Hueco Mountains

Hueco Tanks and Hueco Mountains

DISTANCE FROM EL PASO
32 miles northeast

LATITUDE
31°91'7" N

LONGITUDE
-106°04'4" W

ELEVATION
4,665 feet (1,422 meters)

AREA
860 acres
(348 hectares)

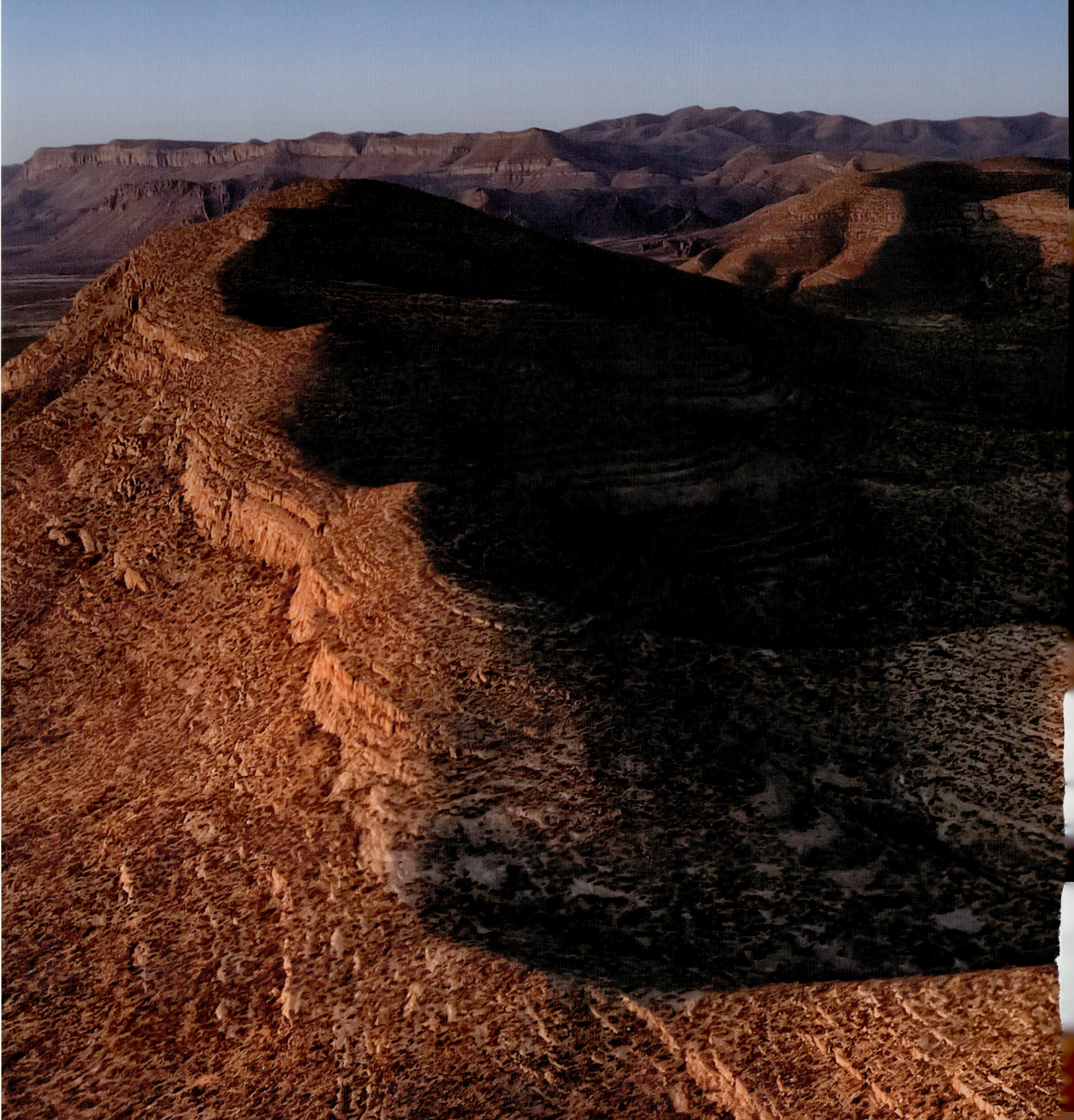

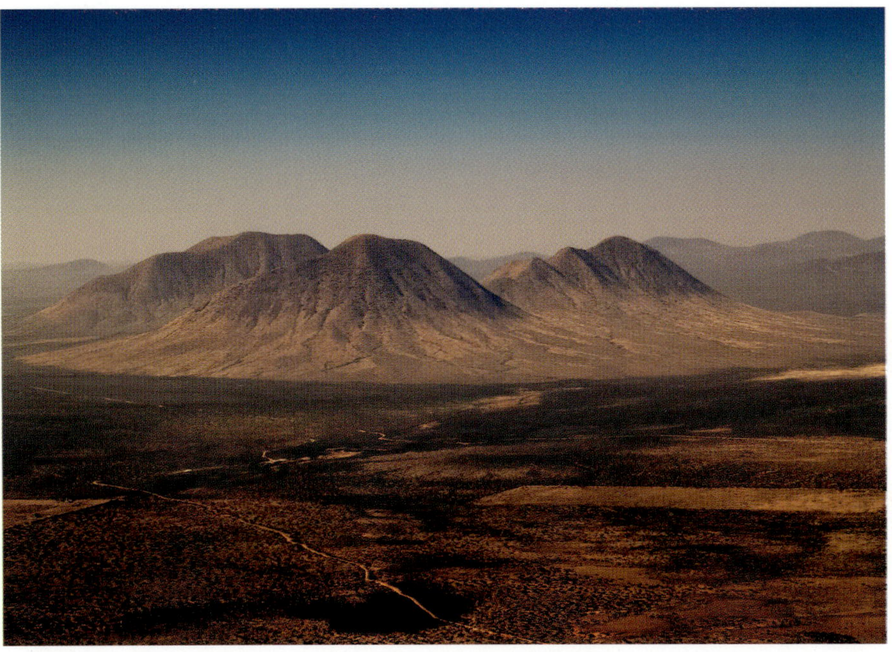

A flaming hot desert day—when the proverbial egg can be fried on a rock—is my favorite time to visit Hueco Tanks. The Hueco Tanks are regarded the world over as one of the best areas in the world for rock climbing. The formidable rocks, which seem to be arranged by pitch and toss, present an obvious but not daunting challenge. At best, I rank somewhere below amateur status as a rock climber, and might very well be a pro at stumbling, whether it's up or down. I can't say I've ever made it to the highest point here. The enjoyment for me is in my clueless but ever-so-careful methodology, negotiating from one level of boulders to the next—not to mention the simple pleasure of breathing the immaculate, flushed air. My improvisational drama comes when reaching an outlook offering an unobstructed view of the glorious, wide-open space sweeping its way to the Hueco Mountains, miles away. Over thirty million years ago, an upheaval of molten rock from the earth's interior created these four-hundred-foot-tall granite hills that seem to spring out of the Chihuahuan Desert floor outside of El Paso. There is an awesome, heart-expanding grandeur in this place.

Long before climbers discovered Hueco Tanks, Native Americans

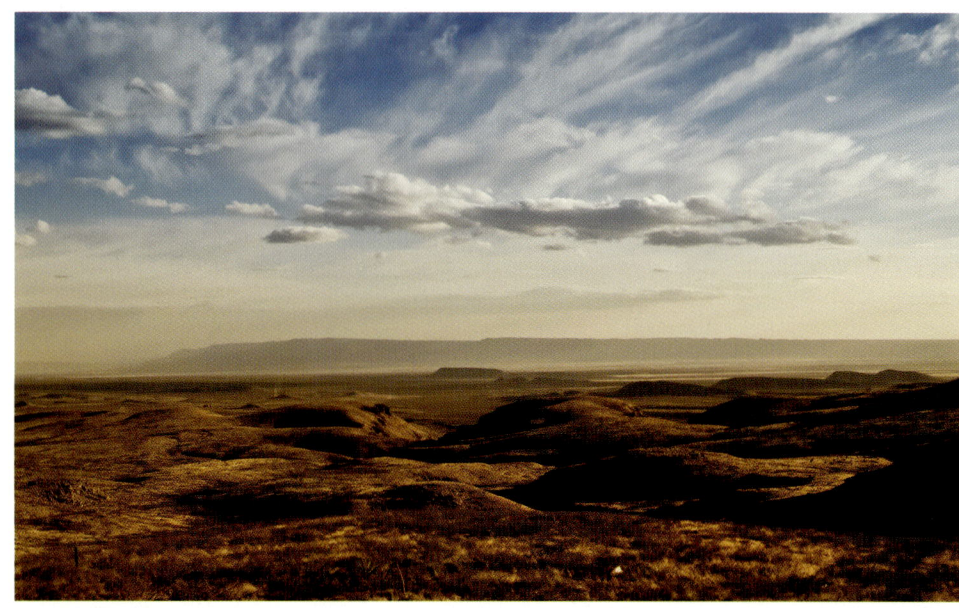

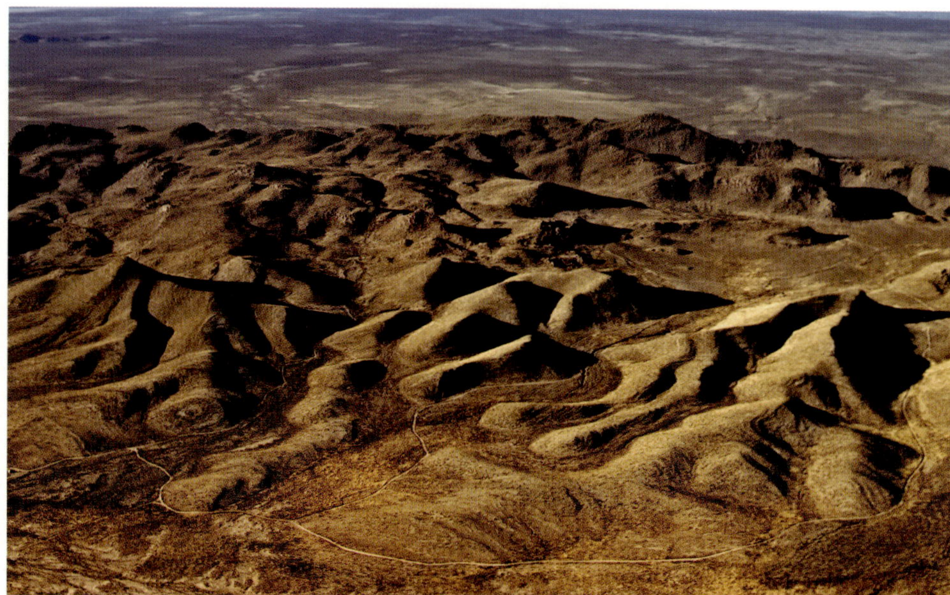

were drawn here because its *huecos*, a Spanish word for "hollow," trap and hold drinkable water—the most valuable desert commodity. Not much more than a century ago, Hueco Tanks held the only dependable source of water between the Pecos River and El Paso.

The Hueco Mountains rise in southern New Mexico and extend twenty-seven miles south into Texas, generally along the El Paso-Hudspeth County line just east of the city of El Paso. The highest point of the range is the Cerro Alto Mountain (6,787 feet).

Lying between the Hueco and Franklin Mountains, the Hueco Bolson, a dropped-down area four thousand feet above sea level, contains sedimentary fill nearly nine thousand feet thick.

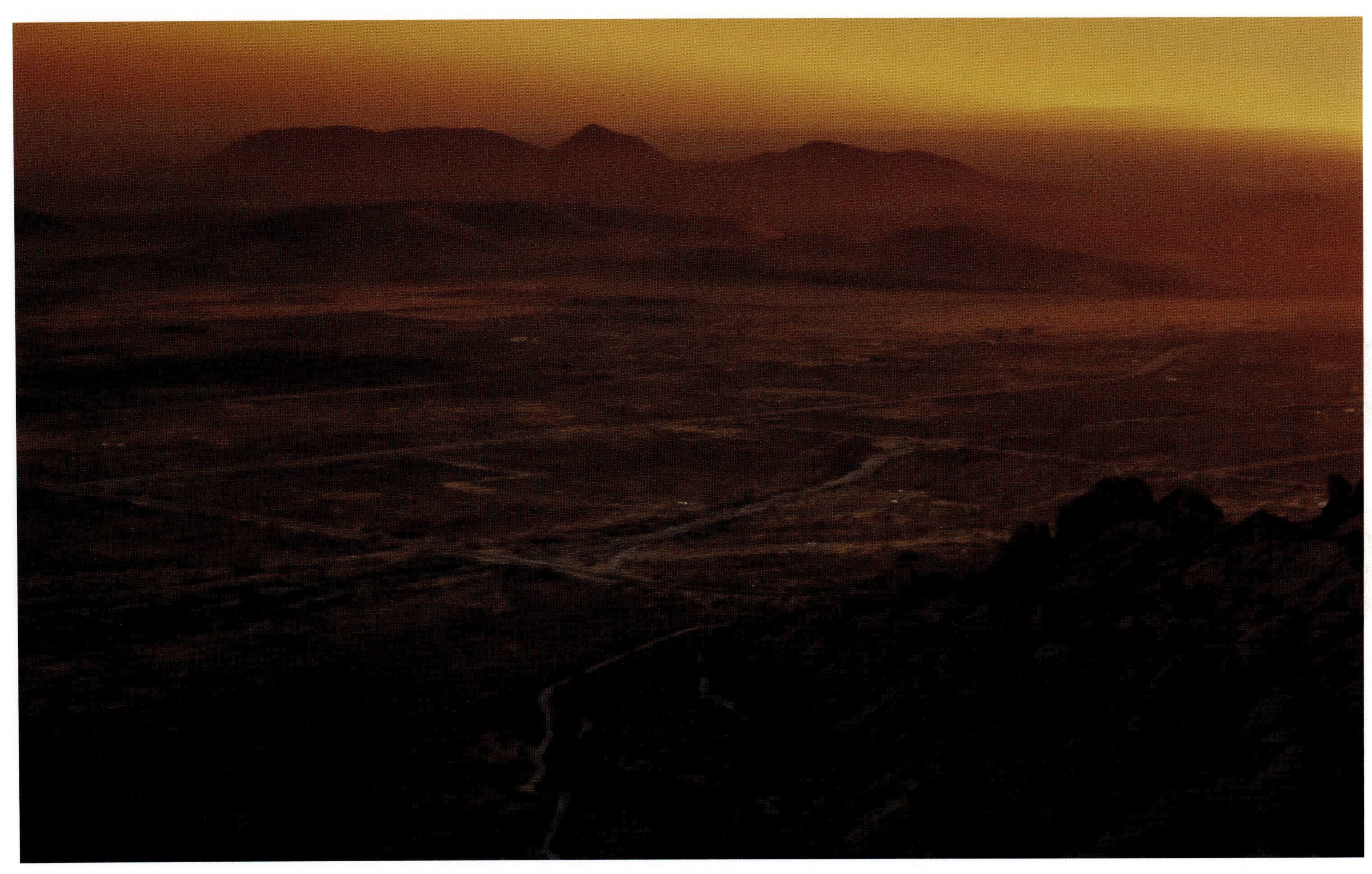

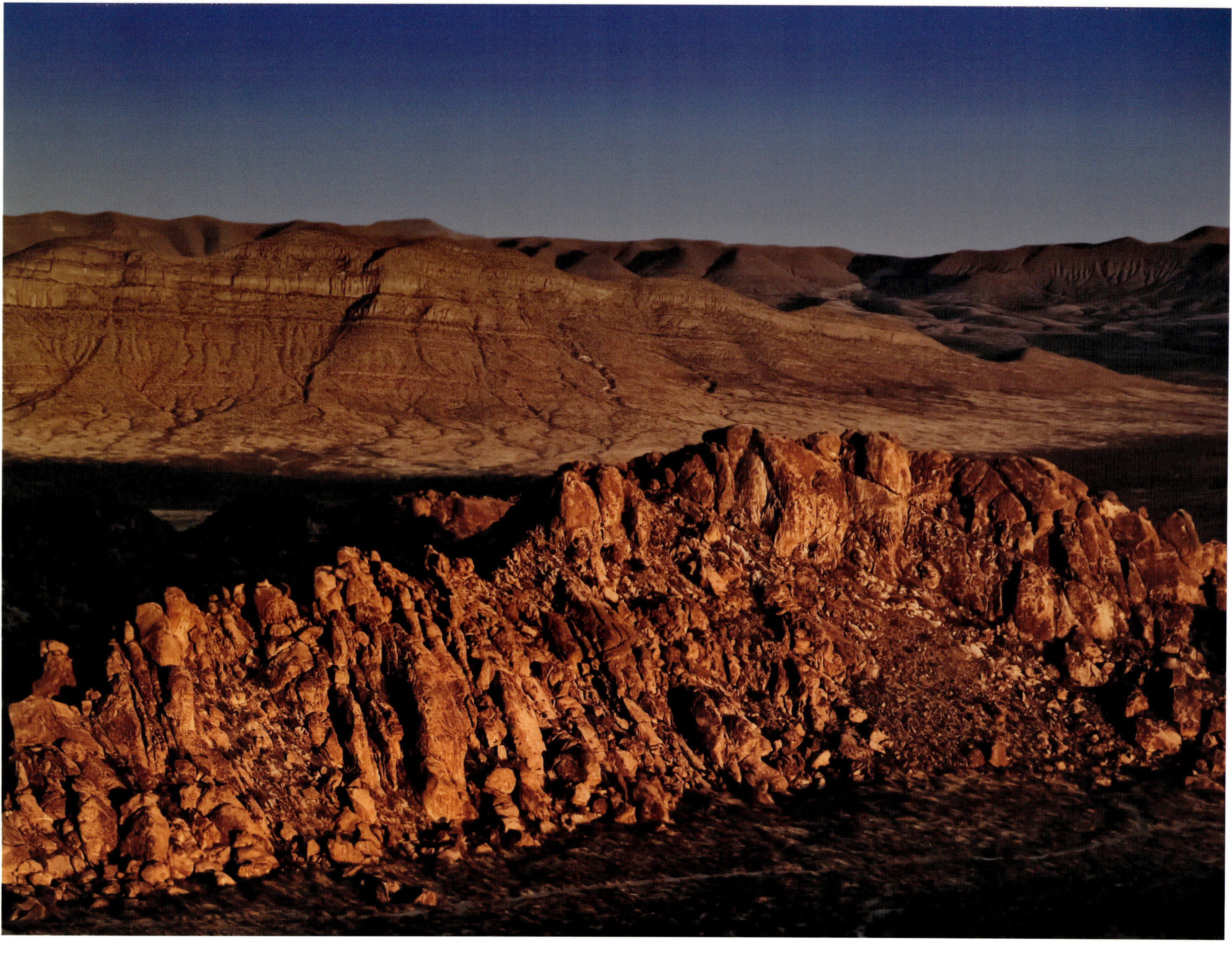

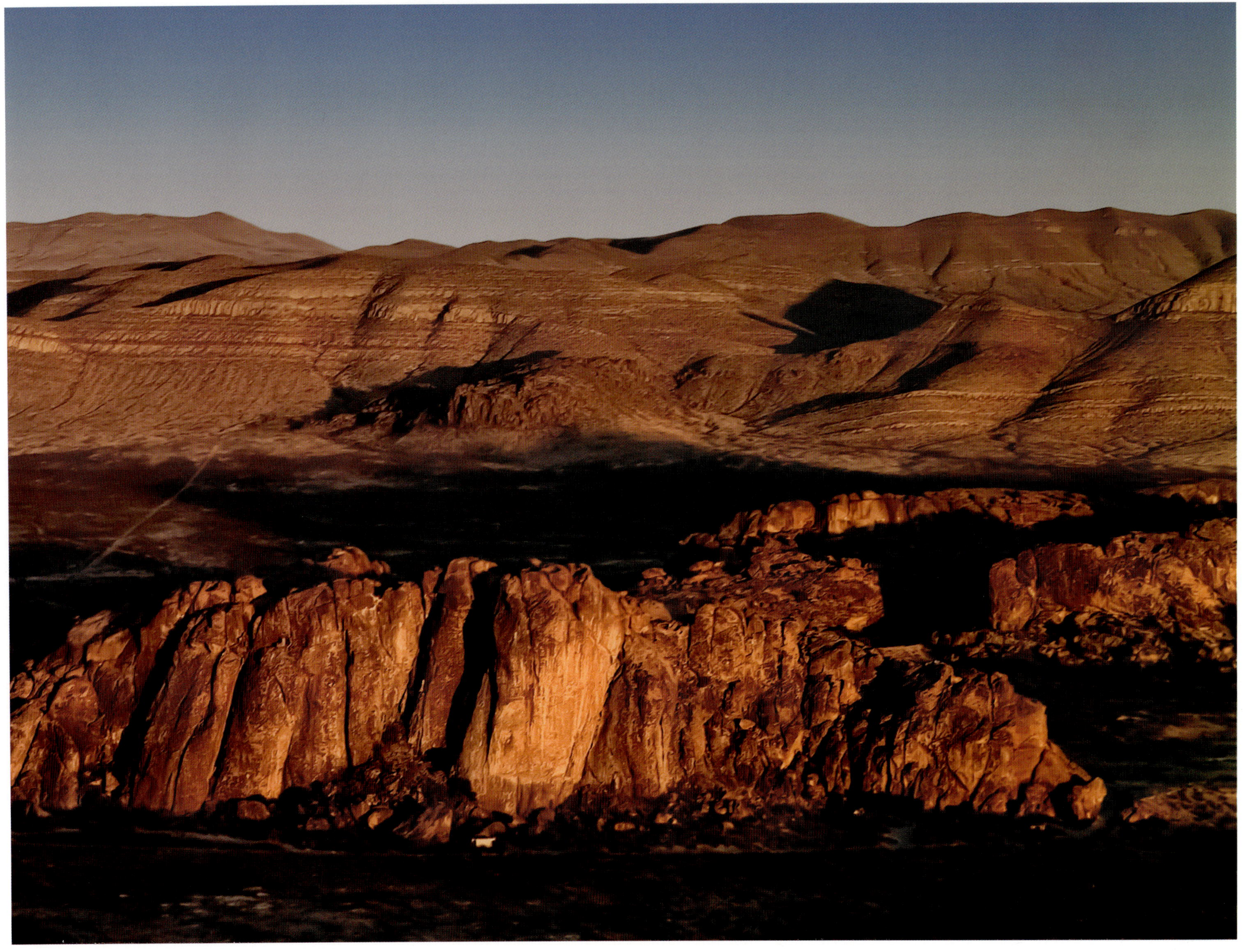

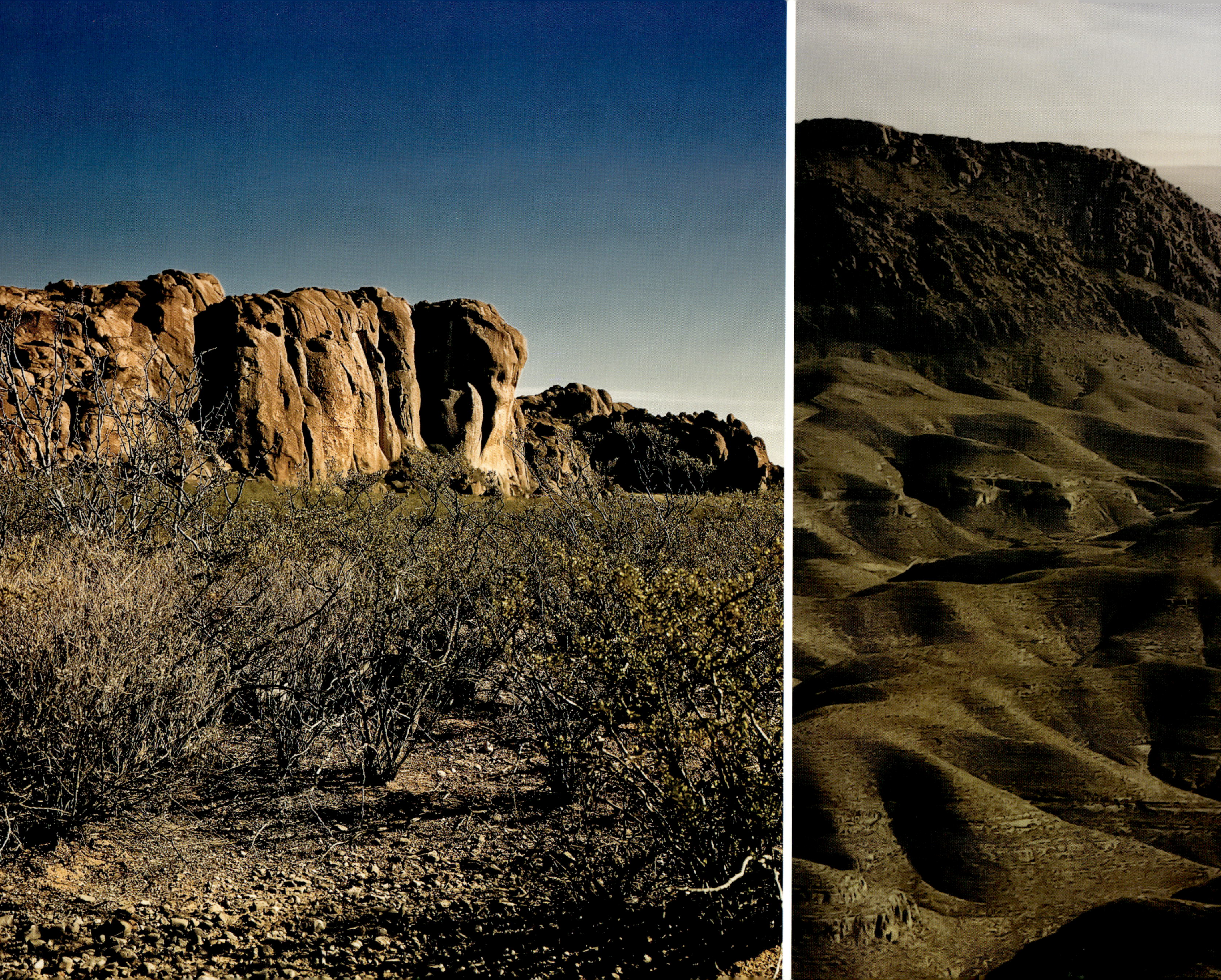

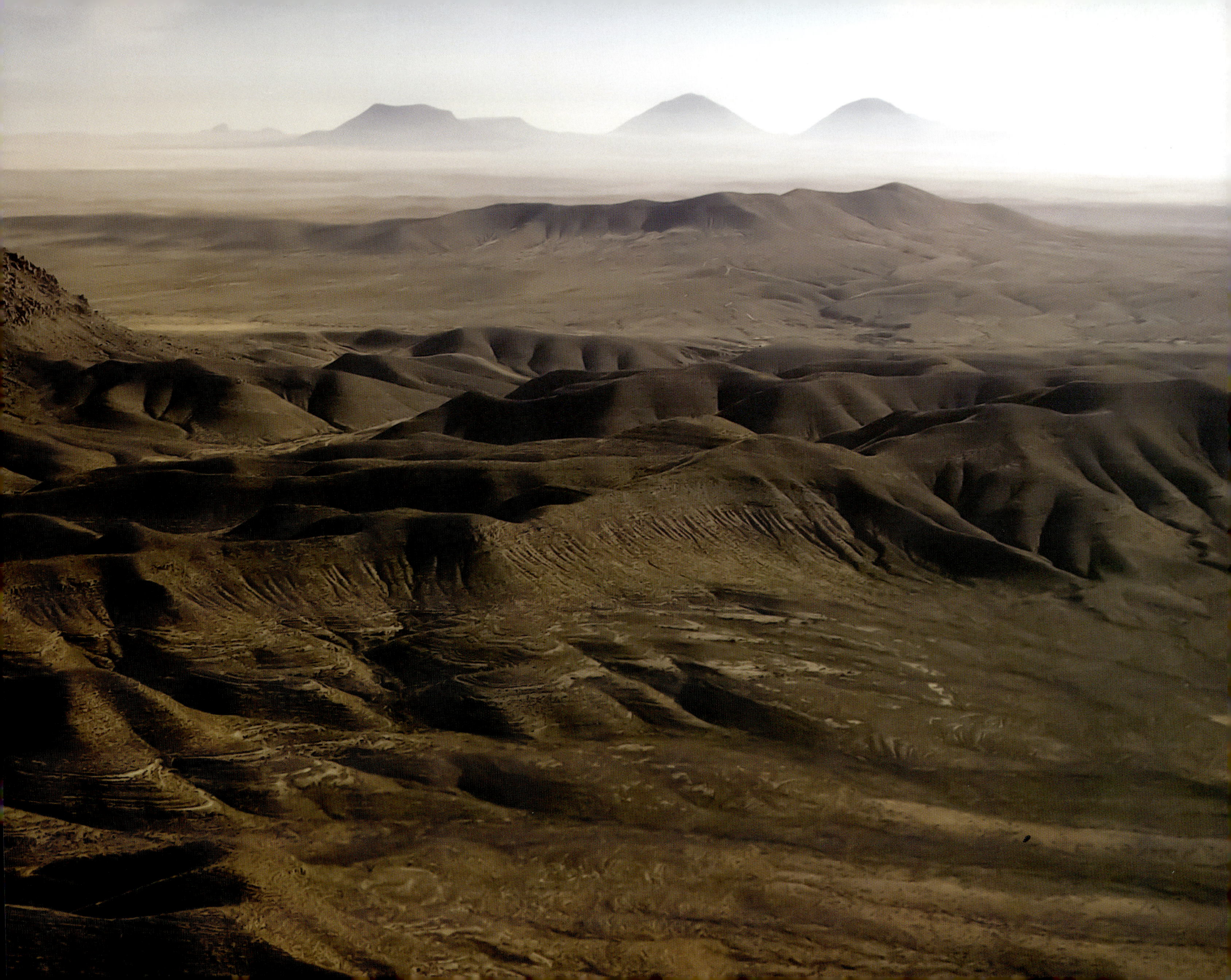

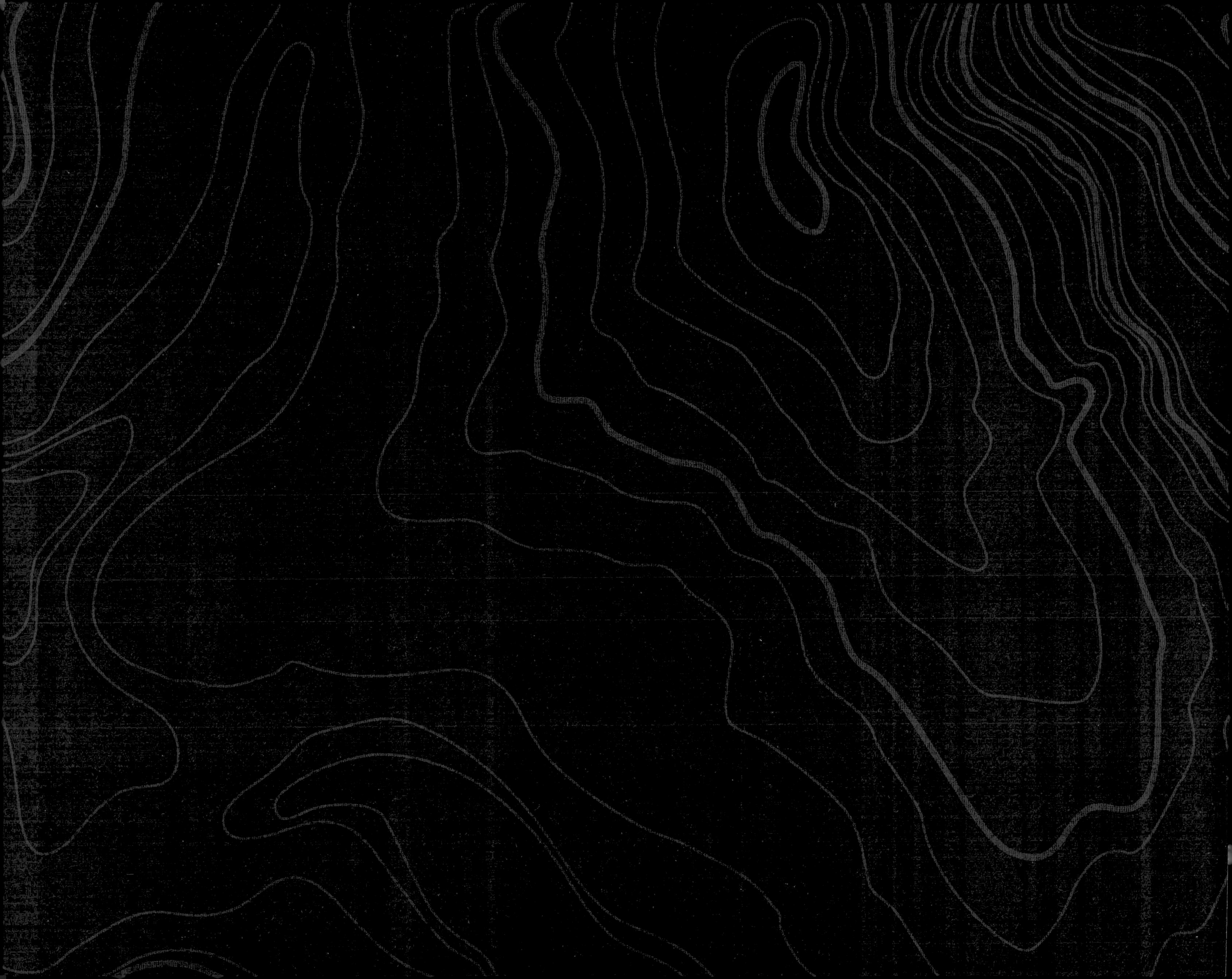

Franklin Mountains

Franklin Mountains

DISTANCE FROM EL PASO
0 miles

LATITUDE
31°54'10"

LONGITUDE
-106°29'36" W

ELEVATION
7,192 feet (2,192 meters)

HIGHEST POINT
North Franklin Mountain

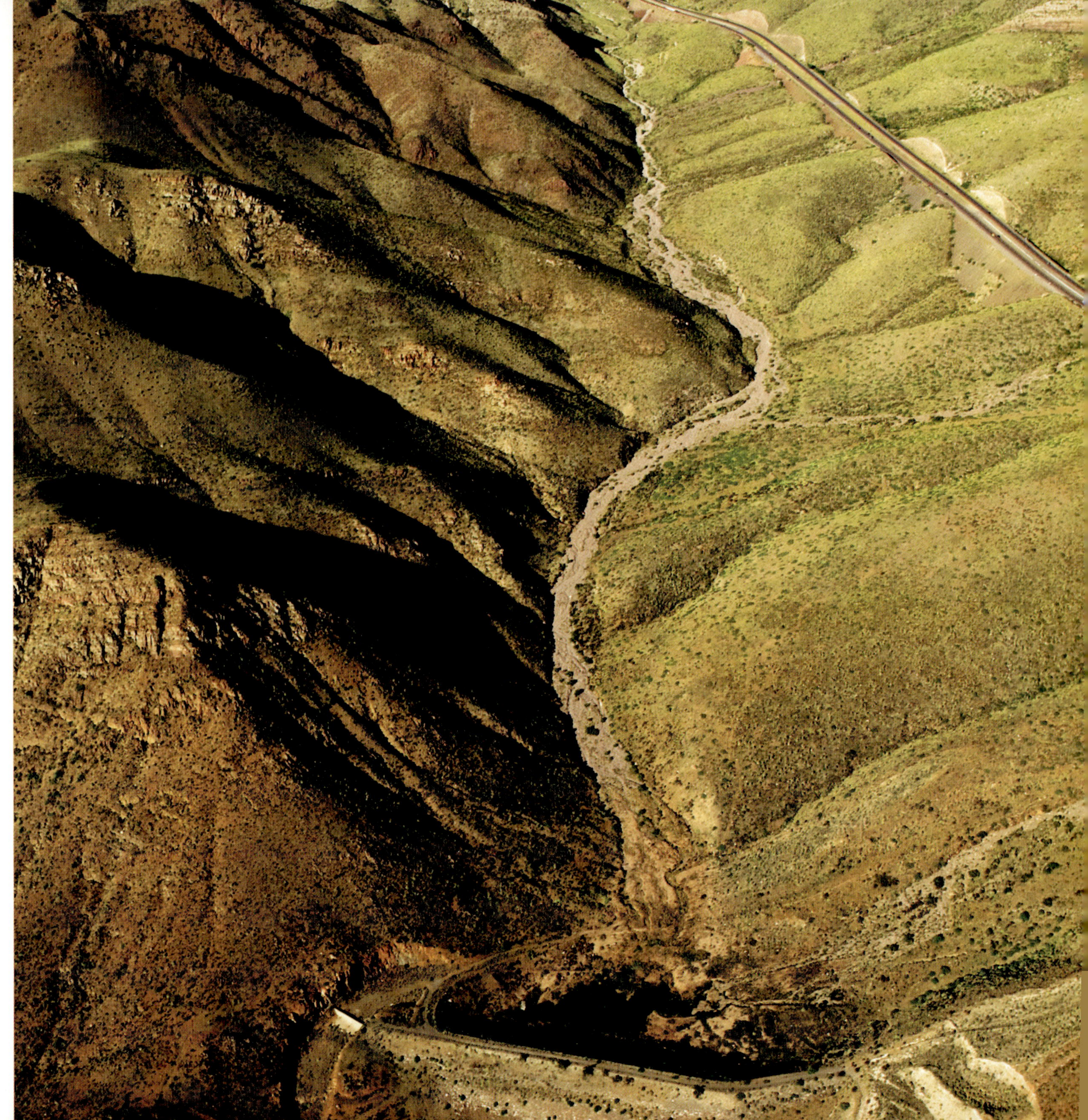

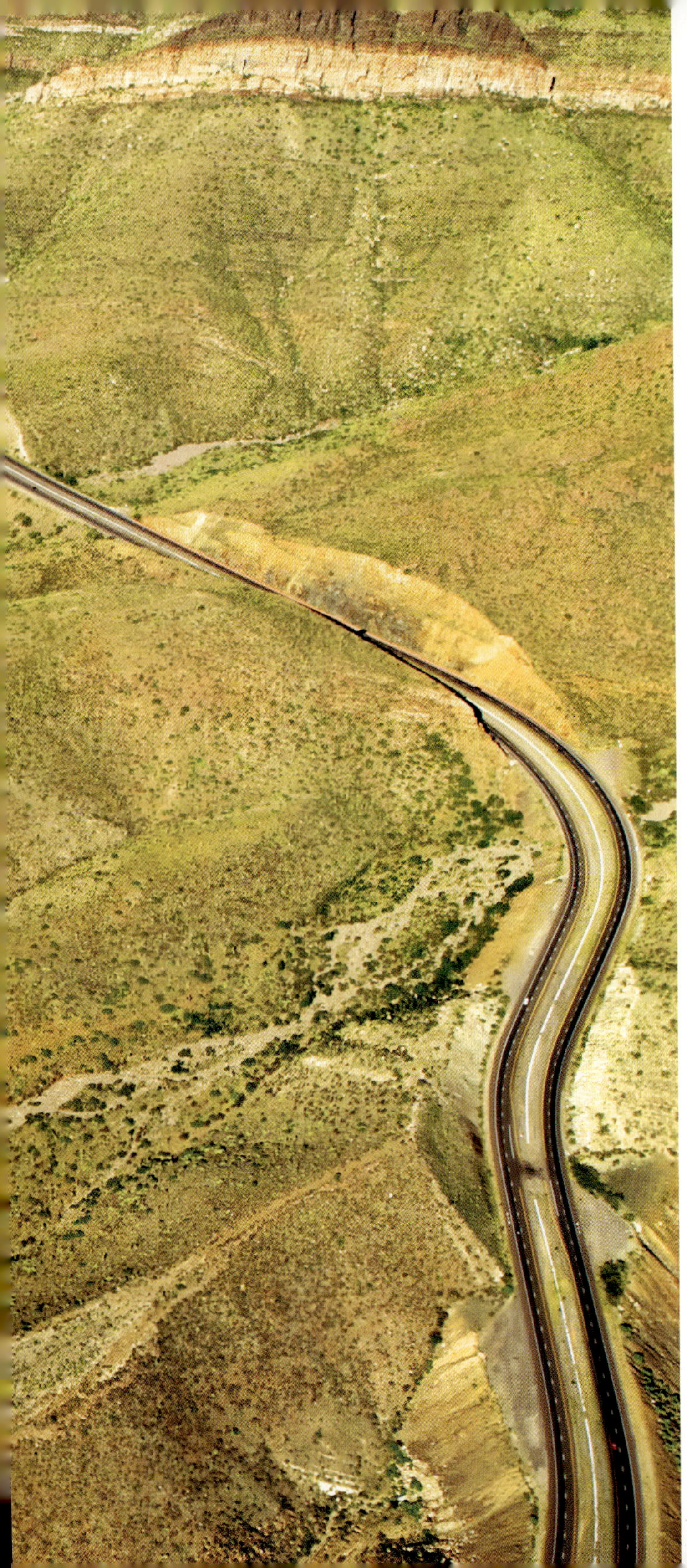

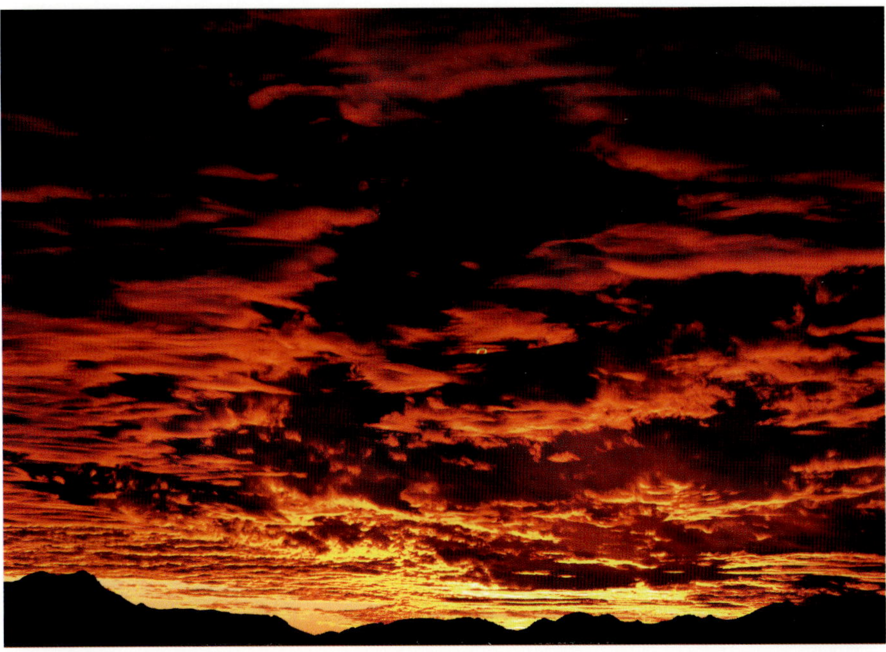

The Franklin Mountains form the northern wall of the Paso del Norte (Pass of the North)—the pass that leads from Mexico to the United States. Native Americans inhabited the area for upwards of eleven thousand years, and over the last several centuries the pass has seen a multitude of soldiers, refugees, settlers, and explorers streaming both ways.

These peaks now form Franklin Mountains State Park, which embraces more than twenty-four thousand acres (thirty-seven square miles), all within the city limits of El Paso. It is the largest urban park in the United States. The Franklin peaks form the southern tip of the Rocky Mountain range. The highest peak is North Franklin Mountain, at 7,192 feet. Other major peaks include Ranger, Comanche, Mount Franklin, South Franklin Mountain, and Anthony's Nose. Major canyons, all draining east or west except for McKelligon, are Vinton, Avispa, Hitt, McKelligon, and Fusselman—the latter named for Deputy US Marshal Charles H. Fusselman, who was gunned down there during a clash with rustlers in 1890.

Formed during the same late Cretaceous period as the Hueco Mountains, the Franklins are called

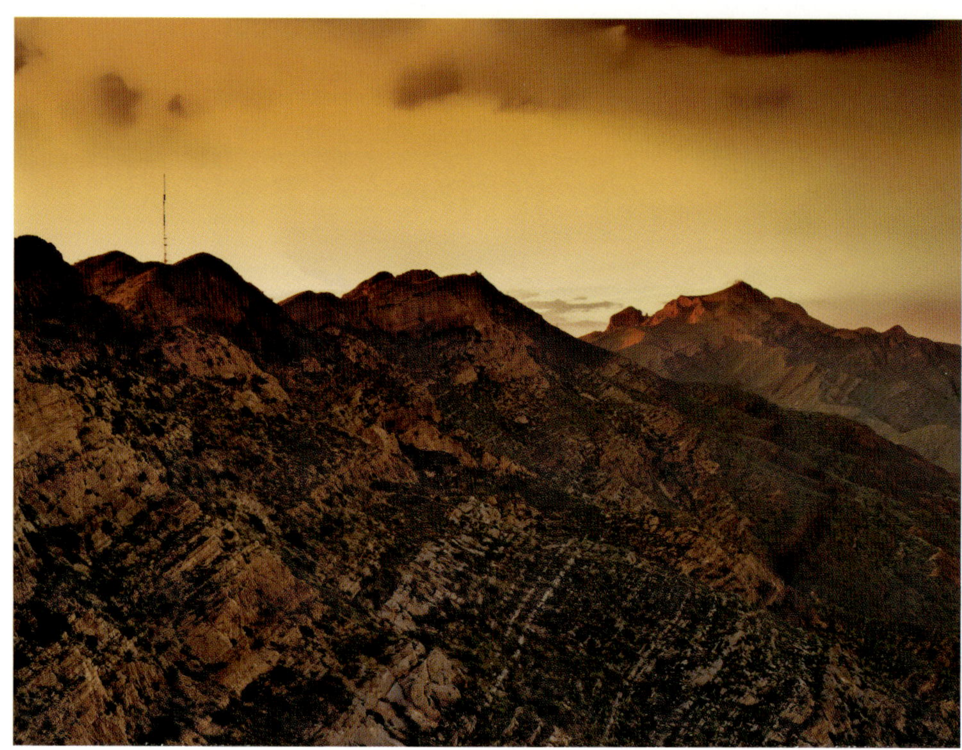

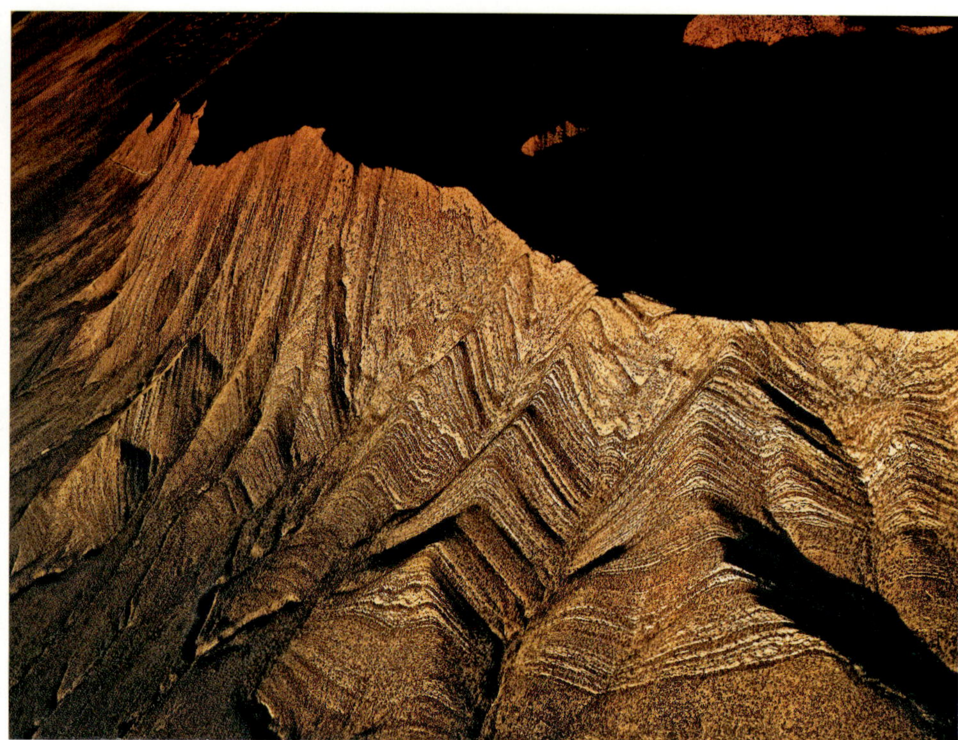

tilted-block-fault mountains by geologists. Their layers reveal rocks from the Precambrian era more than 570 million years old. Plants and animals typical of the Chihuahuan Desert can be found here, along with mountain lions, deer, and the occasional black bear. A few natural springs support stands of native trees such as hackberry, oak, and cottonwood in remote areas of the park.

Standing at the apex of Transmountain Road, or atop the Franklin Mountains, you can observe the magnificent sunsets for which El Paso is known. Suddenly, the fiery ball of the sun seems to slip below the desert floor, and the royal-blue sky rapidly transforms with bursts of splendid golden hues, as if Mother Nature's paintbrush sweeps across the heavens. In an instant, natural fireworks have filled the sky.

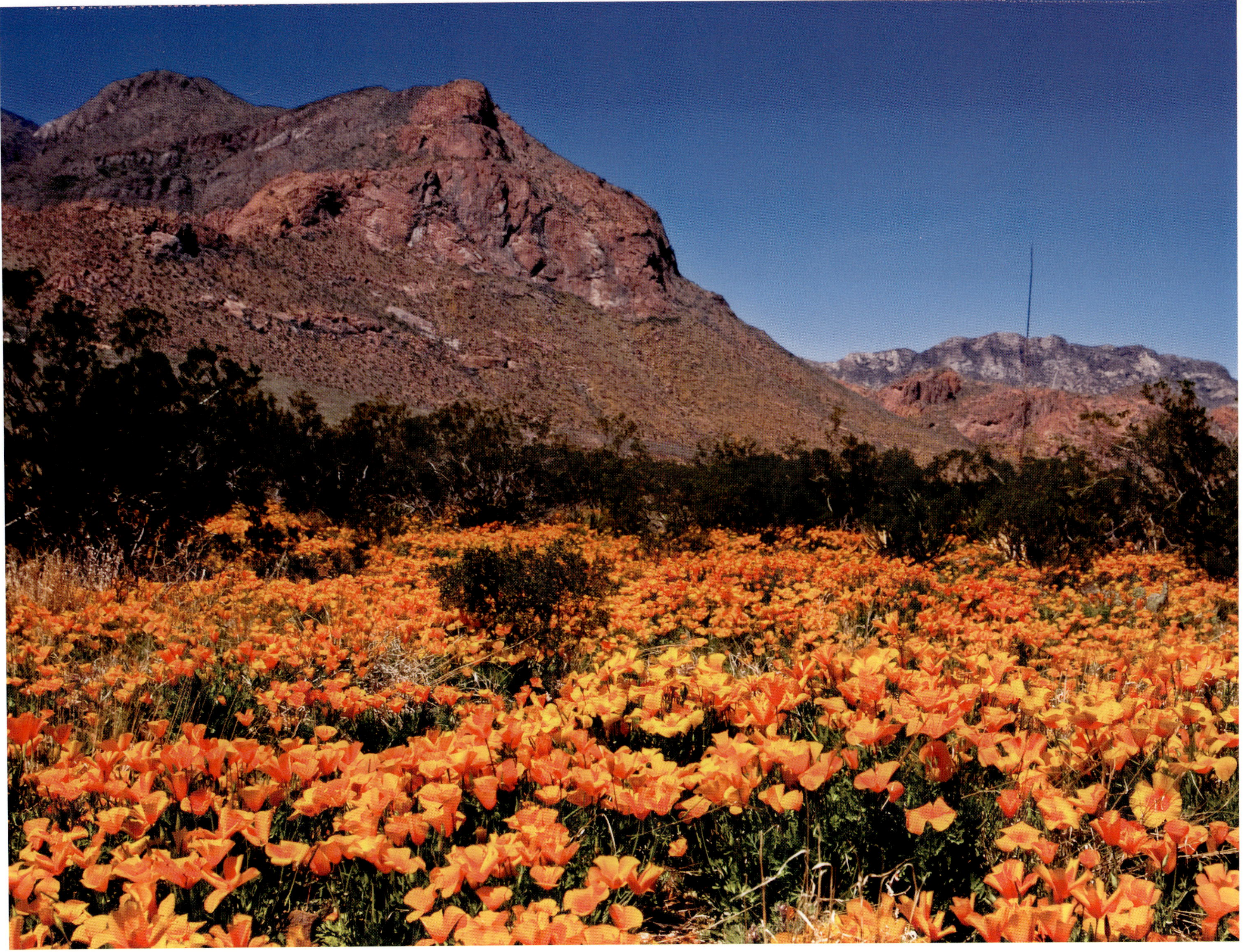

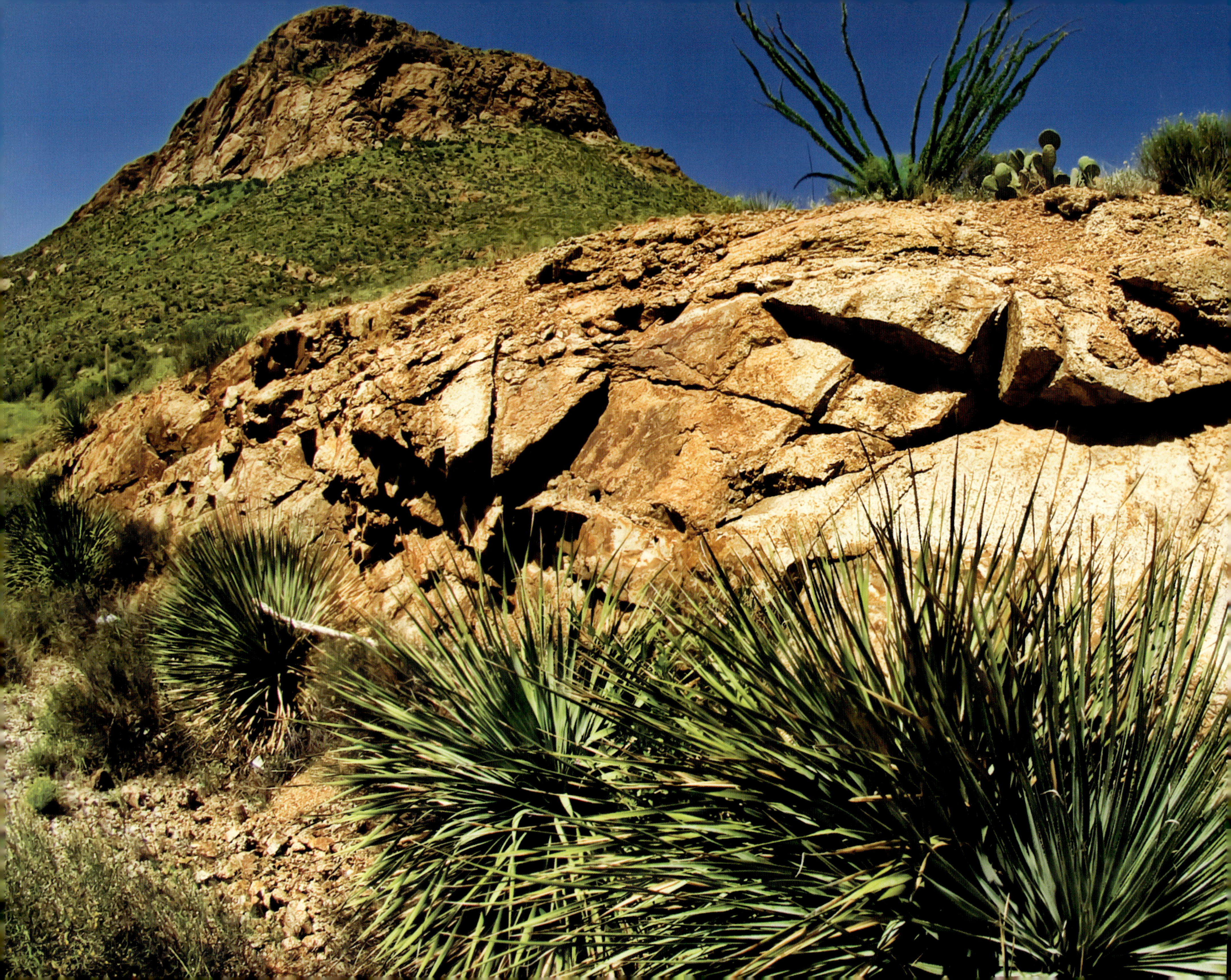

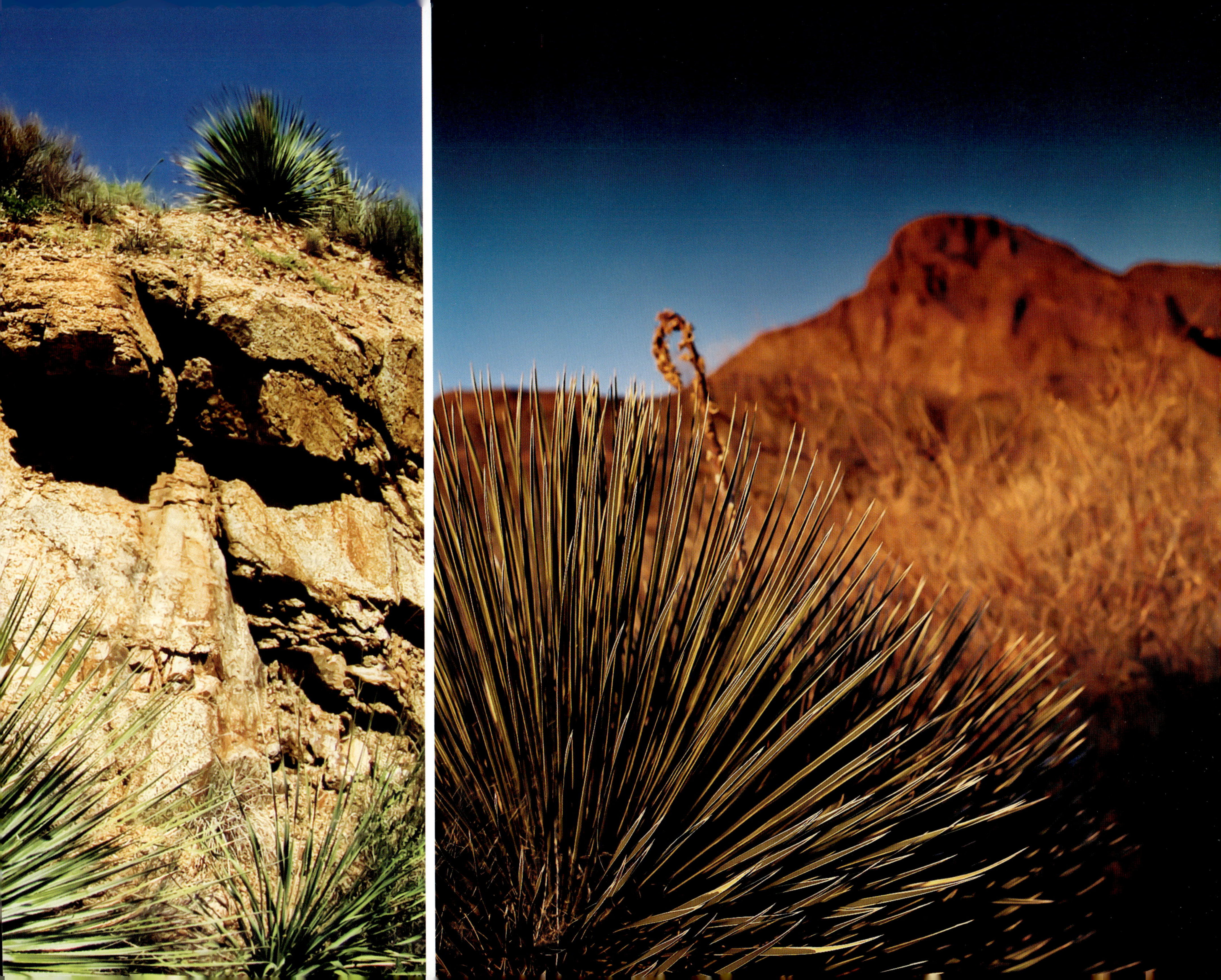

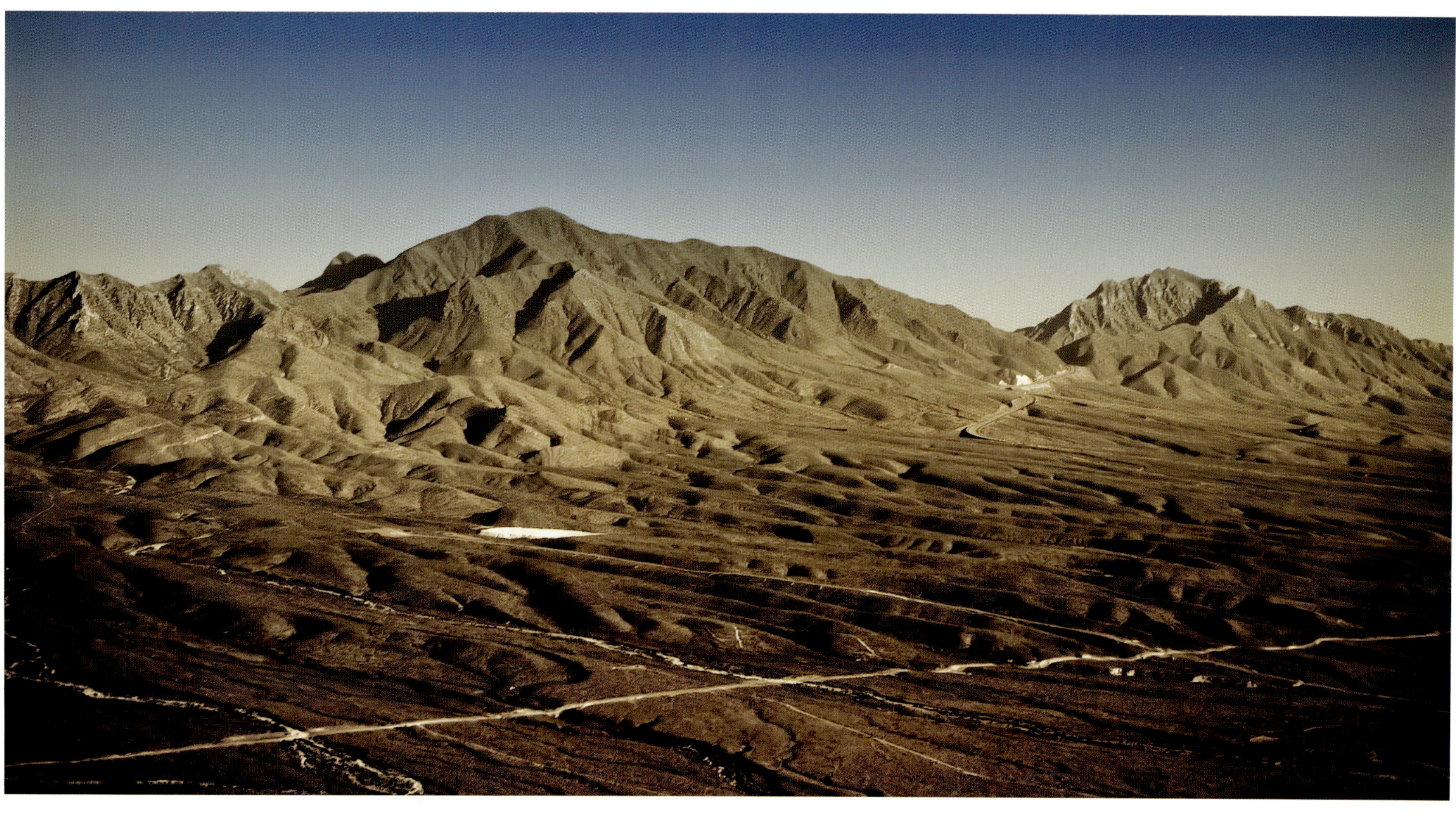

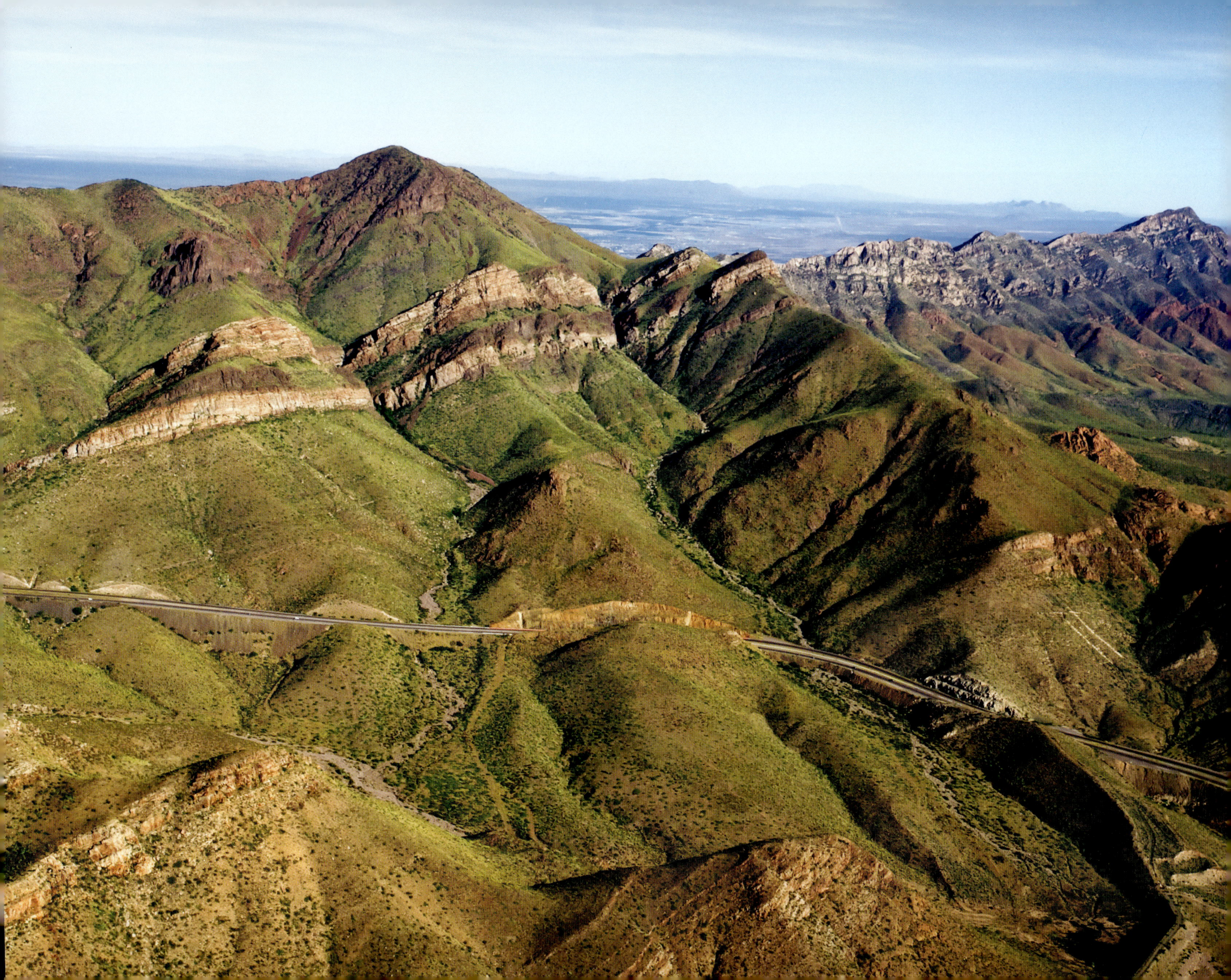

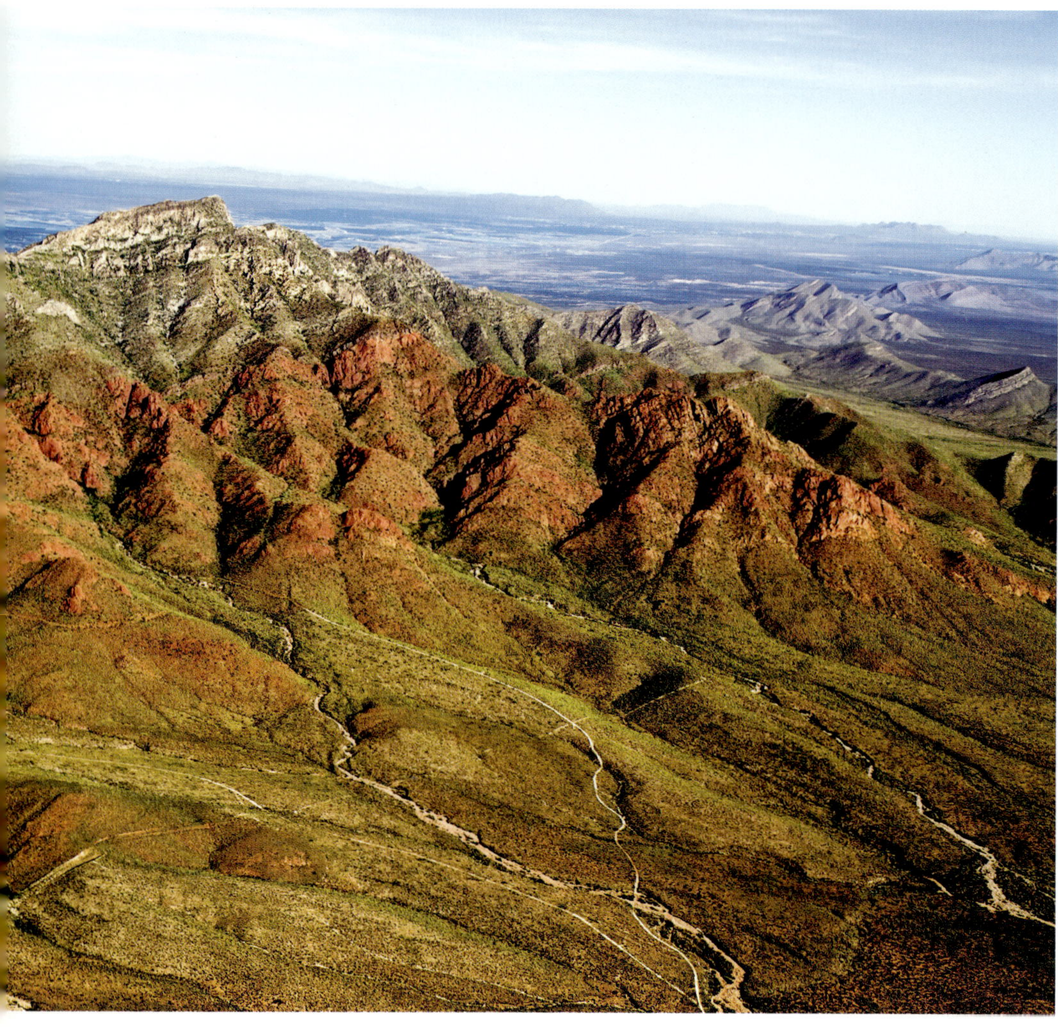

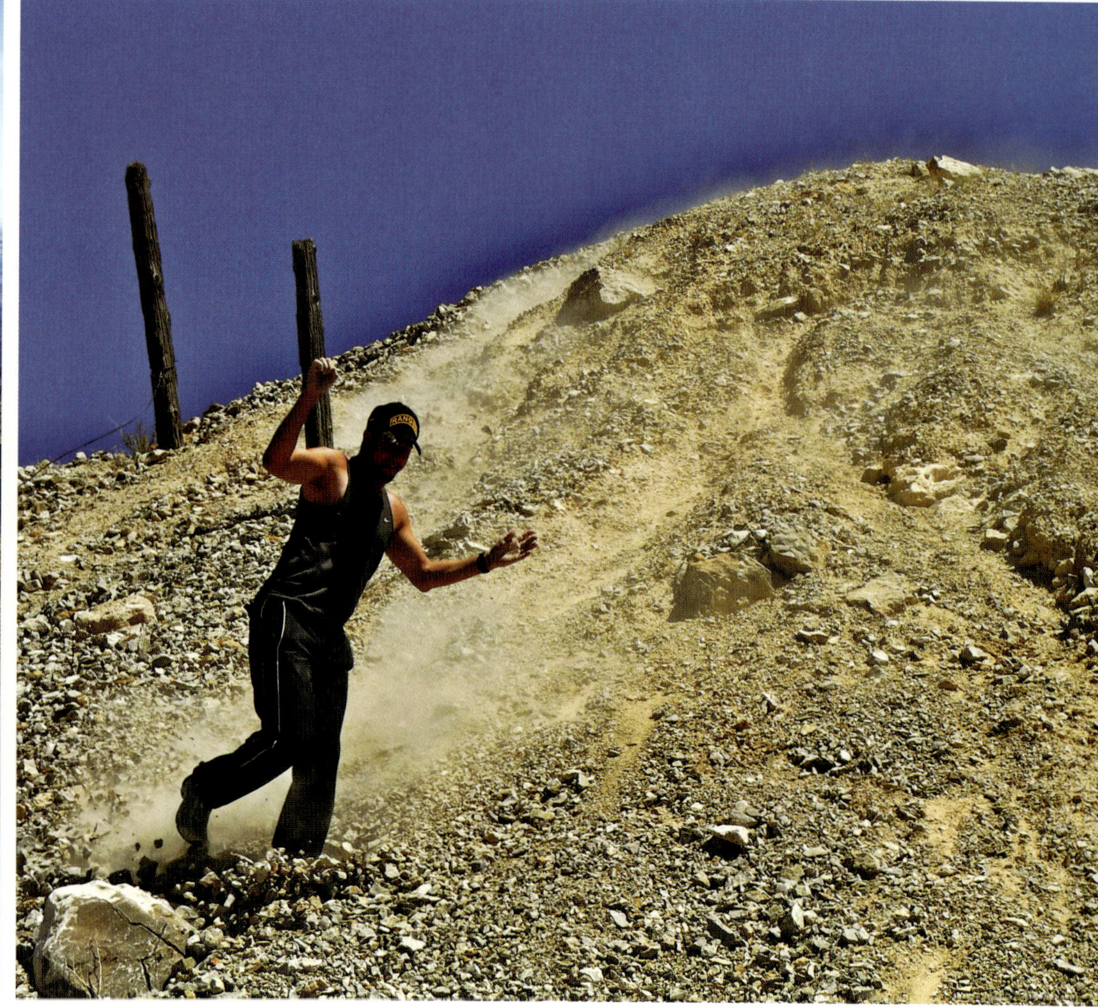

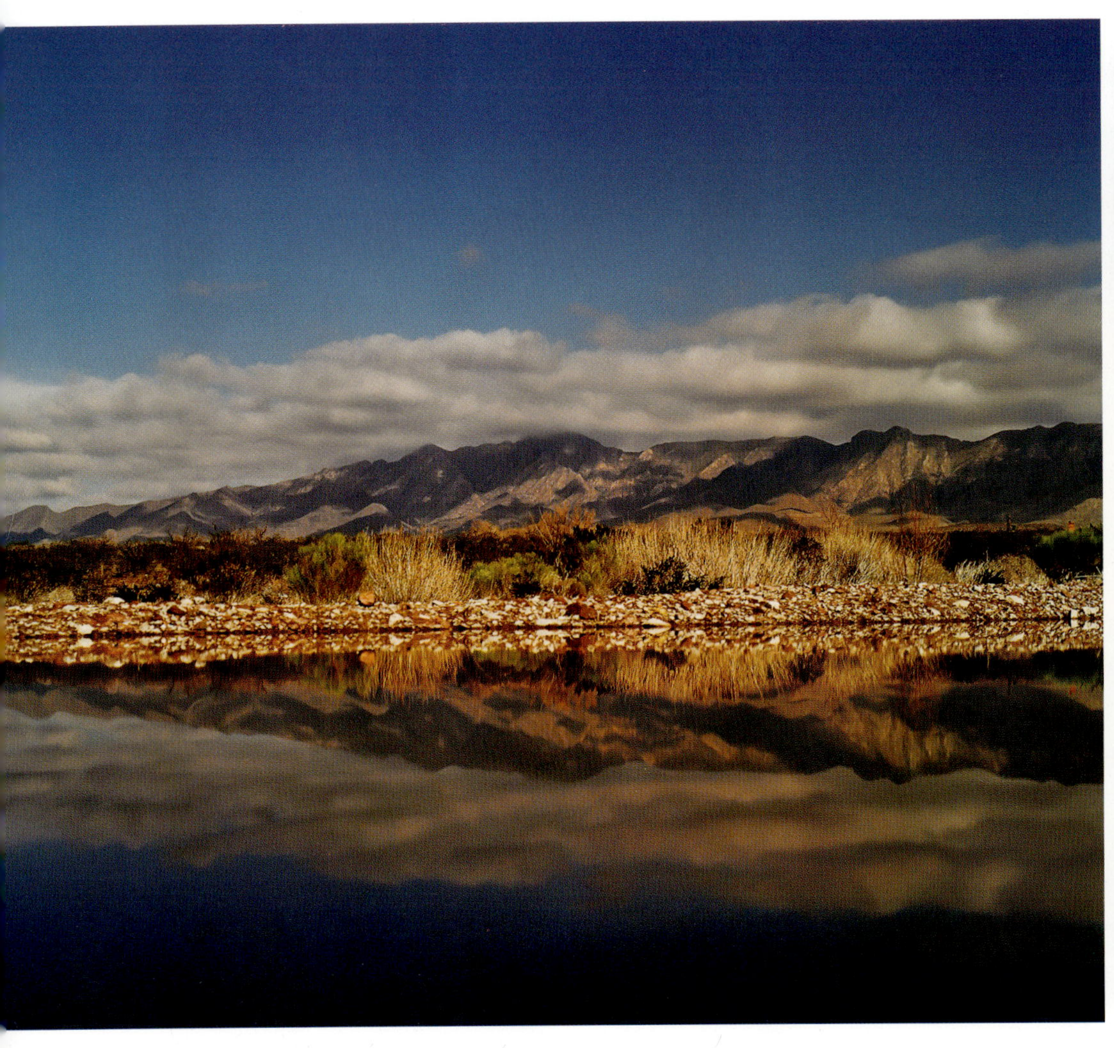

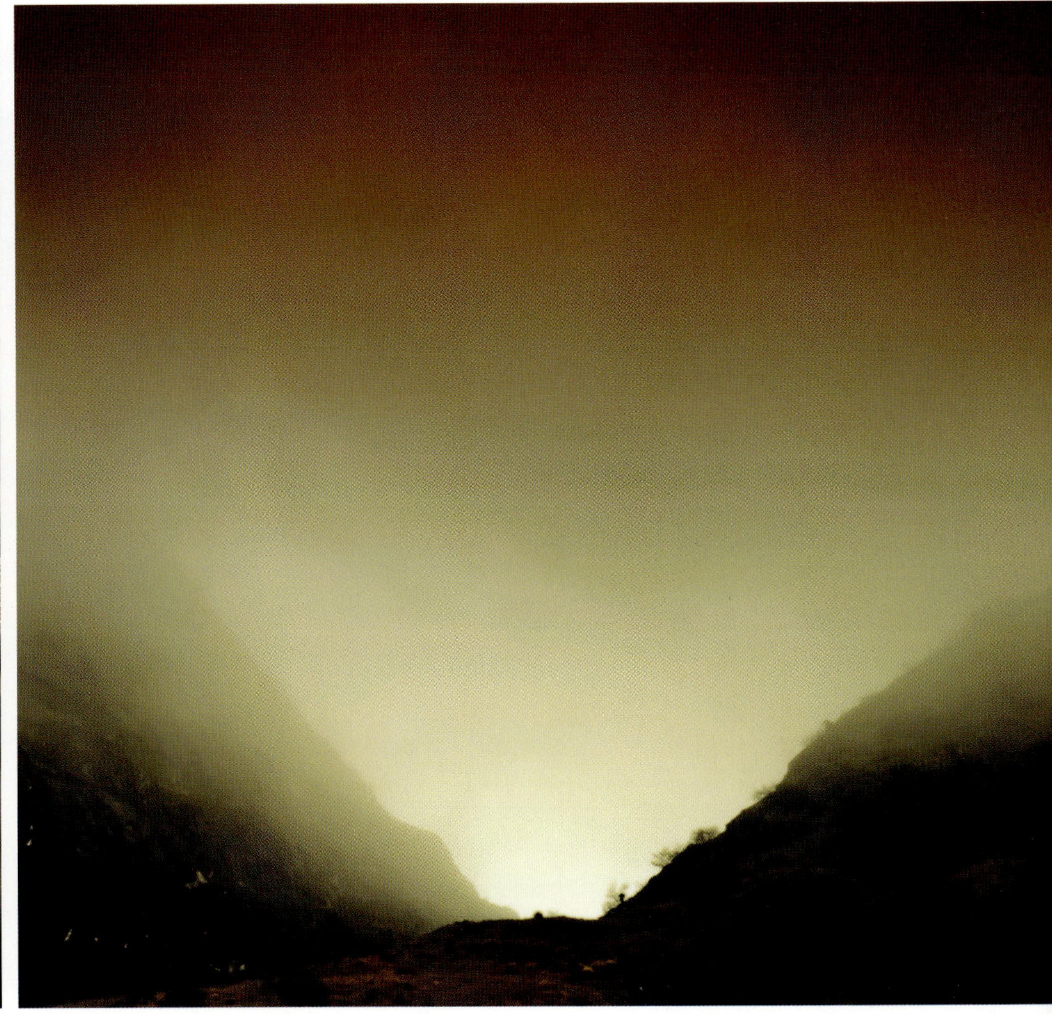

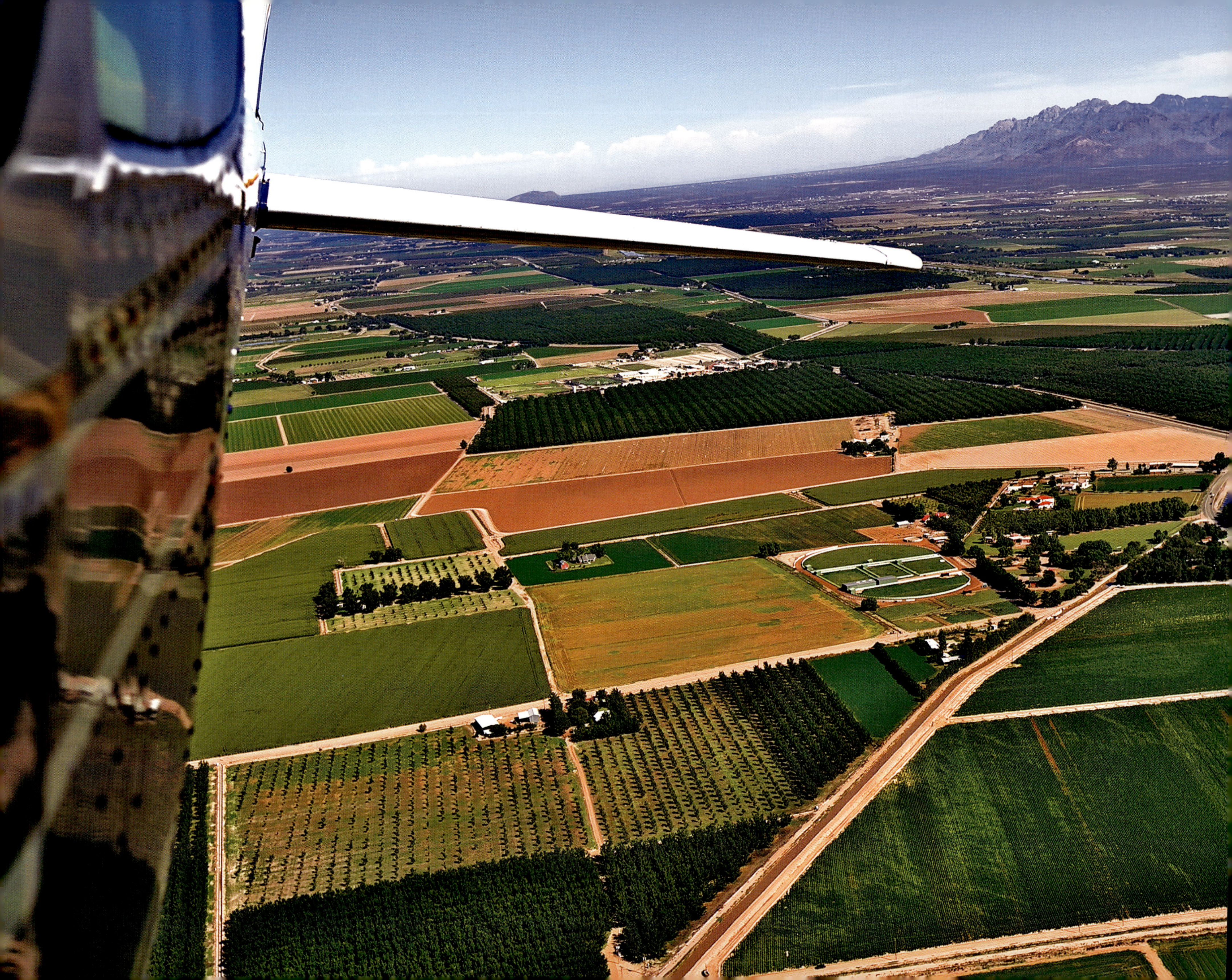

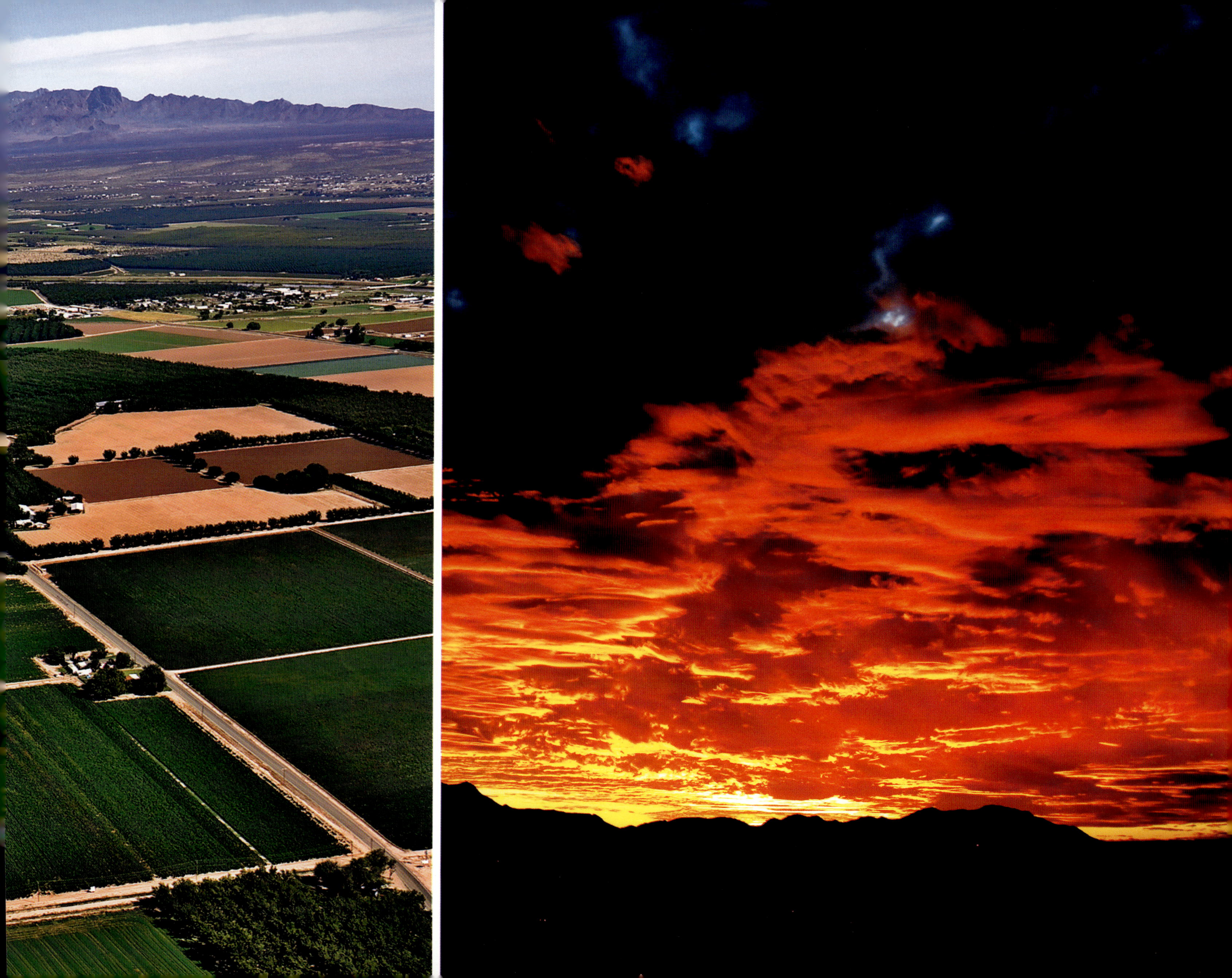

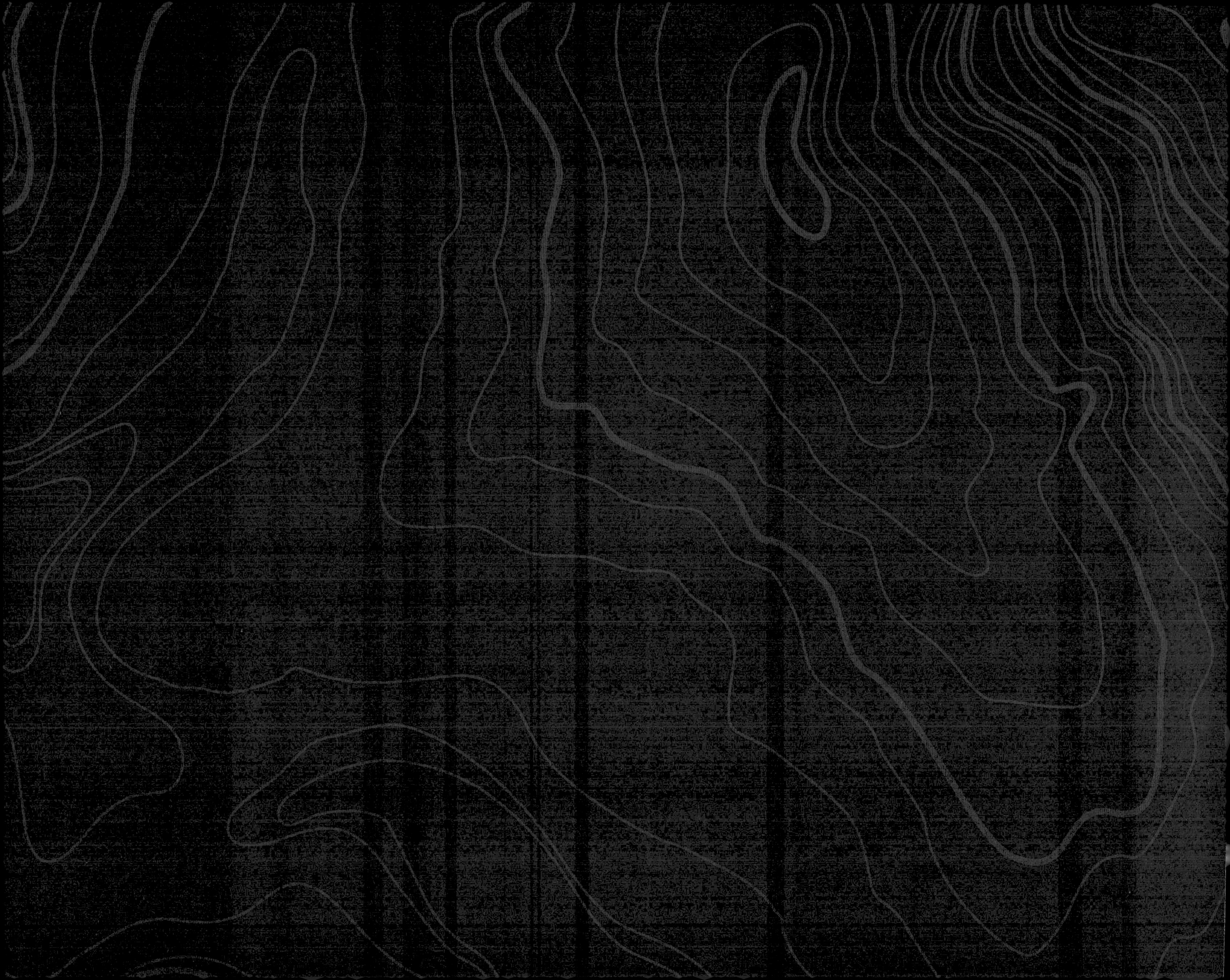

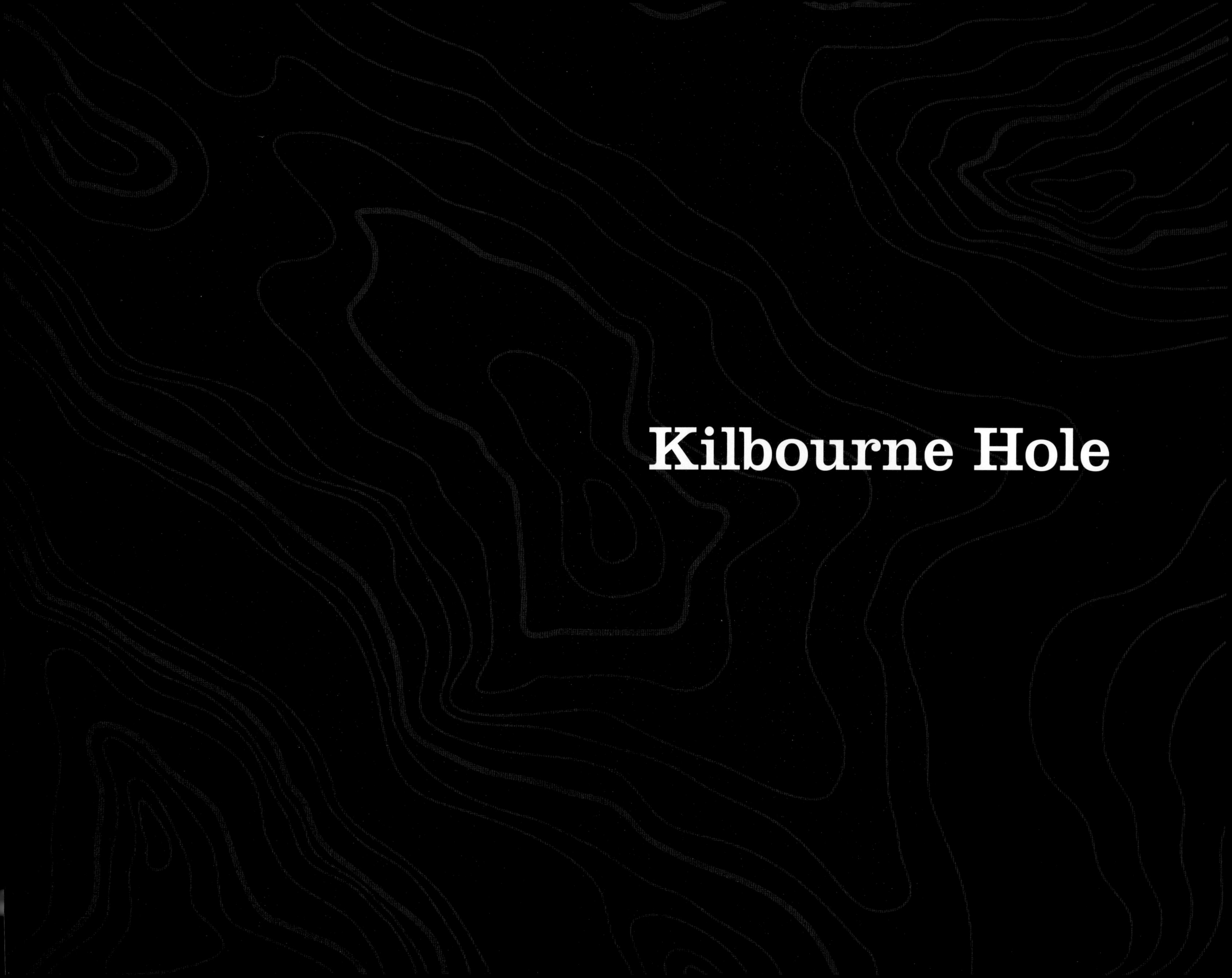

Kilbourne Hole

Kilbourne Hole

DISTANCE FROM EL PASO
30 miles west

LATITUDE
31°58'19"

LONGITUDE
-106°57'53" W

ELEVATION
4,239 feet (1,292 meters)

CRATER DIAMETER
1.5 x 2.1 miles
(2.4 x 3.4 kilometers)

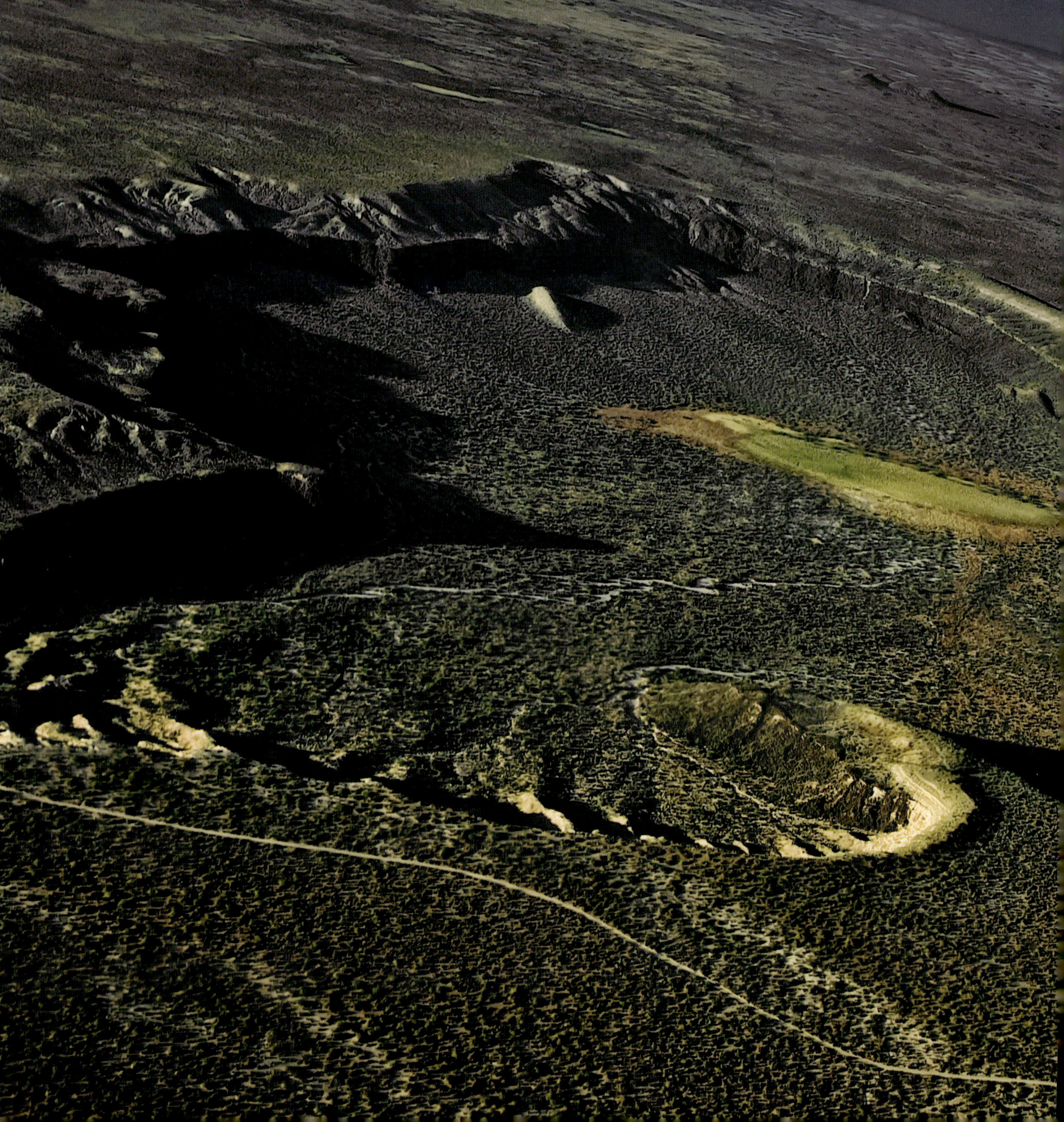

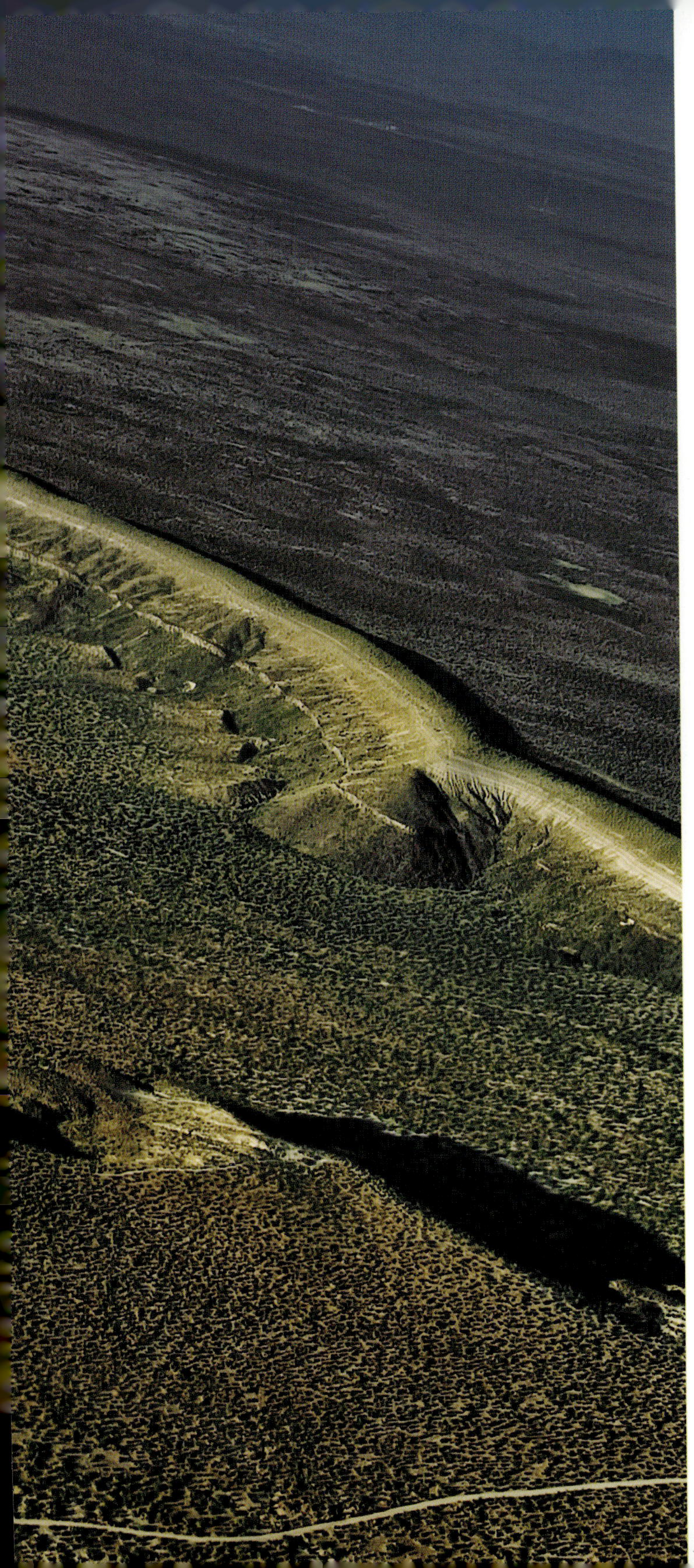

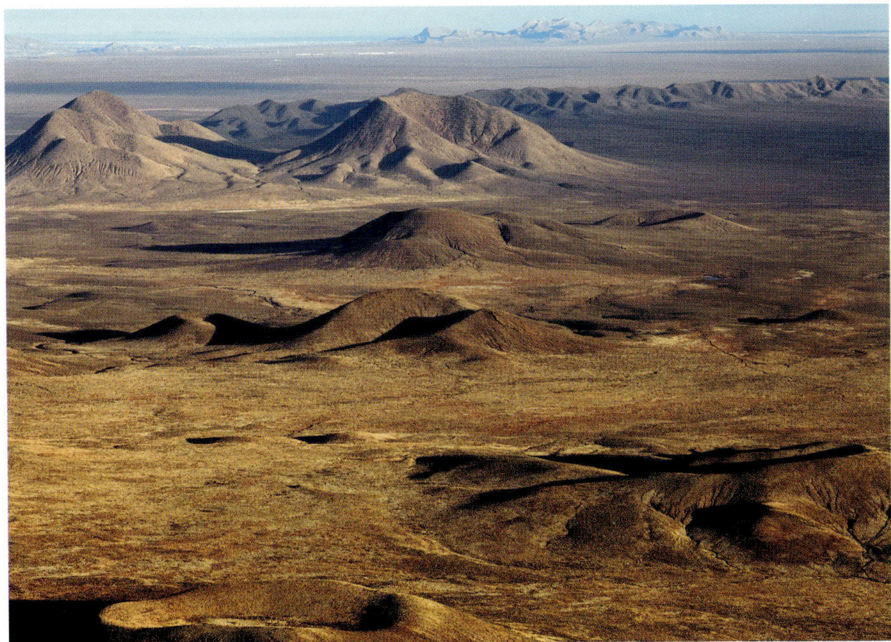

In southern Doña Ana County, in a desert basin between the Rio Grande and the Potrillo Mountains, there lies a crater known as Kilbourne Hole, which is all that remains of an ancient volcanic explosion. Declared a National Natural Landmark in 1975, the crater is 1.7 miles long and hundreds of feet deep. It is believed to be between twenty-four thousand and one hundred thousand years old. Scattered over the site are what look like ordinary rocks, but they are the cooled remains of molten chunks hurled out of the ancient volcano's vent. Cracked open, many of them reveal a sparkling interior of yellow-green peridot.

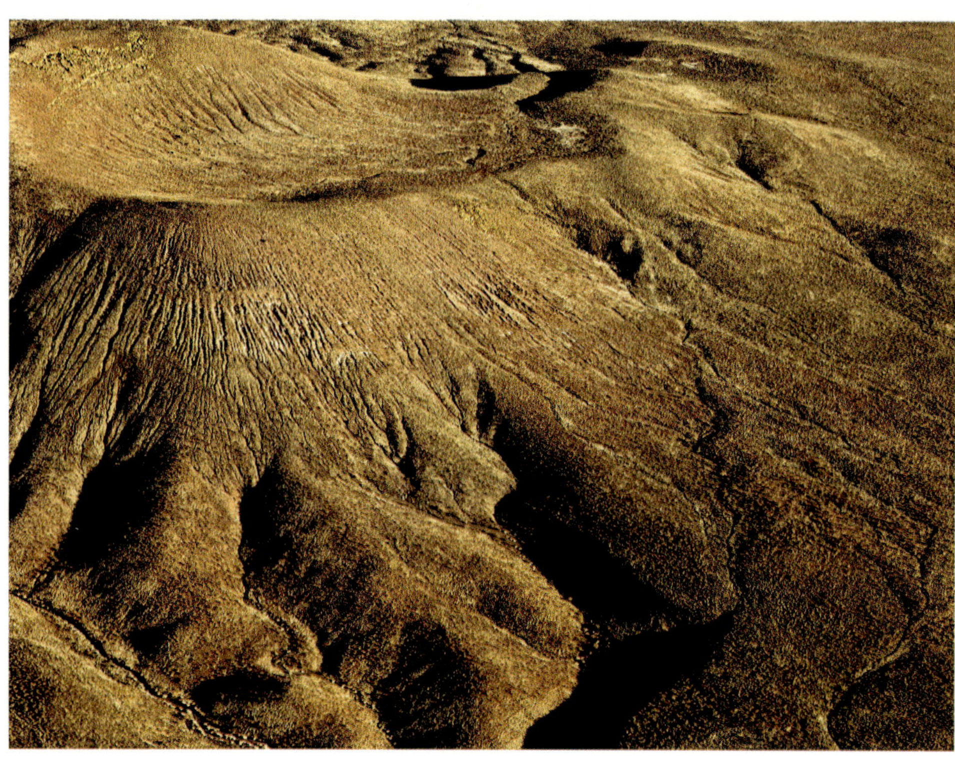

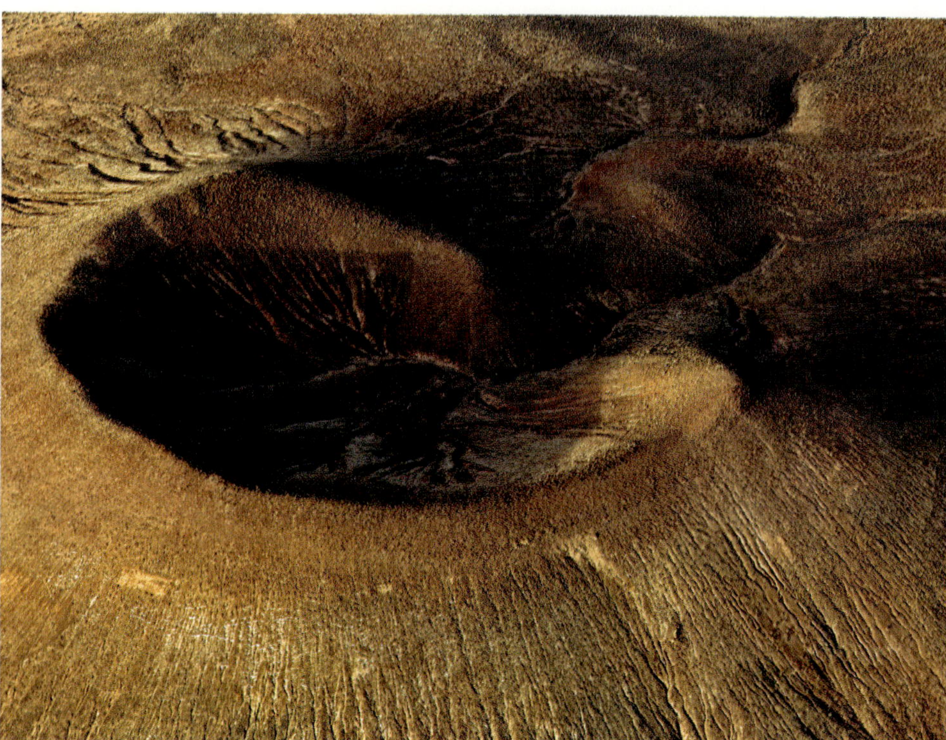

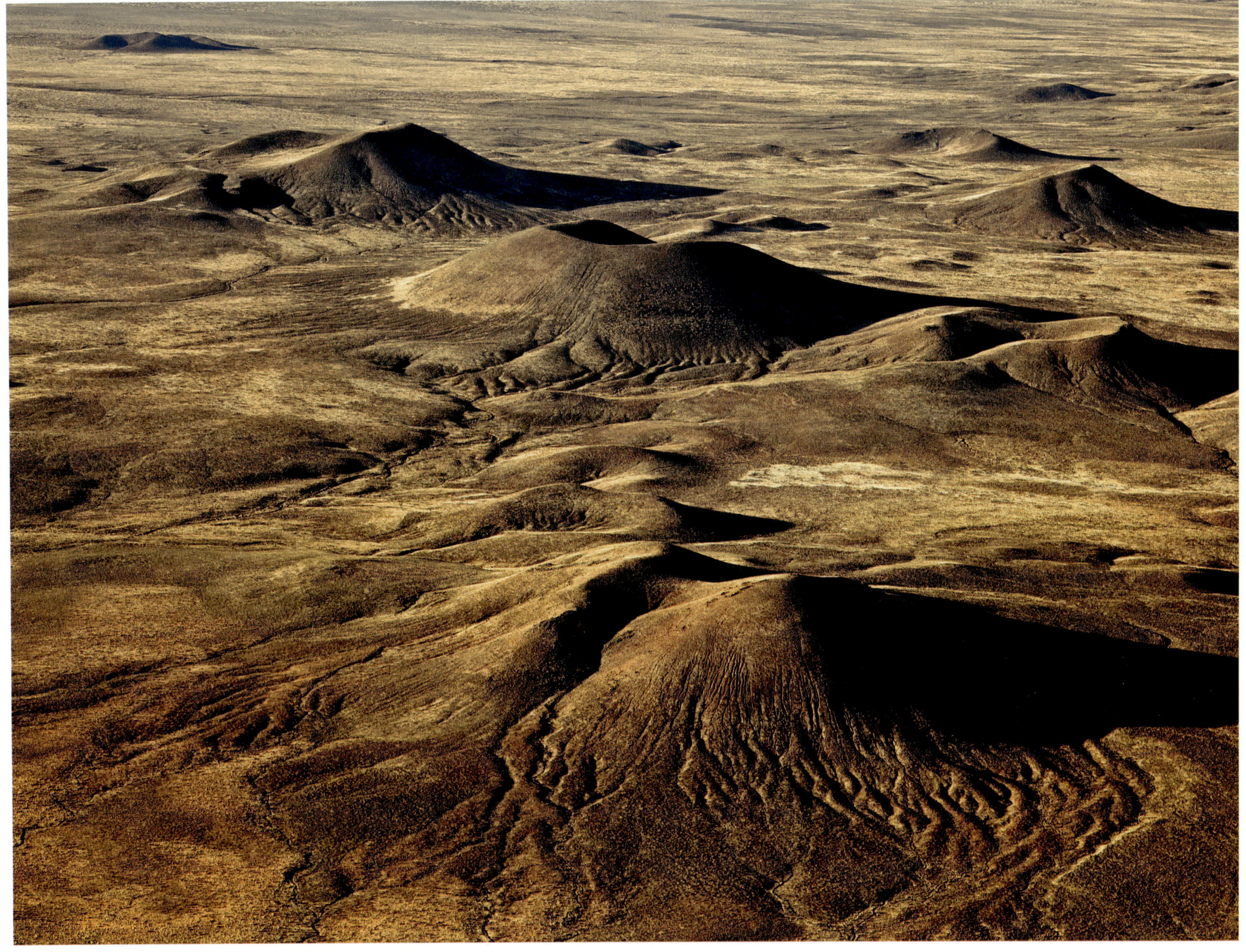

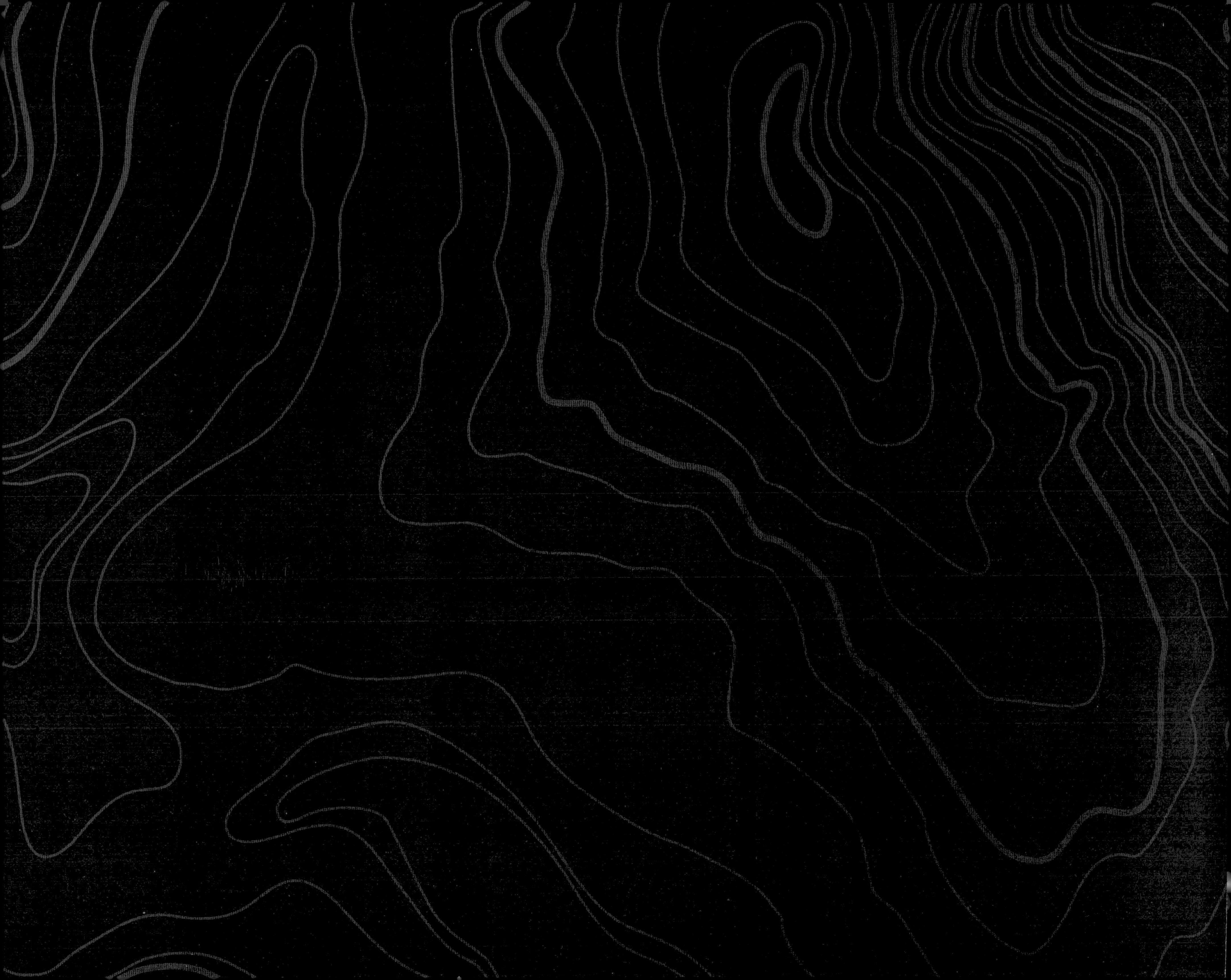

Organ Mountains

Organ Mountains

DISTANCE FROM EL PASO
55 miles northeast

LATITUDE
32°23'35"

LONGITUDE
-106°34'37" W

ELEVATION
8,990 feet (2,740 meters)

HIGHEST POINT
Organ Needle,
at 8,990 to 9,012 feet,
depending upon the
source consulted

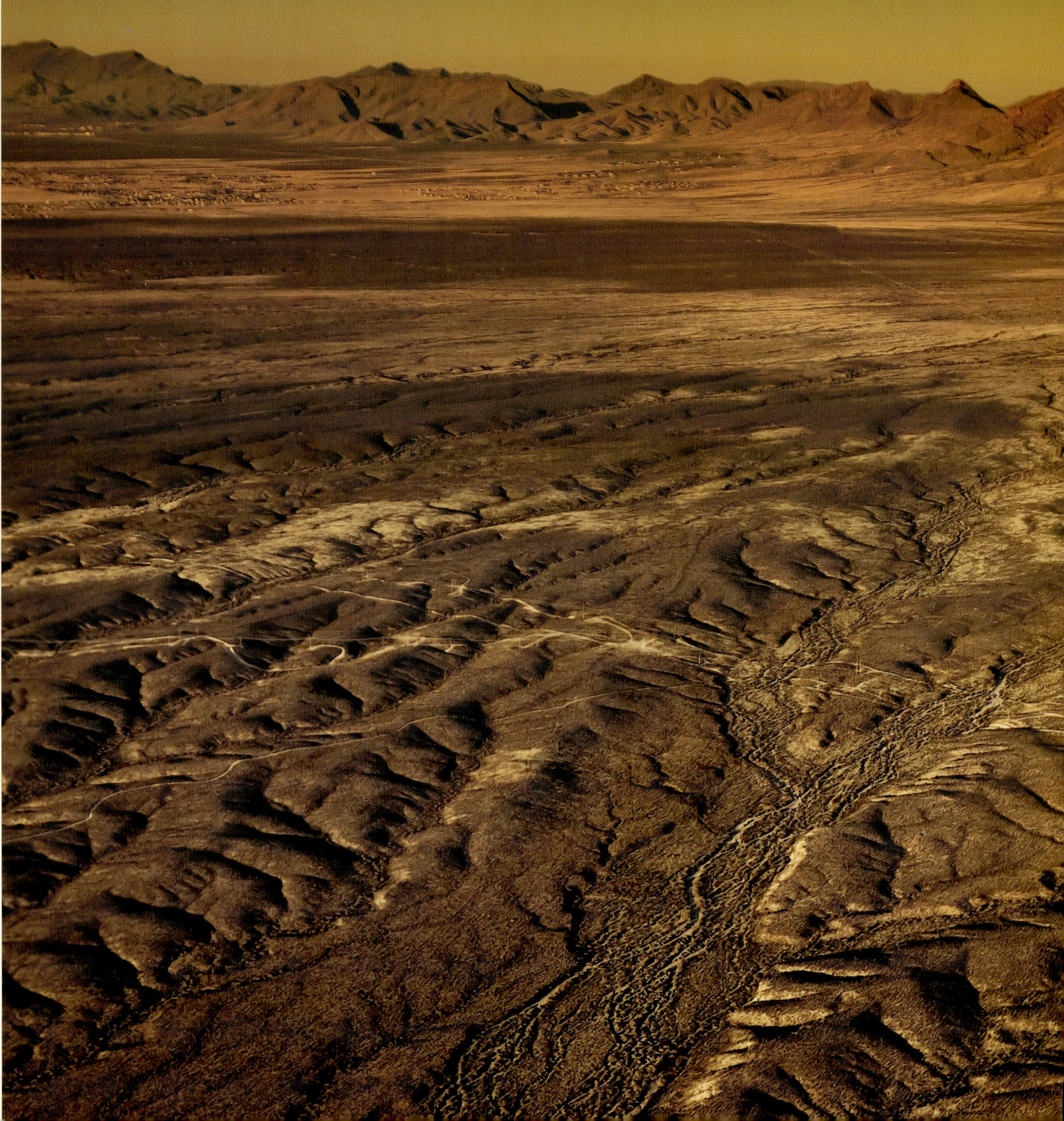

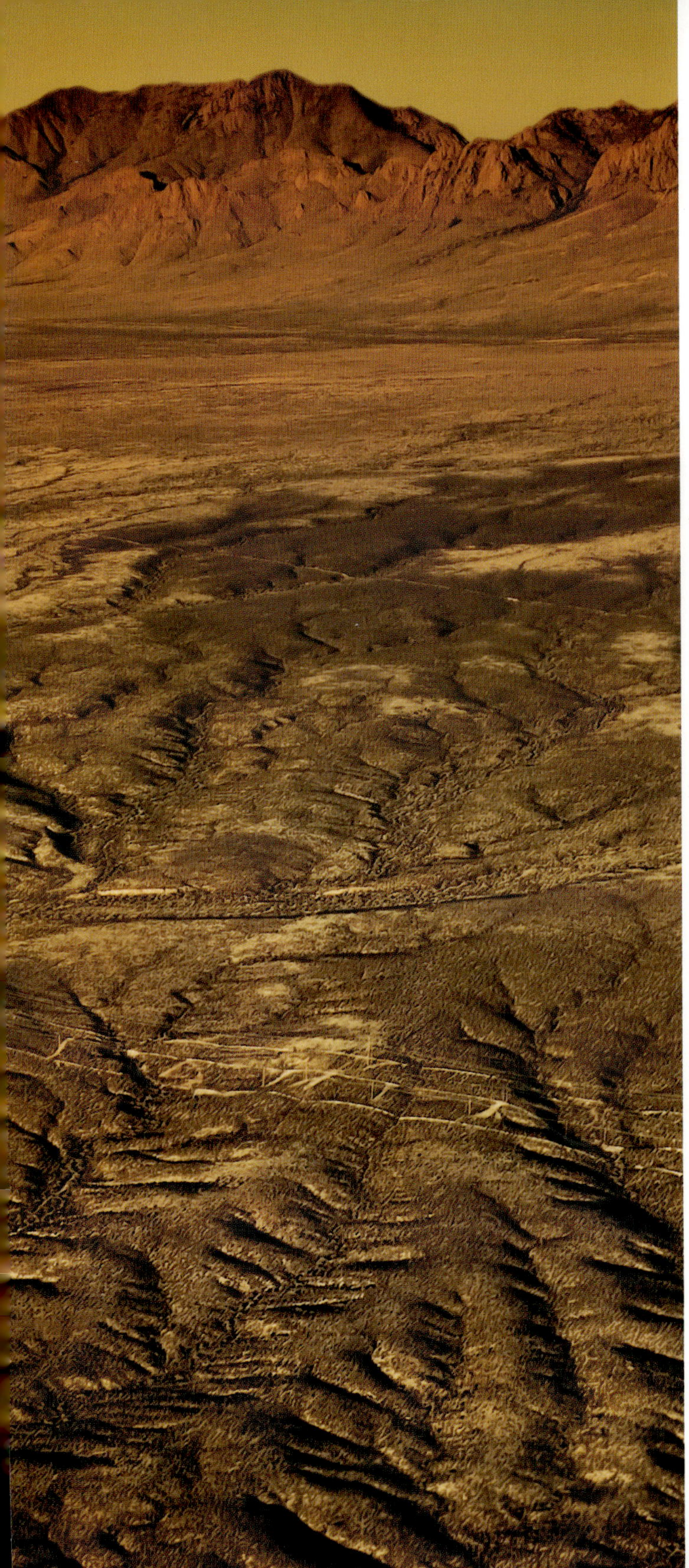

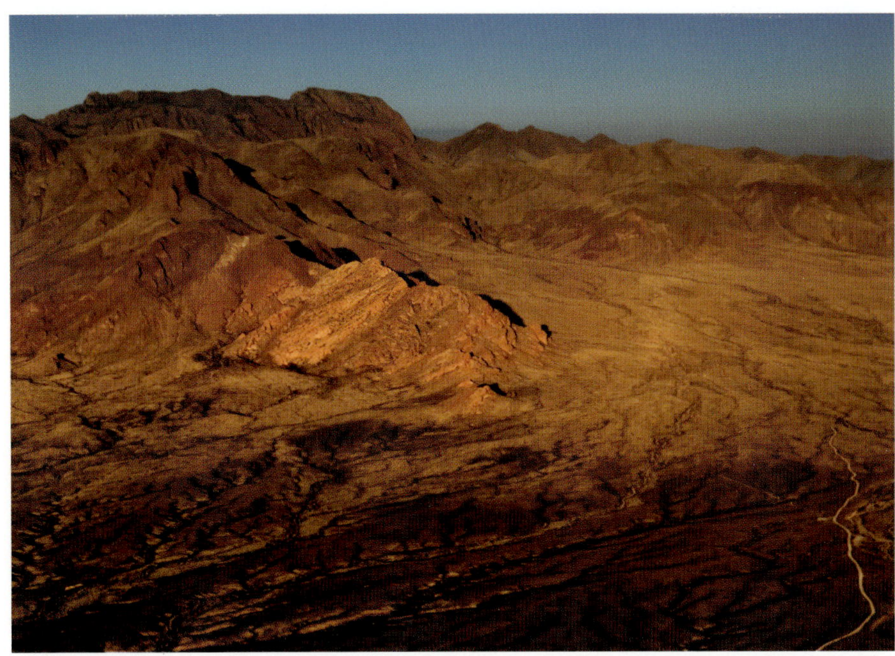

Spanish explorers named this range the Organ Mountains because they thought their pinnacles resembled the pipes of an organ. These spiky peaks lie about ten miles east of Las Cruces, New Mexico, running between the Franklin Mountains to the south and the San Andres range to the north. They are very different geologically from either, as they are primarily igneous rock—granite and rhyolite. At its peak, Organ Point reaches nearly nine thousand feet. Since there is a drop of more than four thousand feet on its western side, it is one of the steepest mountain ranges that can be found in the West.

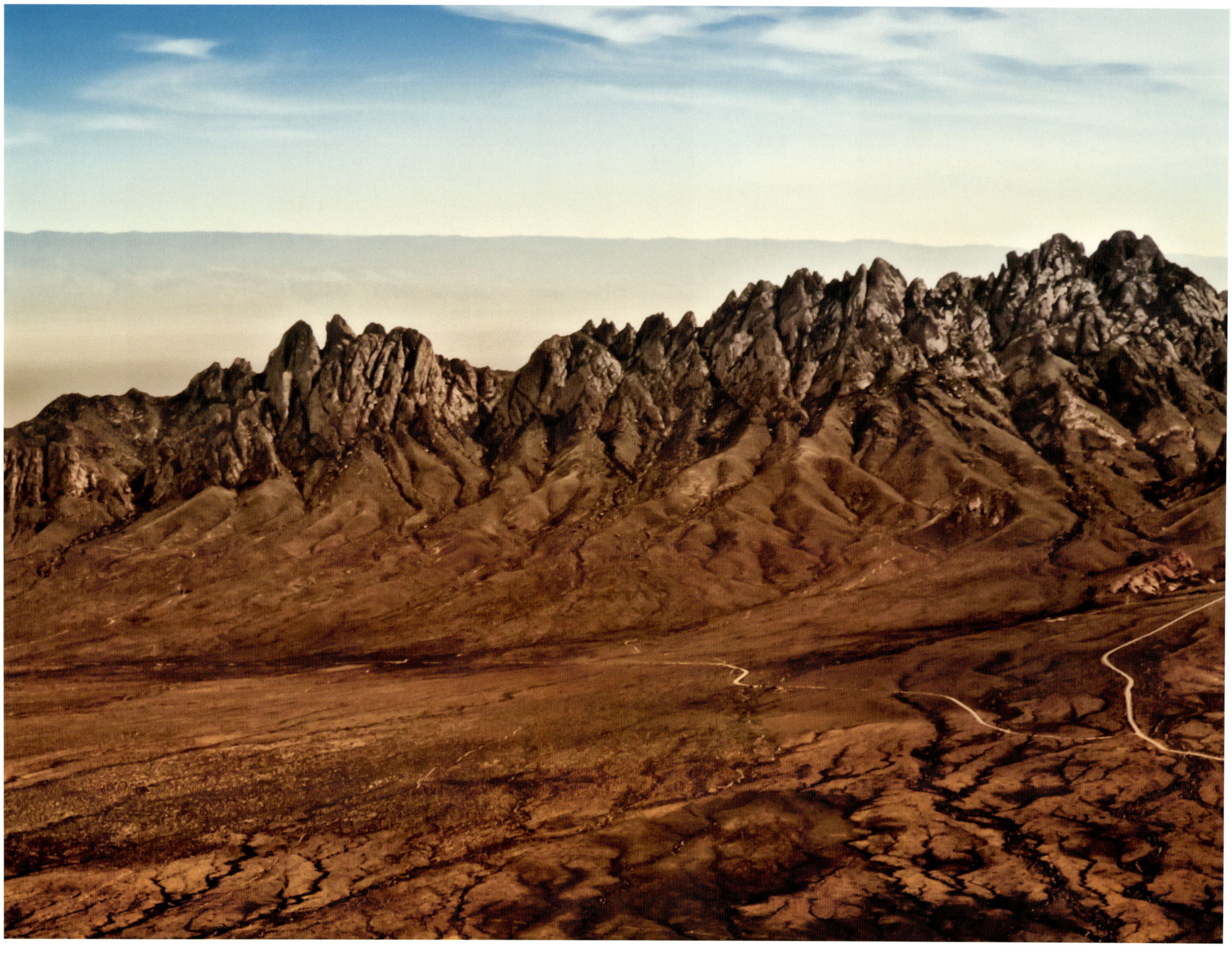

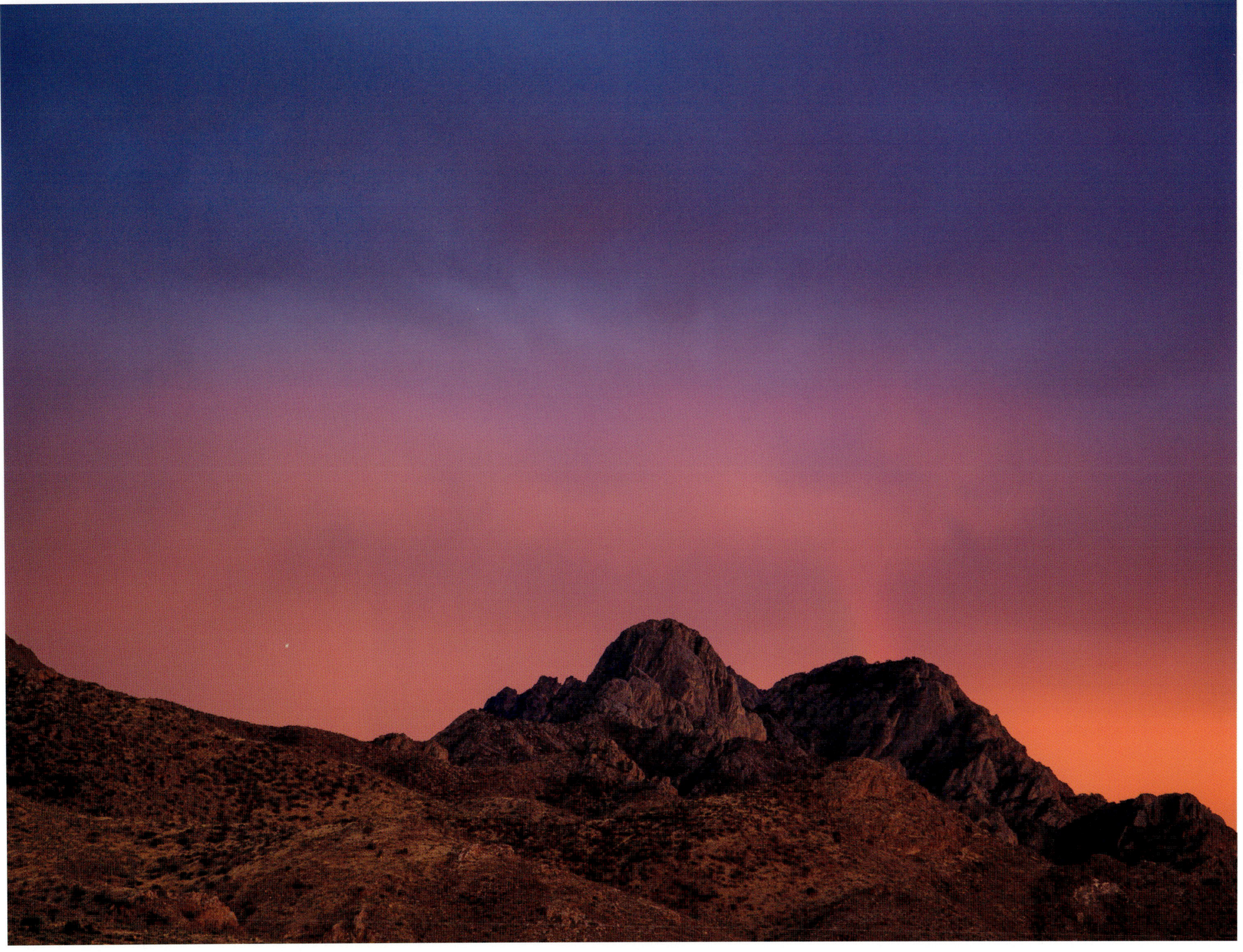

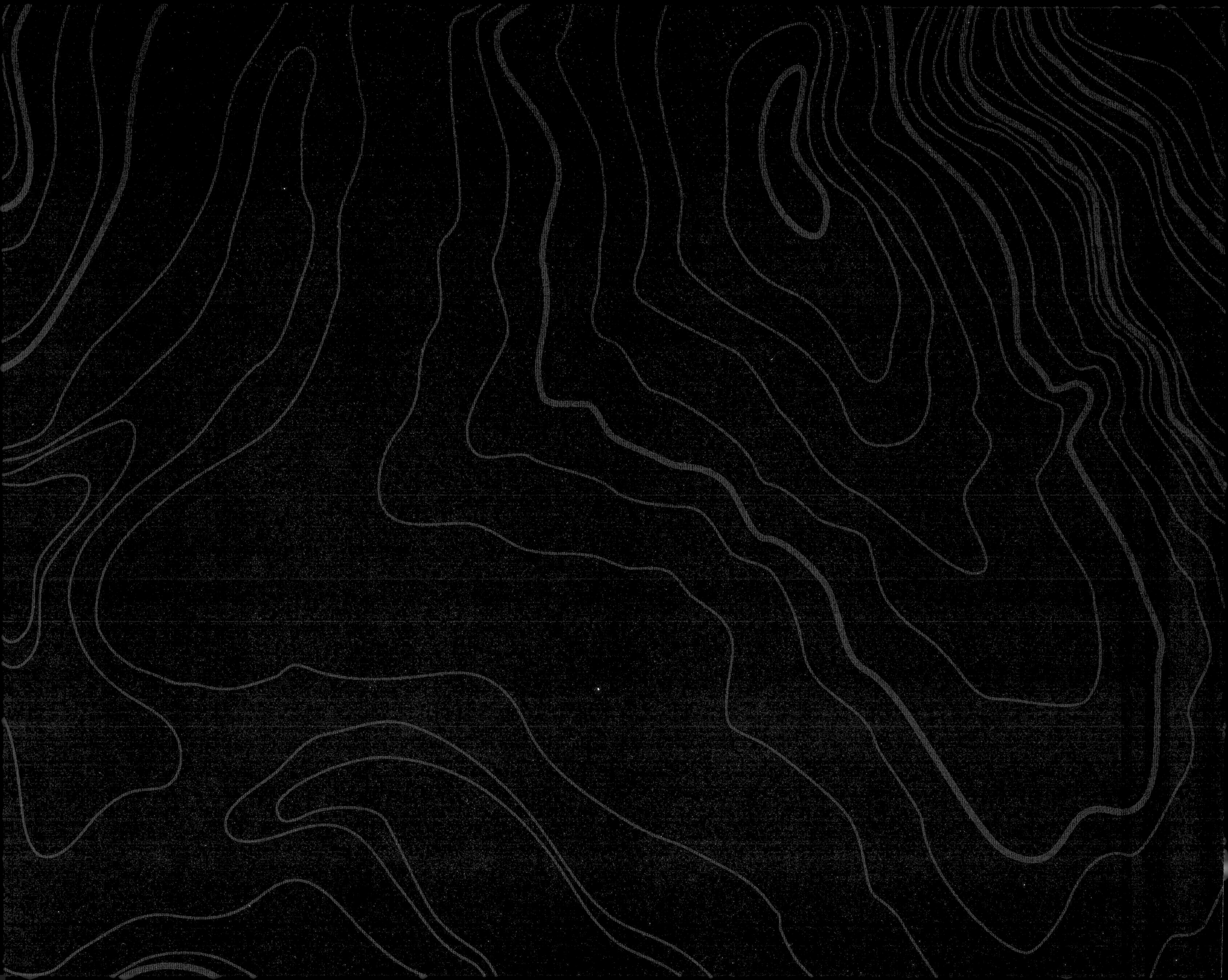

Cloudcroft

Cloudcroft

DISTANCE FROM EL PASO
90 miles northeast

LATITUDE
32°57'17"

LONGITUDE
-105°44'26" W

ELEVATION
8,663 feet (2,640 meters)

AREA
1.497 square miles
(3,877 square kilometers)

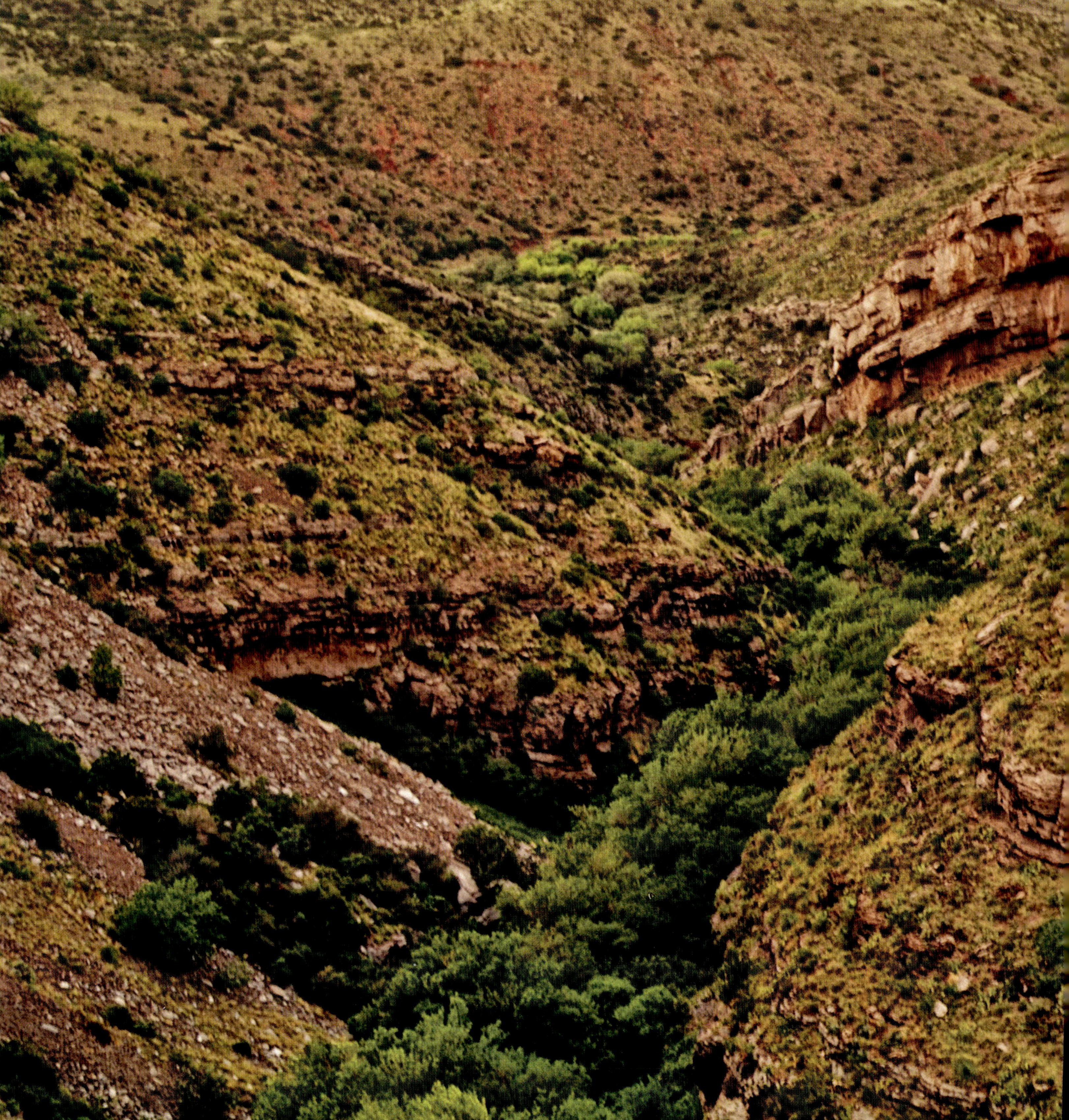

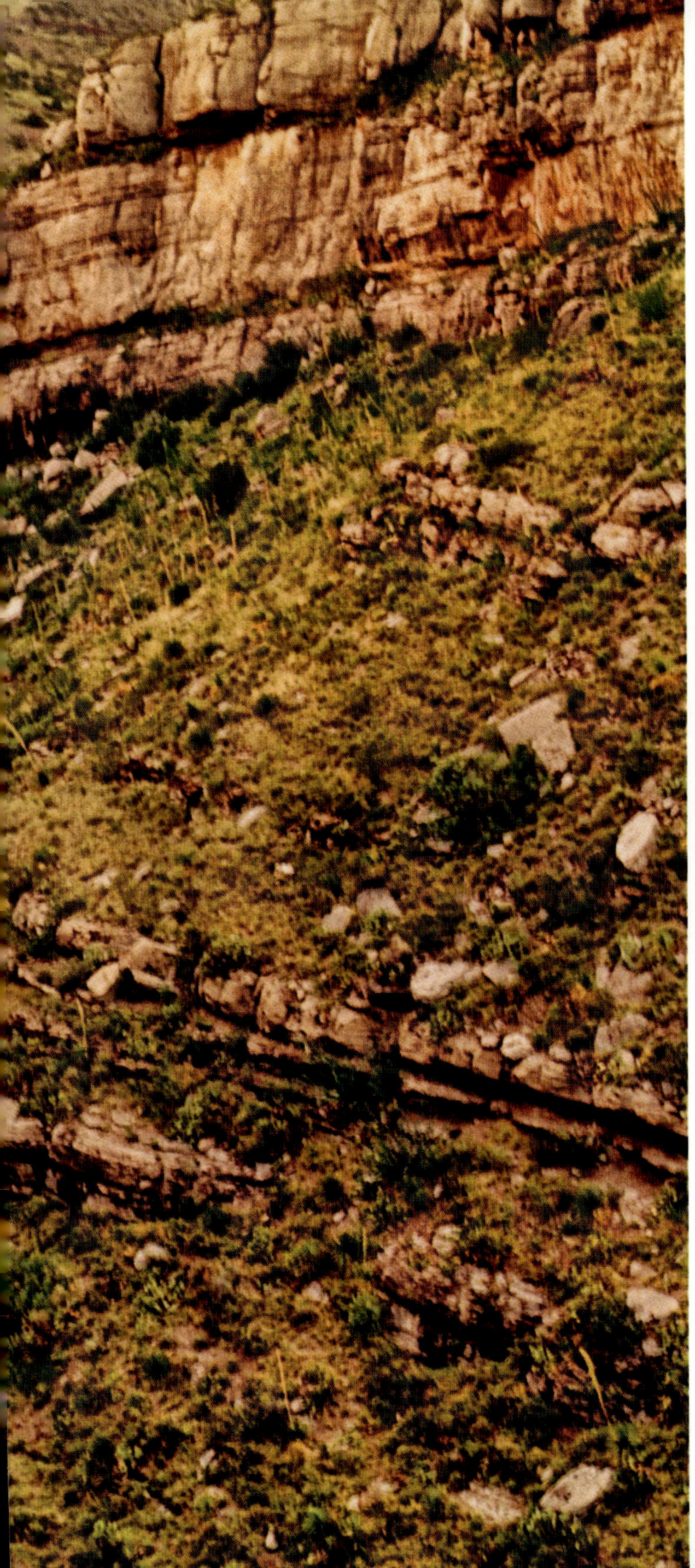

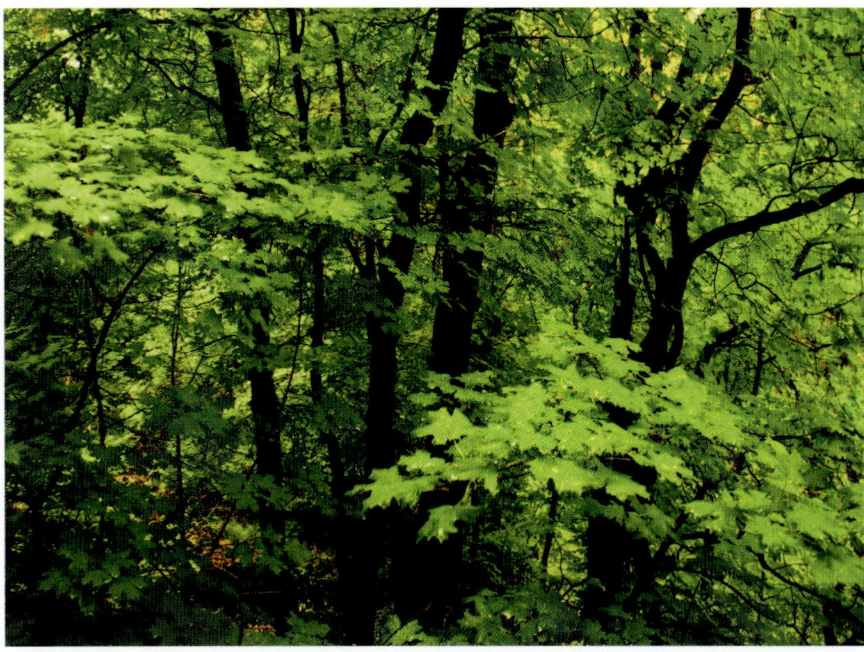

Whether I'm hiking or mountain biking, Cloudcroft is my top spot to escape summer's heat. Nestled up in the Sacramento Mountains high above the desert, this is where I enjoy a glorious view of White Sands in the far distance before starting out on my favorite trek—Trestle Trail. The area's elevation and closely woven pine trees offer immediate relief from the heat. As I descend the winding trail, the air cools almost to a chill. Vegetation becomes denser and more varied, with clusters of vines clinging to any support they can find. The murmur of water can be heard as streams make their way to the high canyon floor. This trail is not to be rushed, as it is here that nature awakens the senses to its idyllic beauty, its euphonic sounds, its savory green and earthy scents. The treat at the end of Trestle is to lie in the tall wispy grasses at the bottom, without a care for anything awaiting outside these mountain walls.

The village of Cloudcroft and its environs lie within Lincoln National Forest, a protected forest in

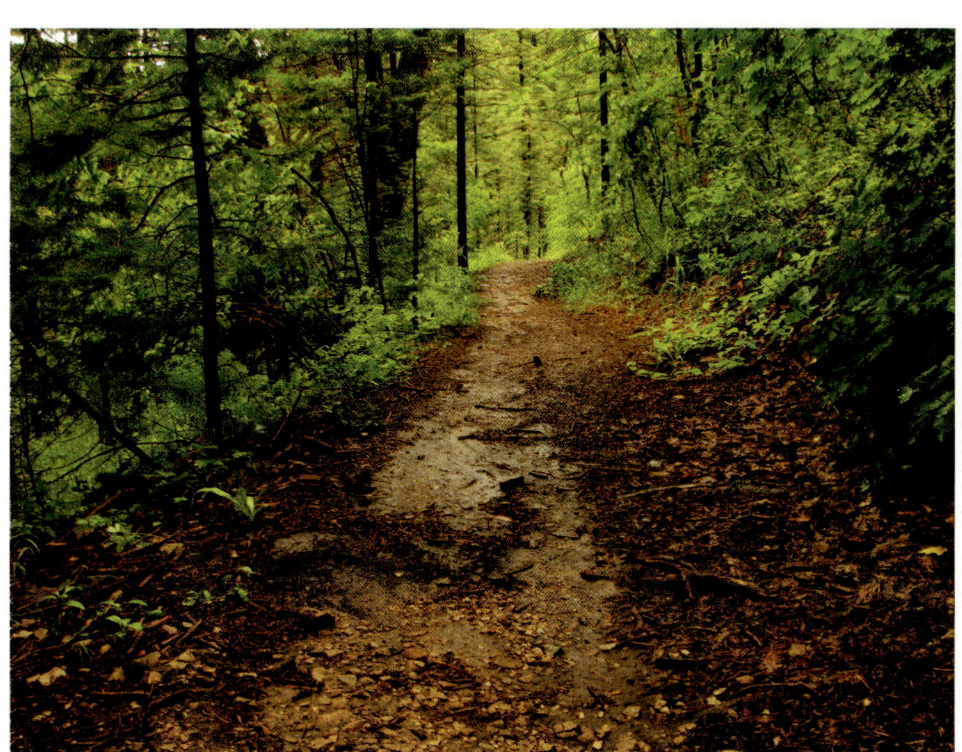

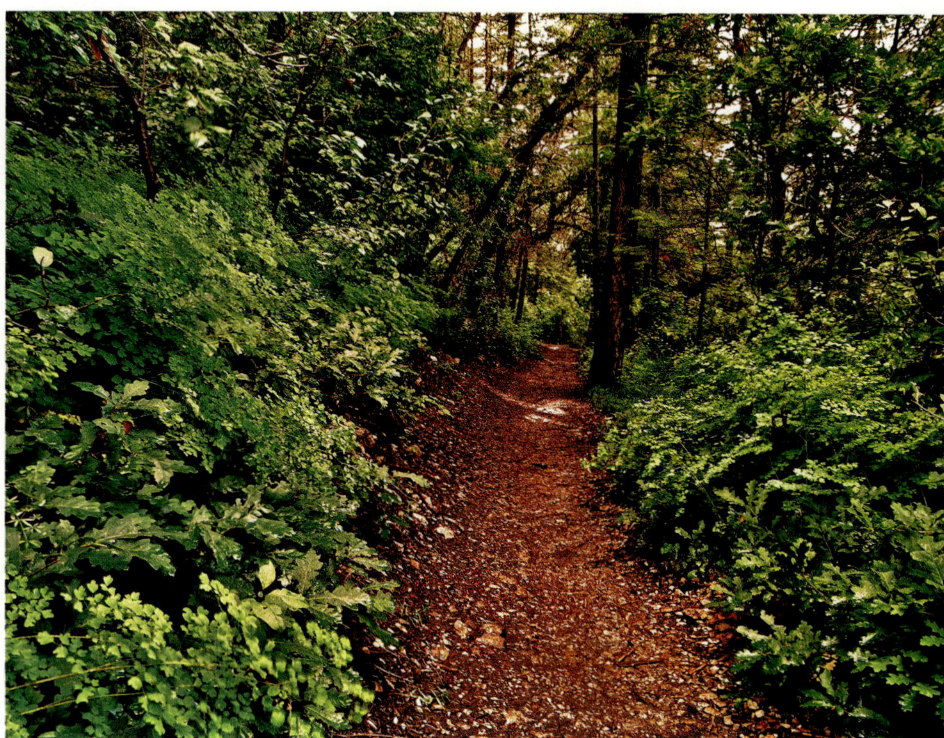

New Mexico that encompasses more than a million acres. The birthplace of Smokey Bear—known to generations of children as the embodiment of forest fire prevention—the forest was named in honor of Abraham Lincoln. The name Cloudcroft, which means a pasture for the clouds, suggests the area's high elevation compared to that of the surrounding desert. The town of Cloudcroft was put on the map in 1898, when a railroad crew discovered that the area wasn't just an accessible source of timber—it was a place that could attract visitors. In the winter, Cloudcroft offers sports such as cross-country skiing, snowmobiling, and ice skating. Winter or summer, the area confounds the expectations of those who believe the Southwest is invariably hot and dry.

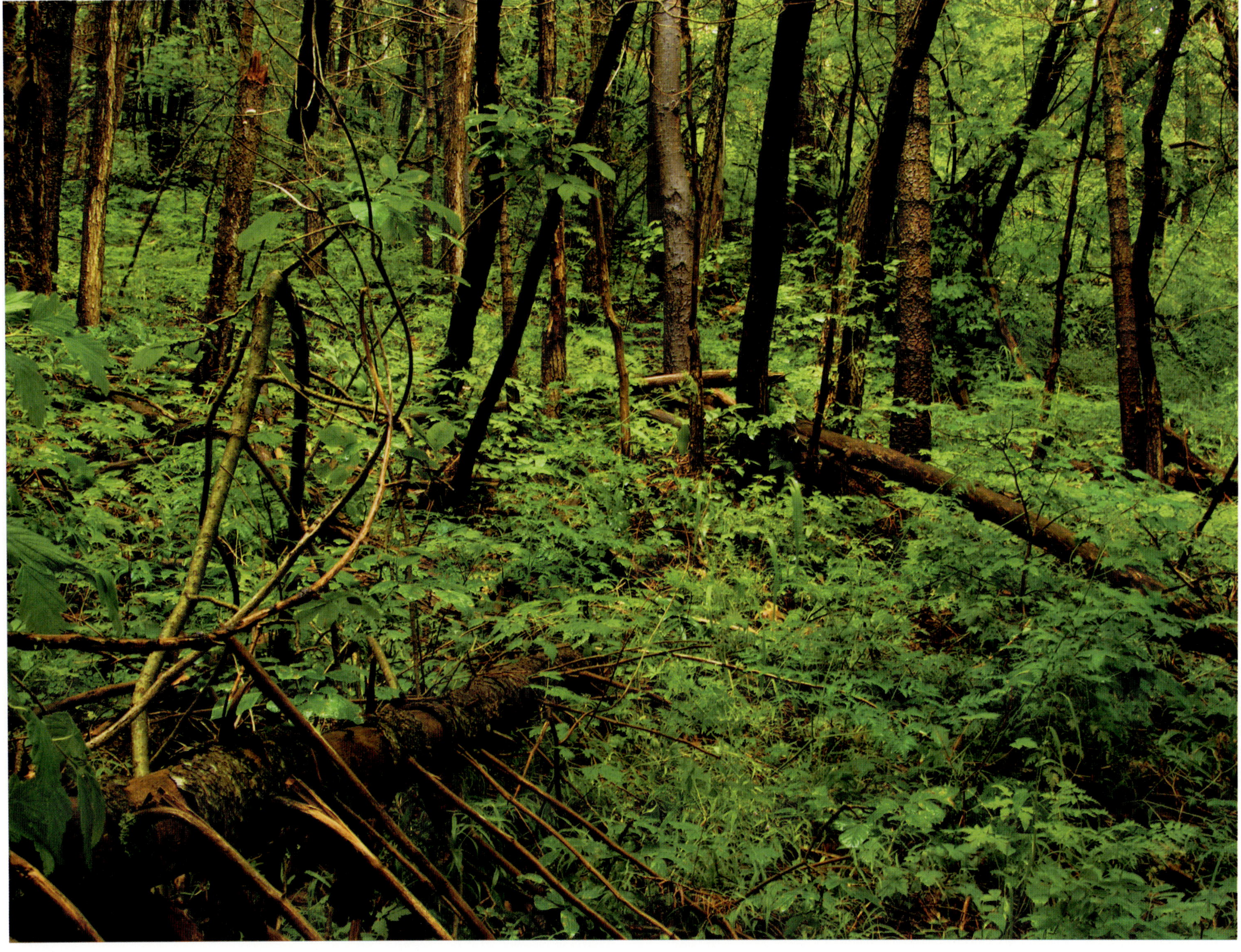

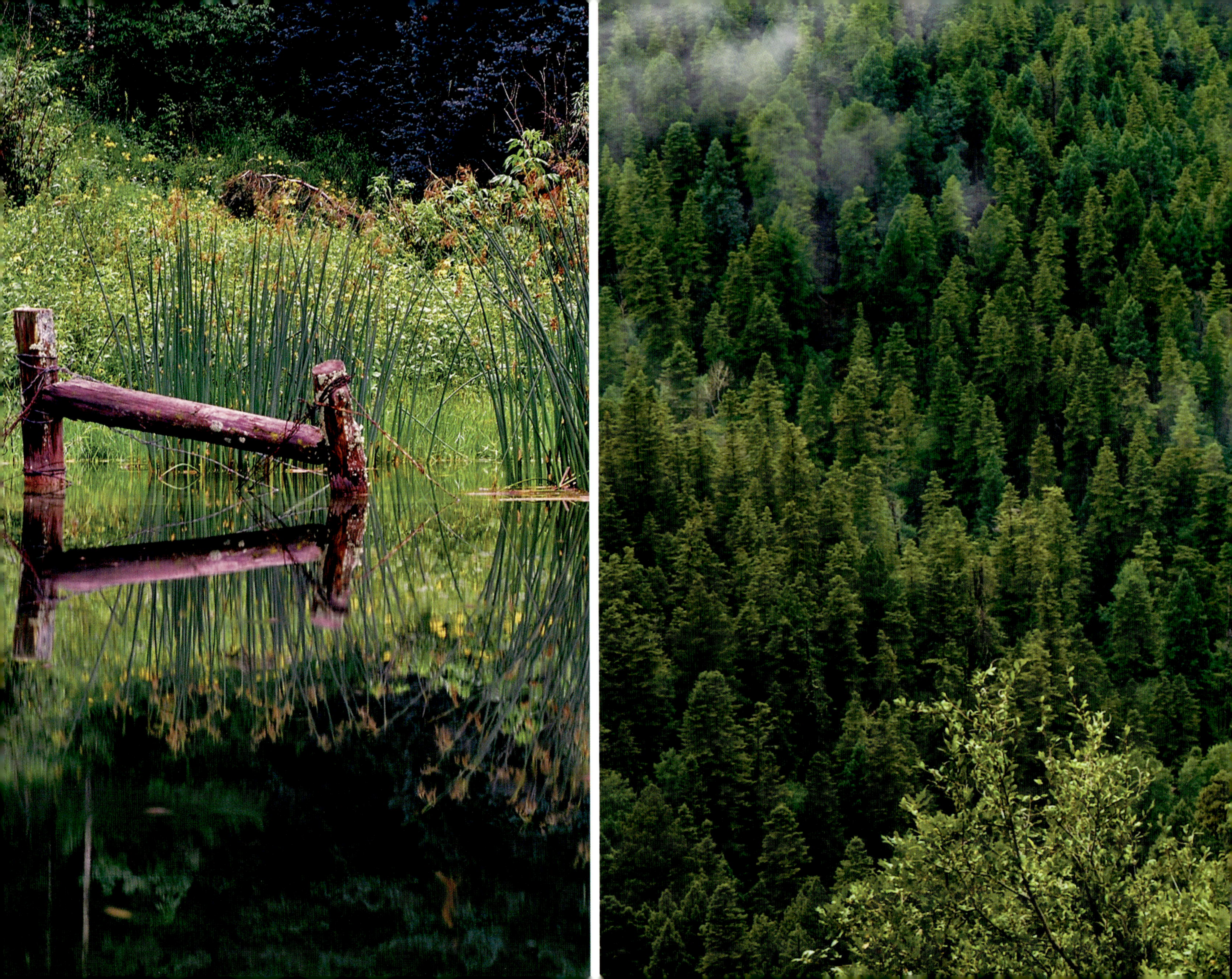

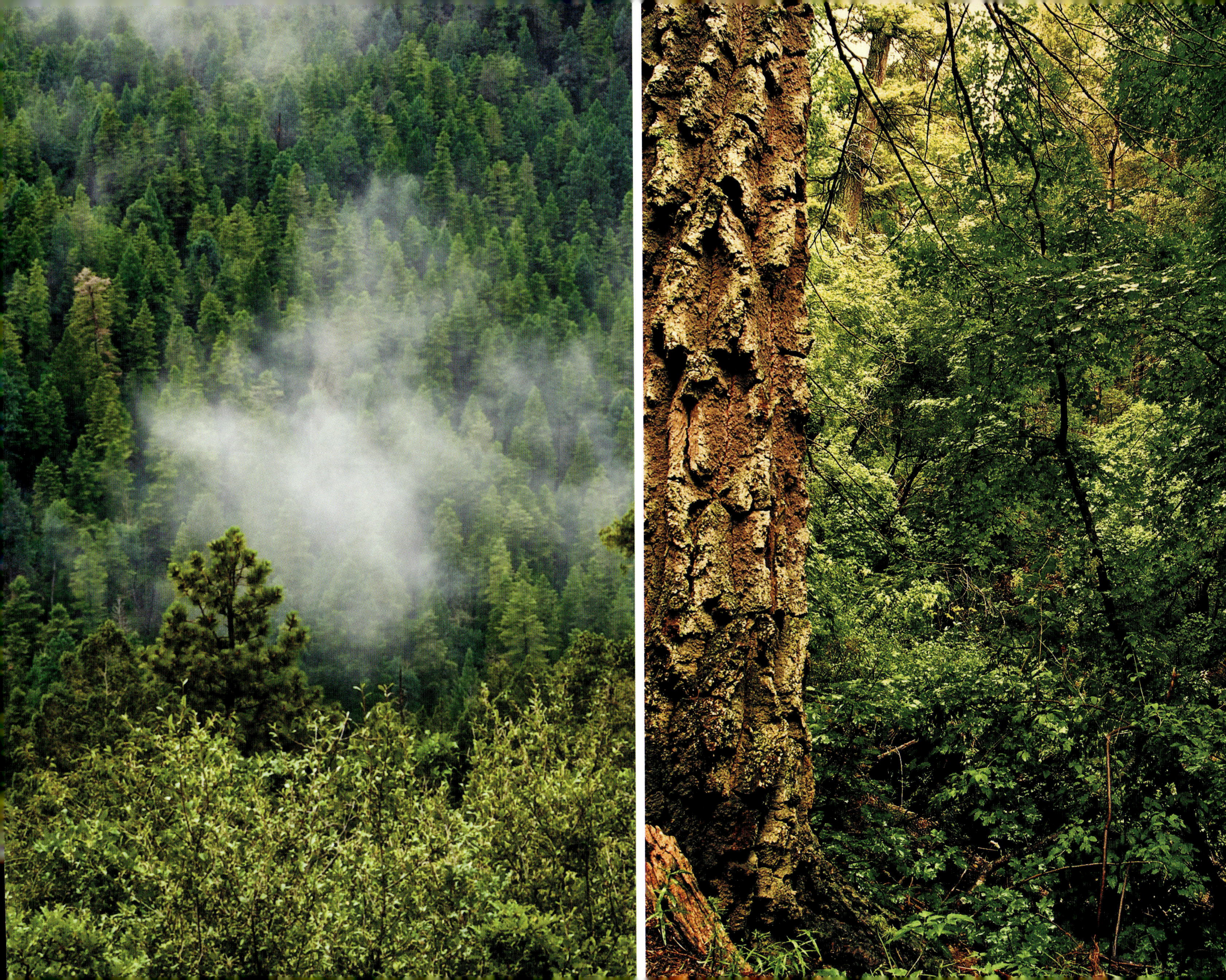

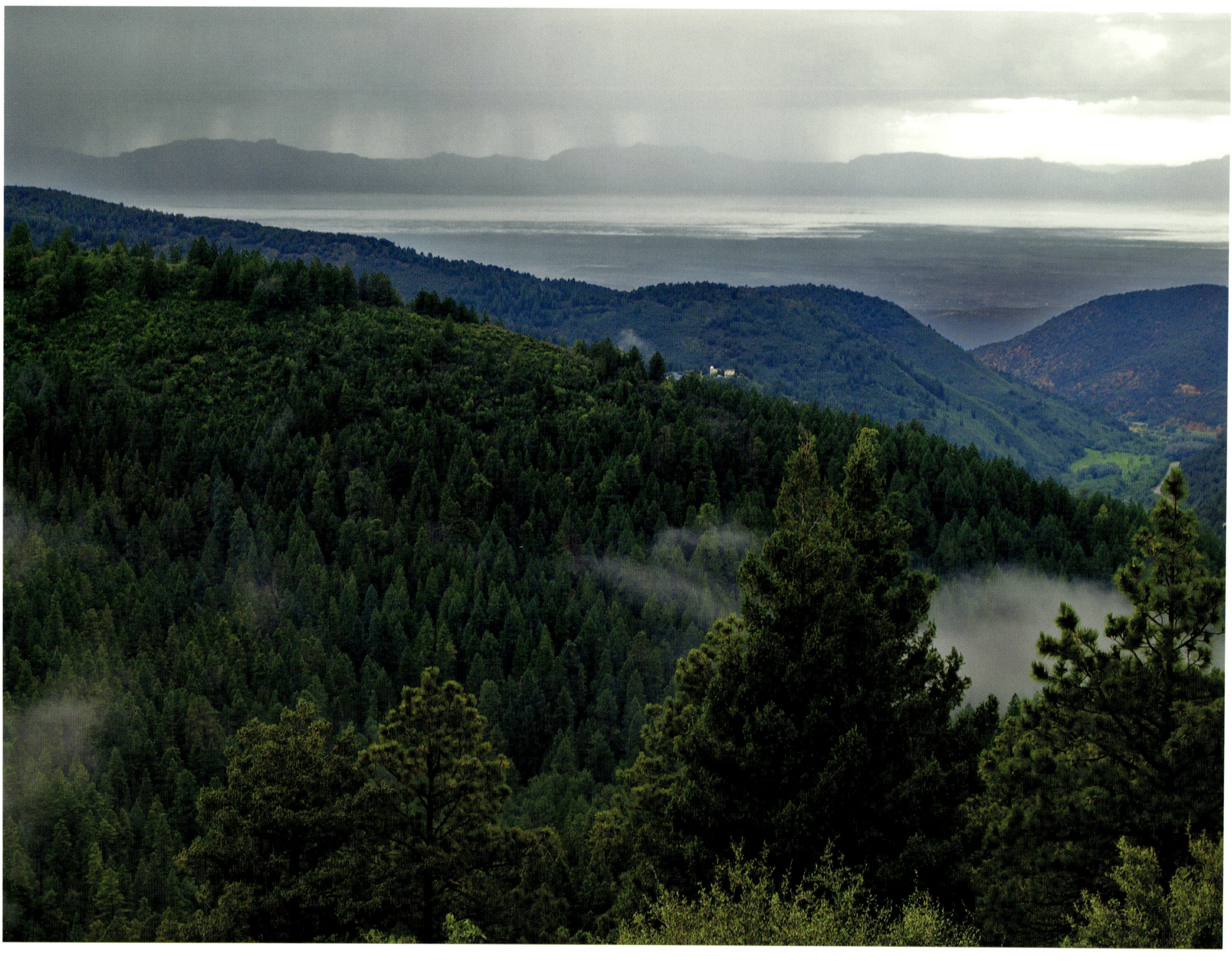

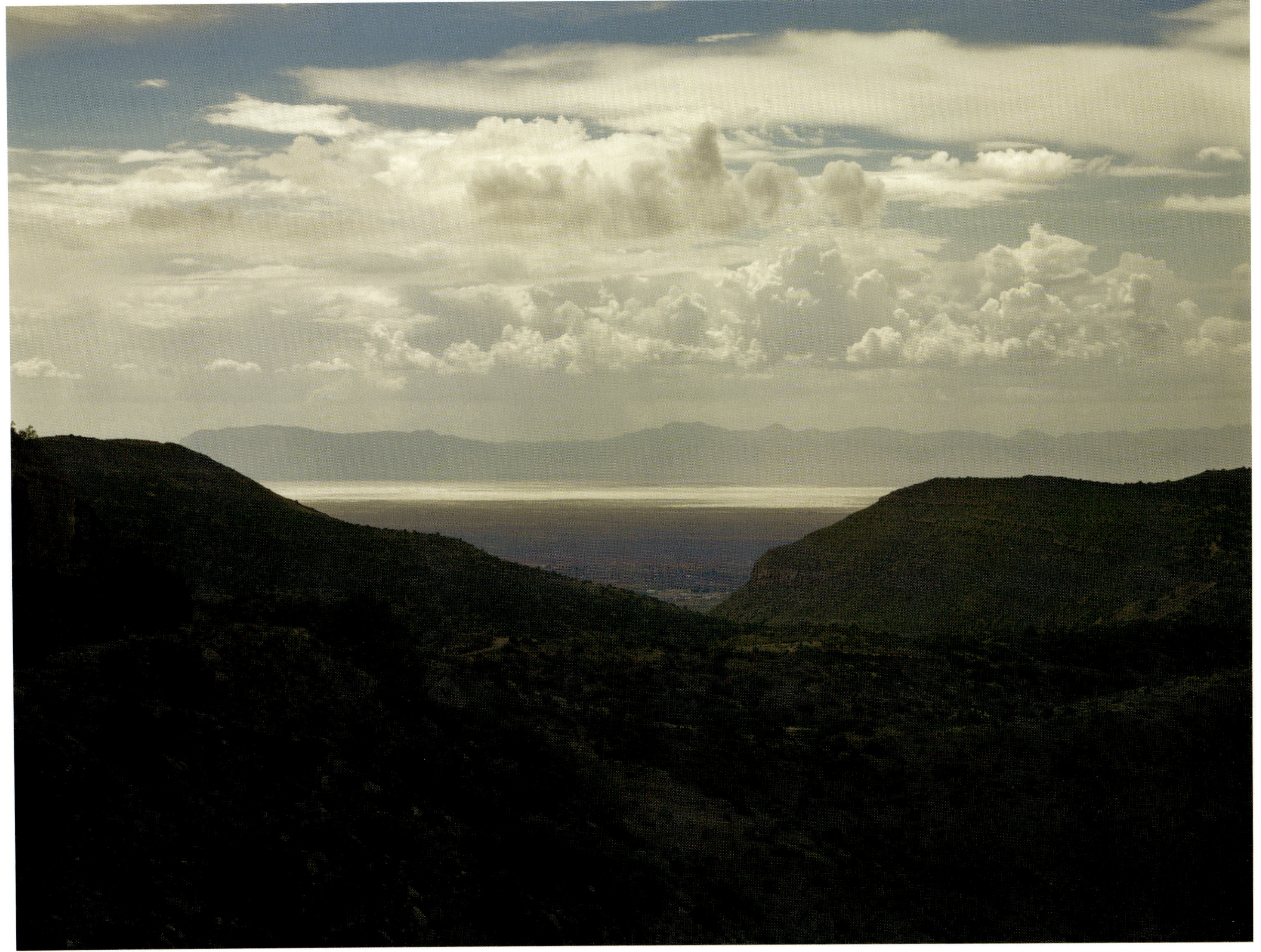

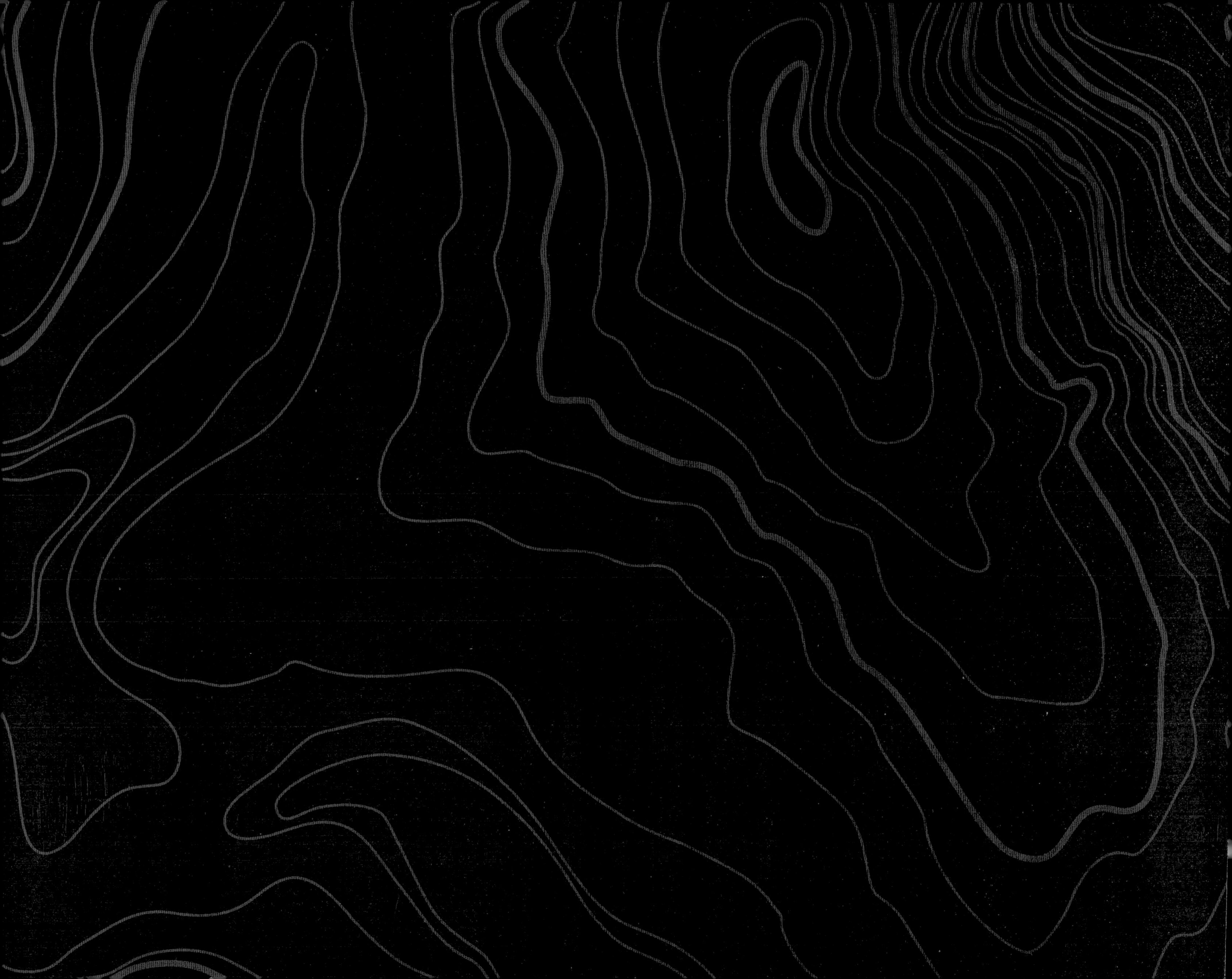

White Sands National Monument

White Sands National Monument

DISTANCE FROM EL PASO
95 miles north

LATITUDE
32°46’47” N

LONGITUDE
-106°10’18” W

ELEVATION
4,235 feet (1,291 meters)

AREA
275 square miles
(712 square kilometers)

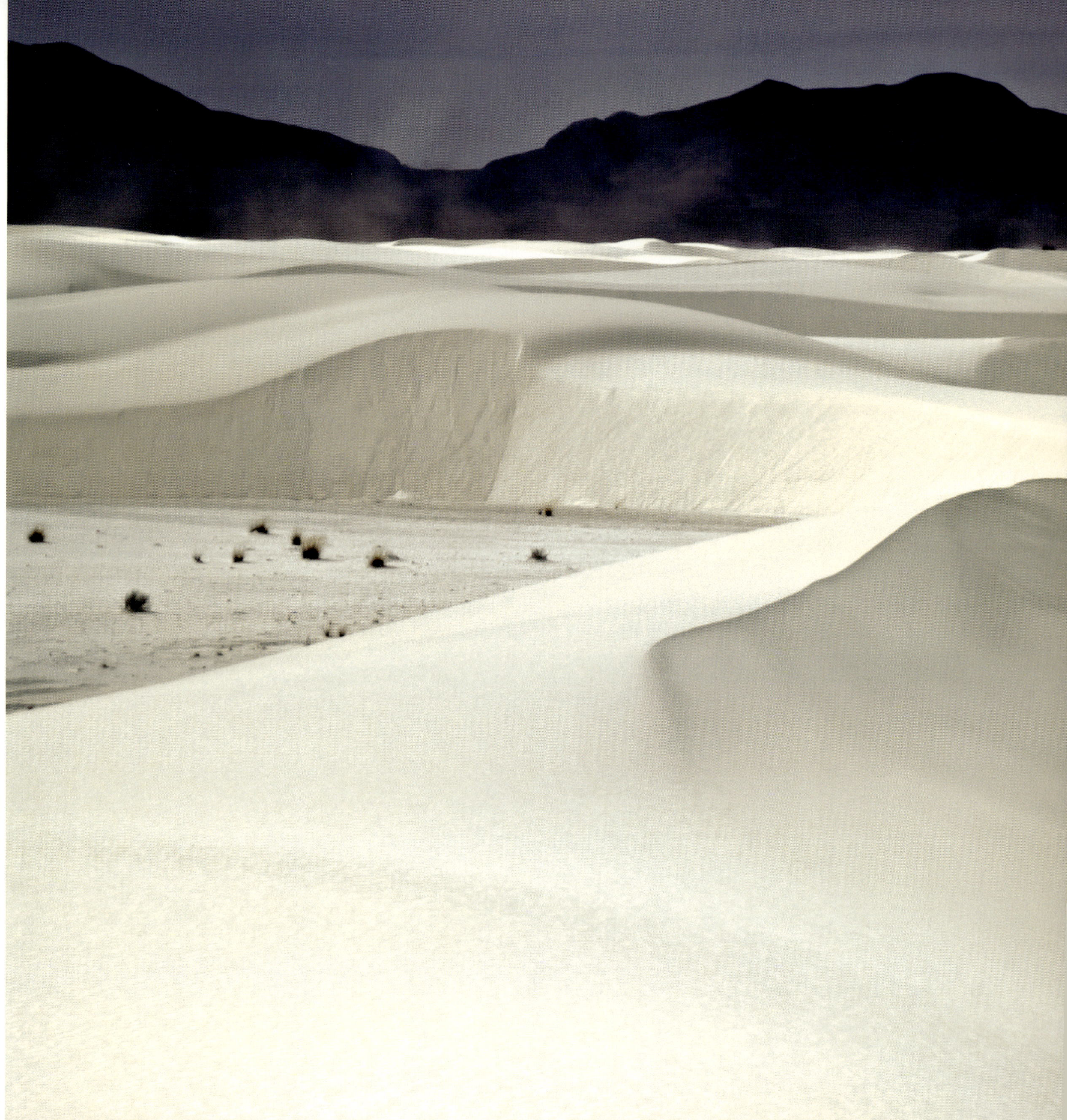

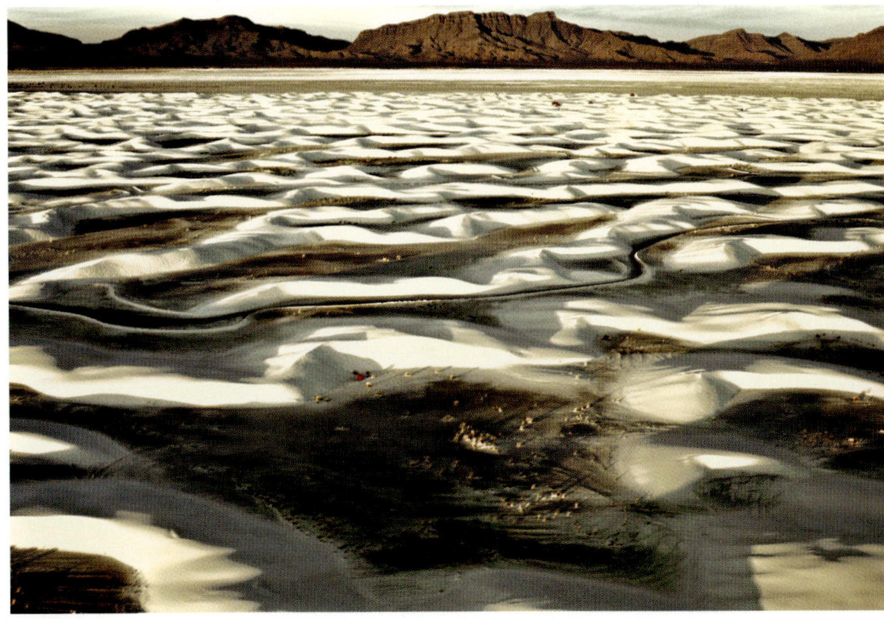

Snow white and mysteriously beautiful, New Mexico's White Sands National Monument is the world's largest gypsum dune field, with huge, wave-like dunes that constantly roll across some 275 square miles of desert in the Tularosa Basin. These pristine waves affect me more than any other place in this world. Here I am in awe of the dune's ever-changing natural beauty. I like the notion of the blowing wind shifting the sands into different formations, as this reflects my own life. Not much ever remains the same for me over time, and I look forward to change.

White Sands touches deep within my soul, often serving as a healer—a place of solace, if you will. When life becomes hectic, the pure silence of the dunes provides calm, allowing my mind and spirit to become centered once again. There are no distractions, and what sometimes appears impossible in other surroundings reveals itself to be the opposite.

This is where I retreated to make some sort of sense of my father's sudden passing at an all-too-young age, and where, saying goodbye one last time, I was able to let go. Only me, the dunes, and unfiltered thoughts of a man who worked so hard to give me so much. Too, after being diagnosed with a virus that will never leave my body, it was the white sands I kicked, pounded, yelled at, then cried over from fear and disappointment. And it was among the graceful dunes that my partner of twenty-four years and I reconnected, strengthening our relationship well beyond words.

Yes, I've spent countless hours hiking White Sands as far as possible, seen more than a million stars overhead, watched the sand illuminate under the full moon, and have had the good fortune to view the area from overhead, hanging out of a small plane. The dunes of White Sands have a personal hold on me. I may go in with a heavy heart from time to time, but I always leave knowing I am not running from anything; instead I am running toward the day with eyes wide open. For this, I will be forever grateful.

Gypsum sand is rare because gypsum is usually dissolved by rain and carried out to sea. But the deposits of gypsum washed down from the San Andres and Sacramento Mountains that ring the Tularosa Basin are trapped there, for the basin has no outlet to the sea. When shallow pools left by the rain evaporate, they leave on the surface a layer of gypsum in a crystalline form called selenite, which forms in crystals that can be well over a foot long. Whipped by constantly blowing winds and exposed to extreme temperature changes, the crystals are eventually pounded into a fine-grained sand that gathers in brilliant white drifts moving across the desert floor. Because the terrain is in constant motion, only a few plants and animals survive here, adapting to the changing conditions in unique ways.

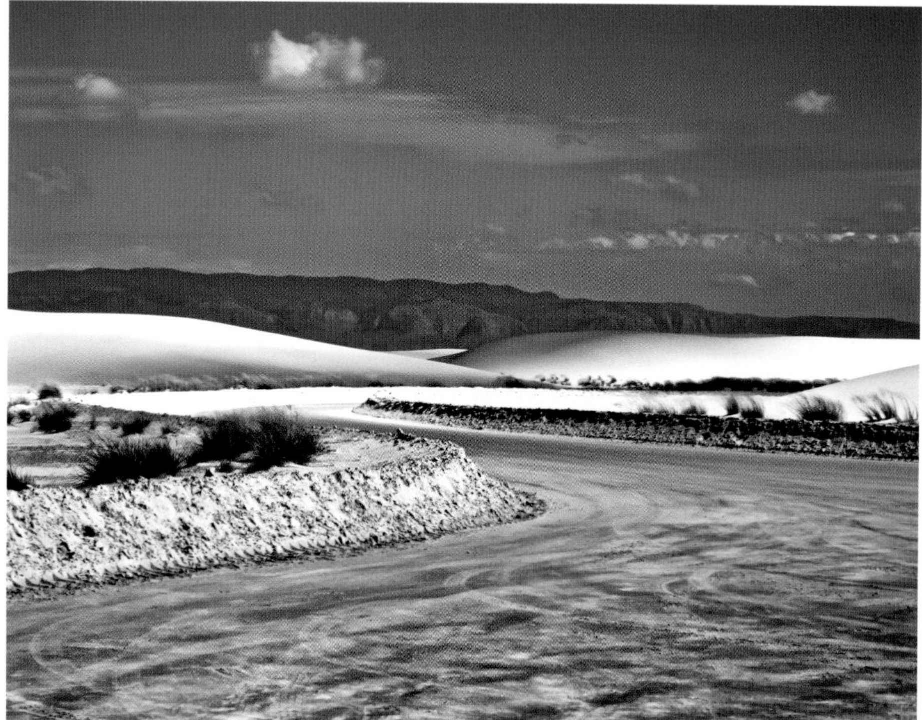

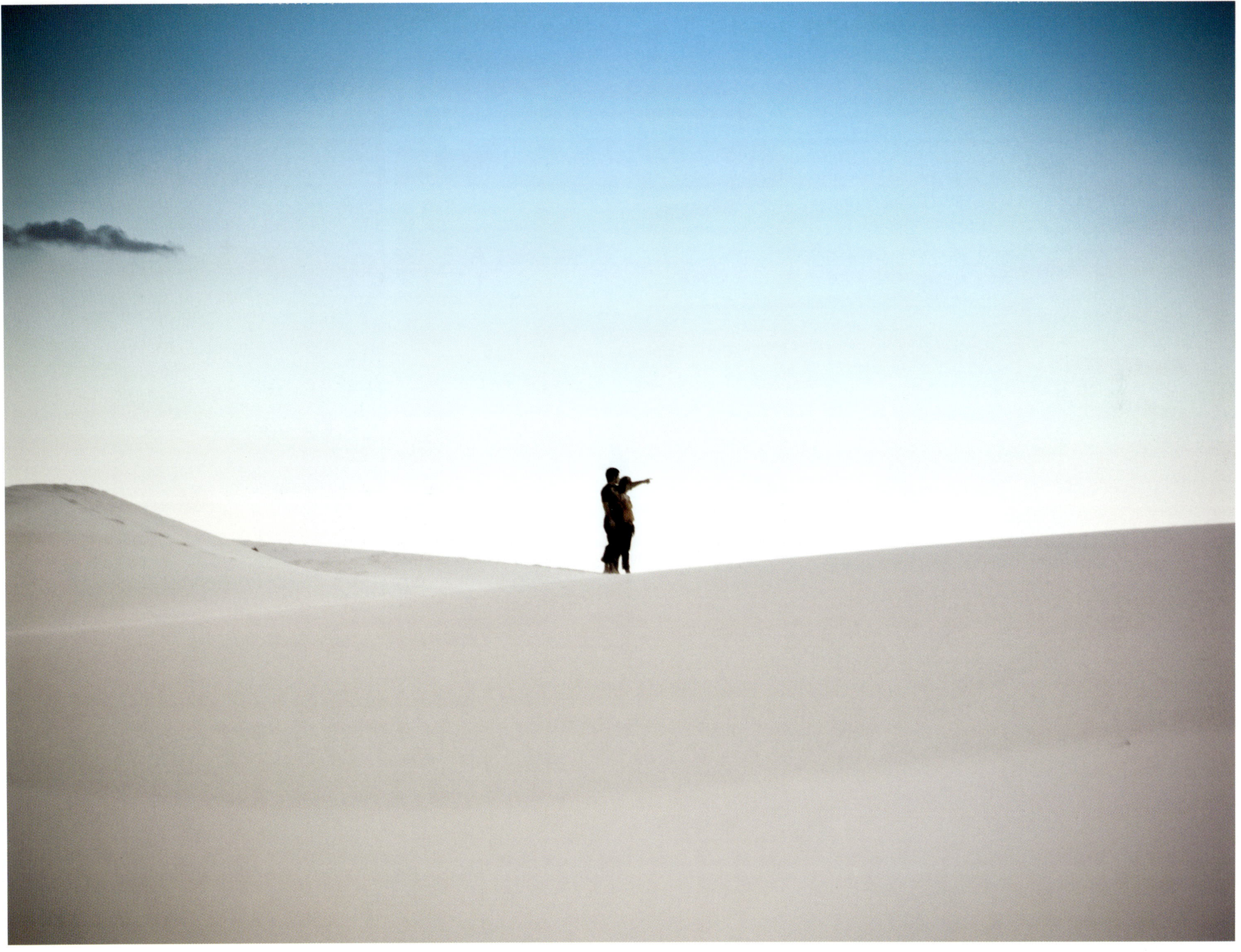

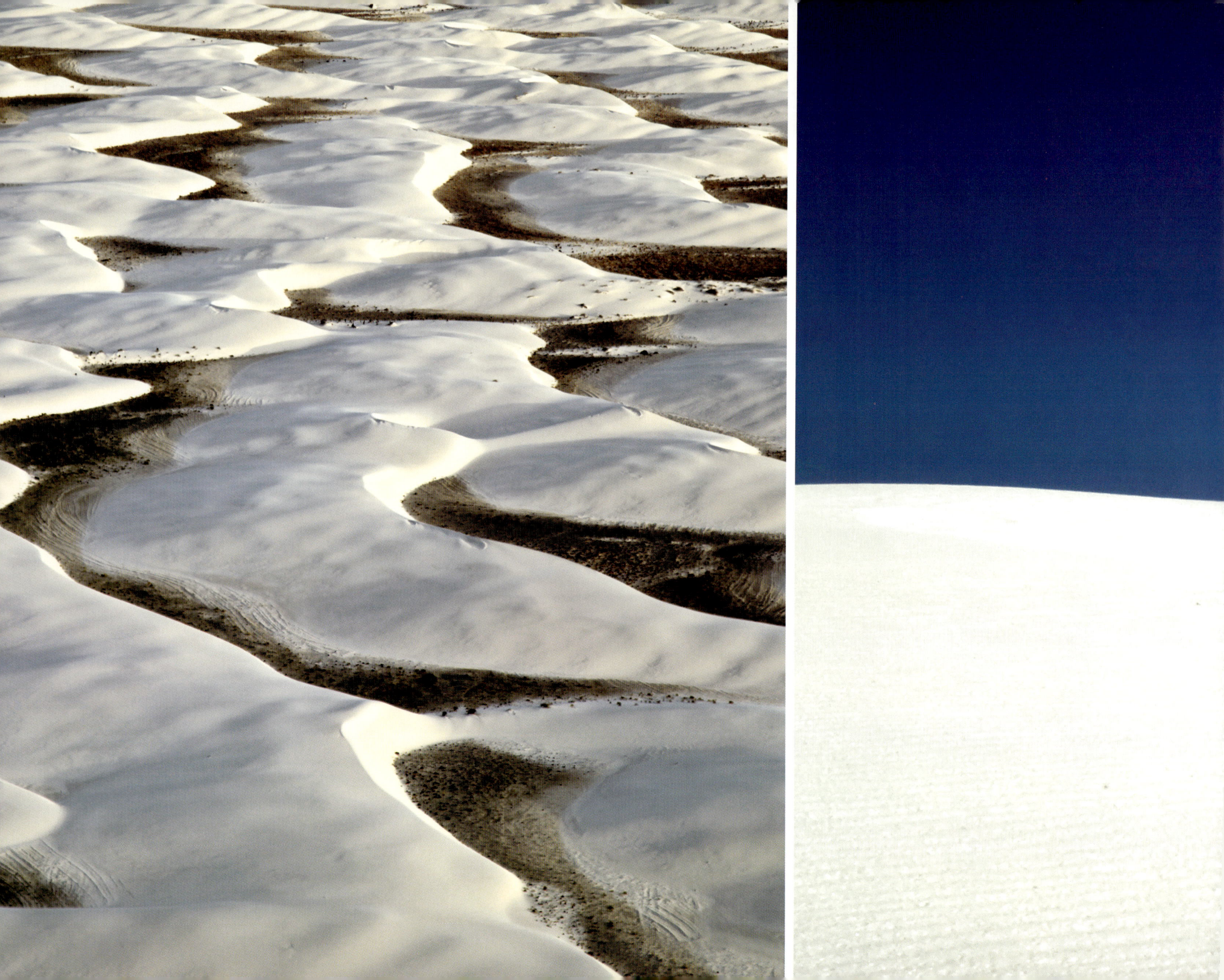

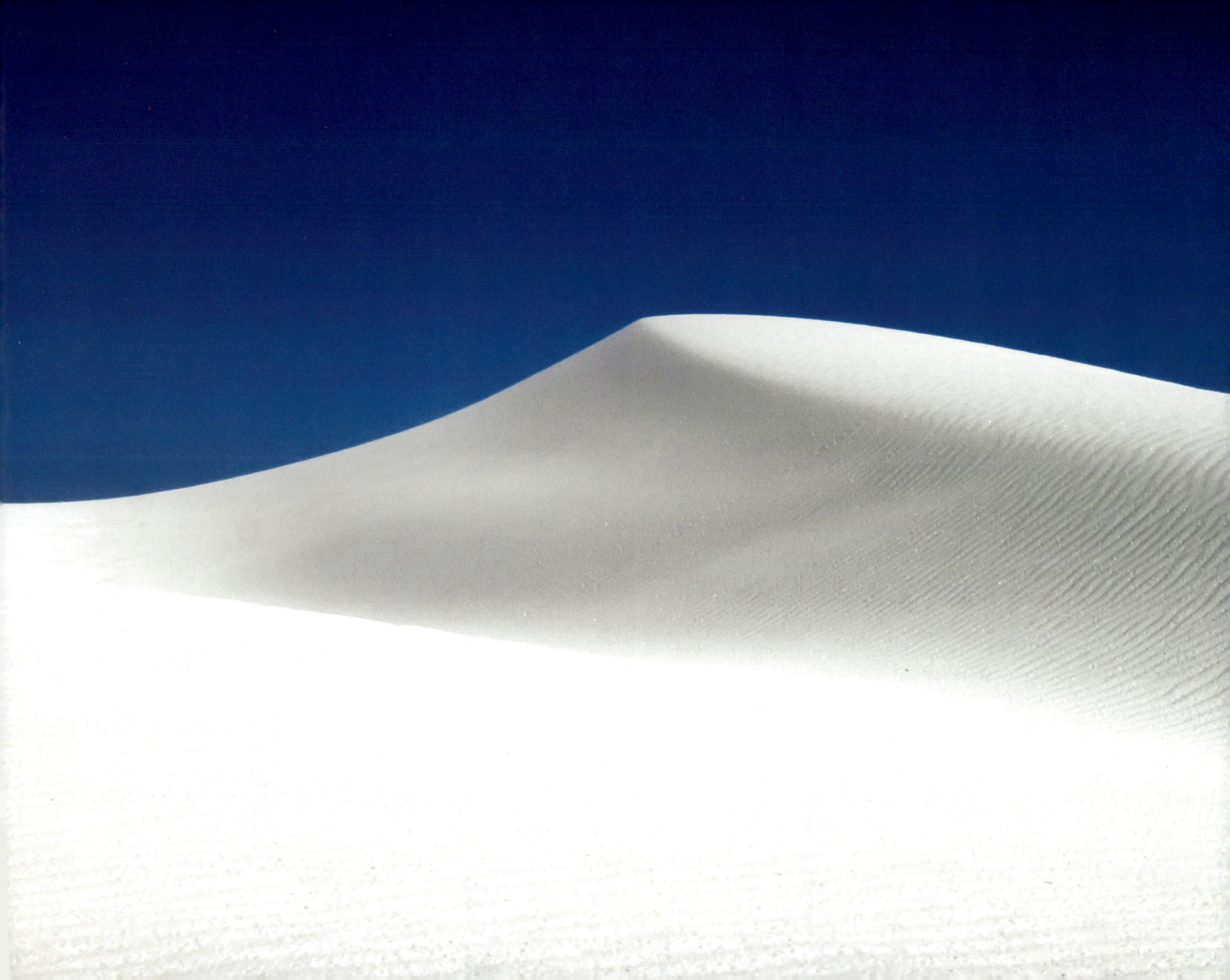

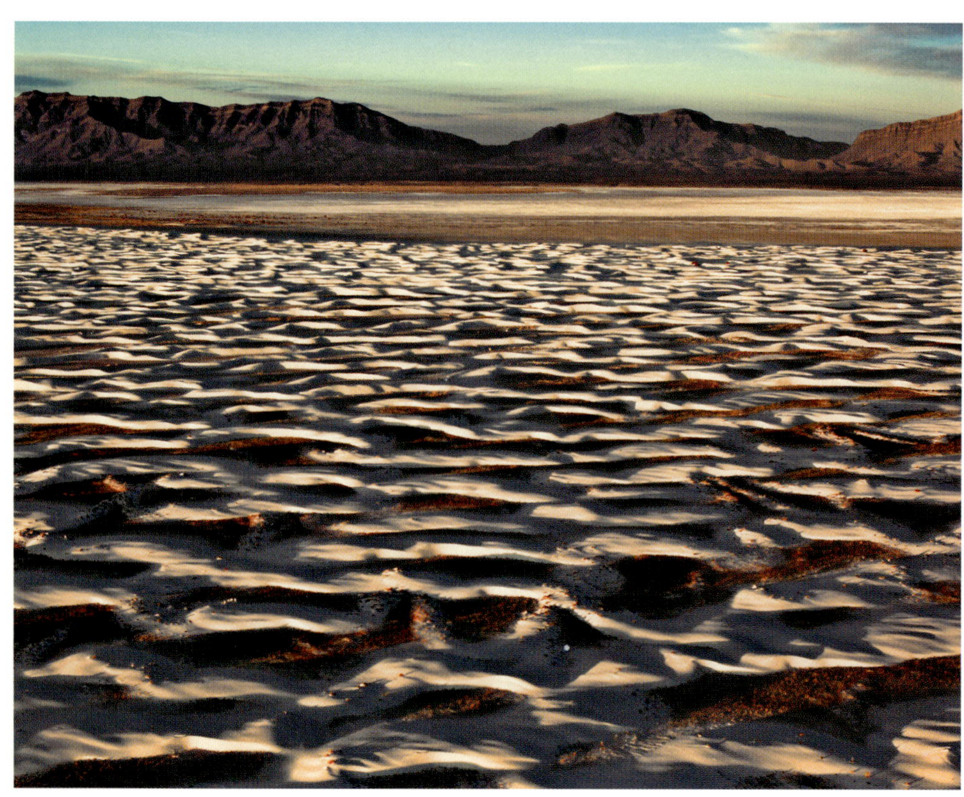

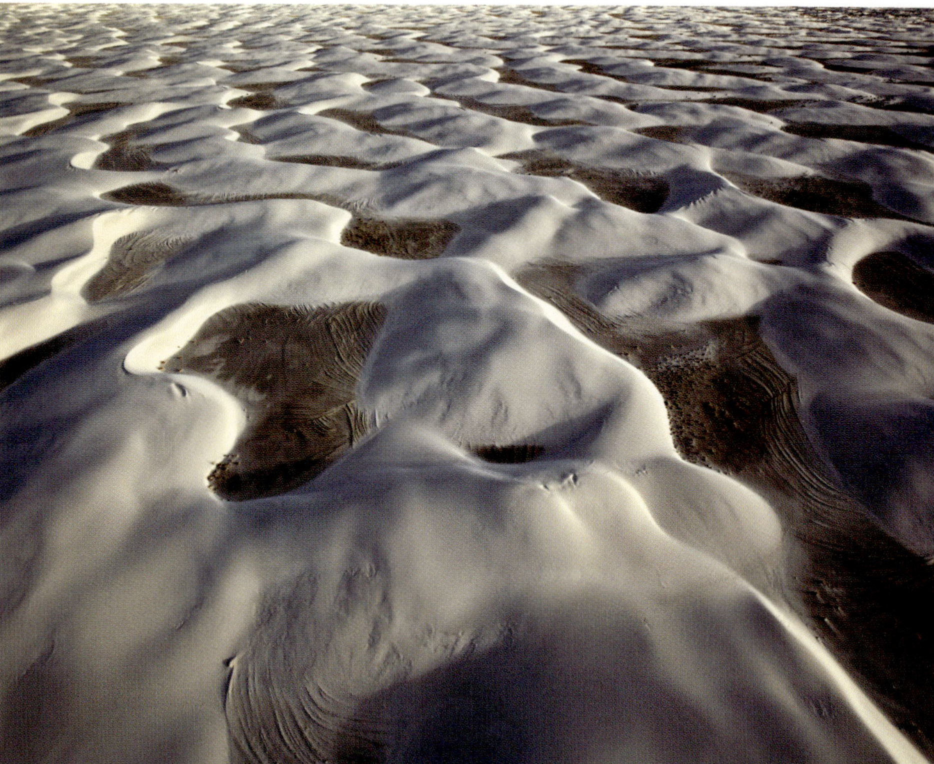

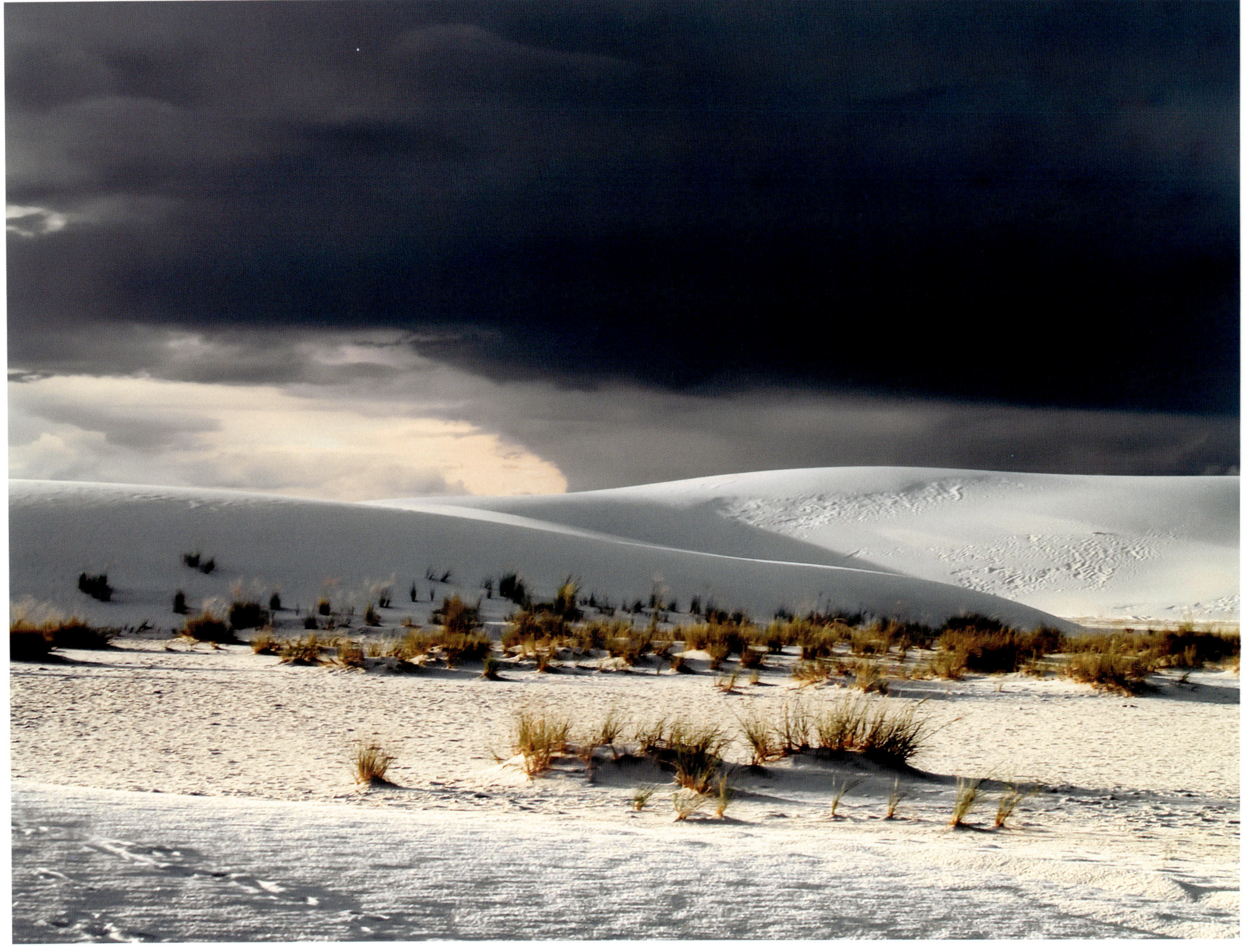

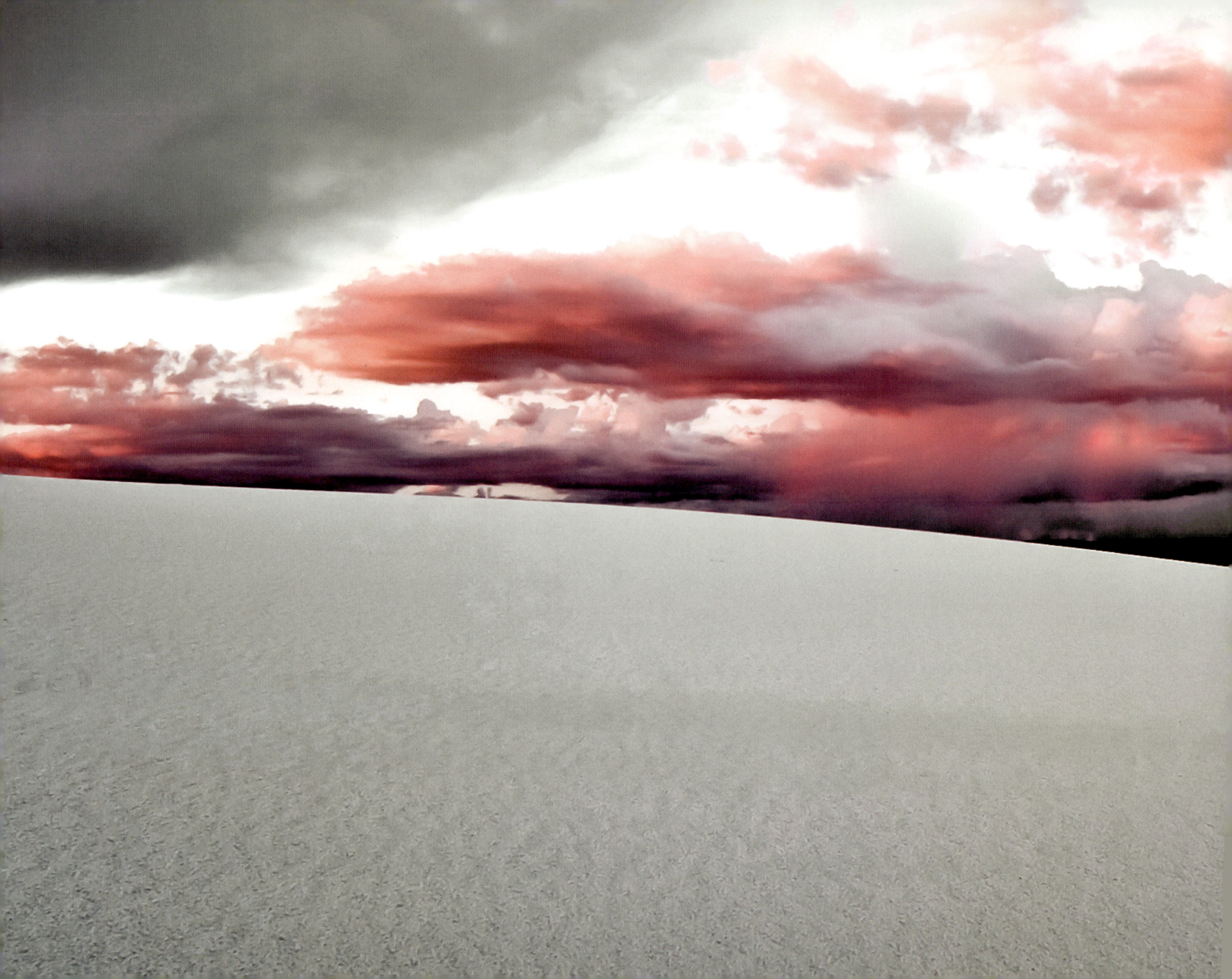

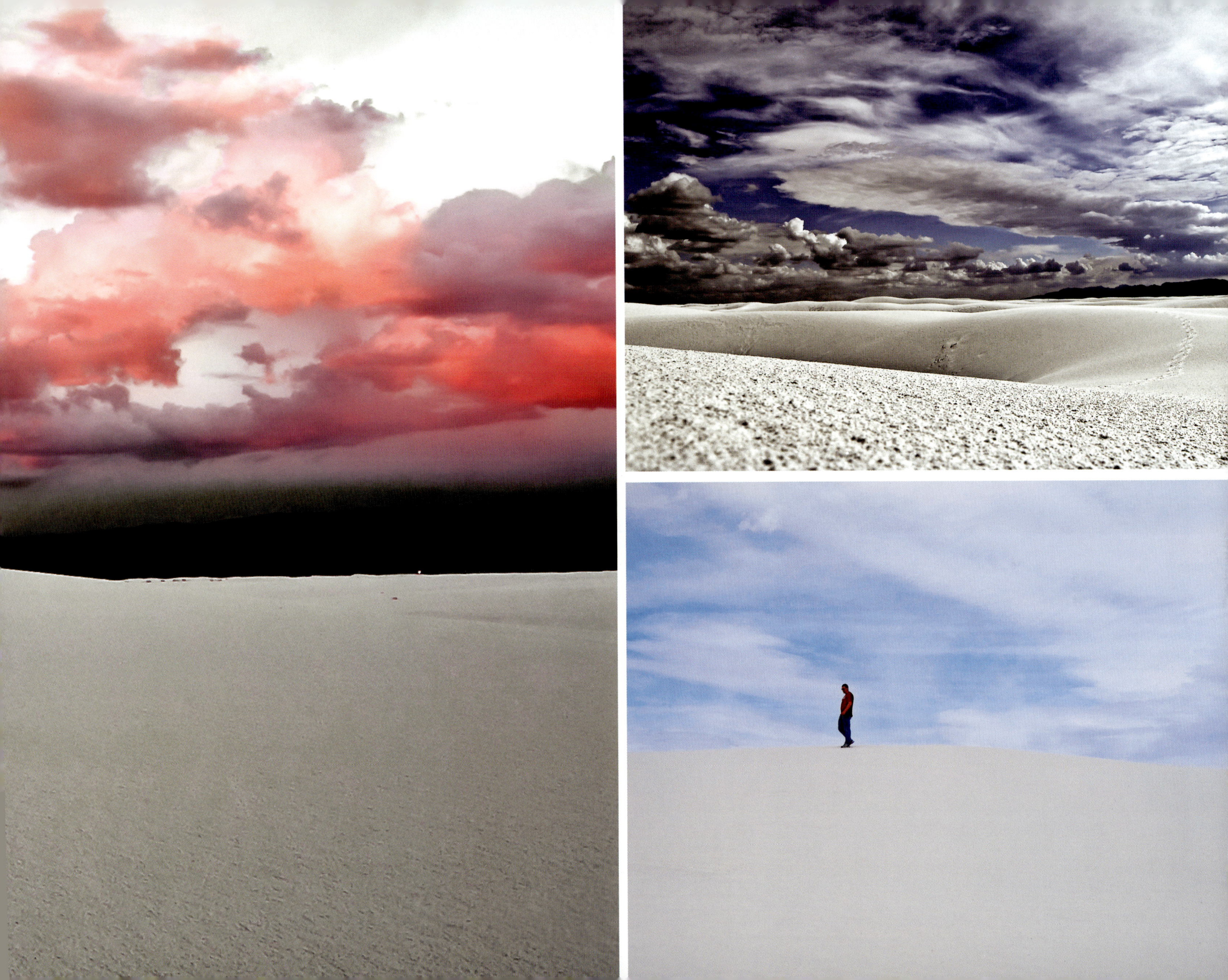

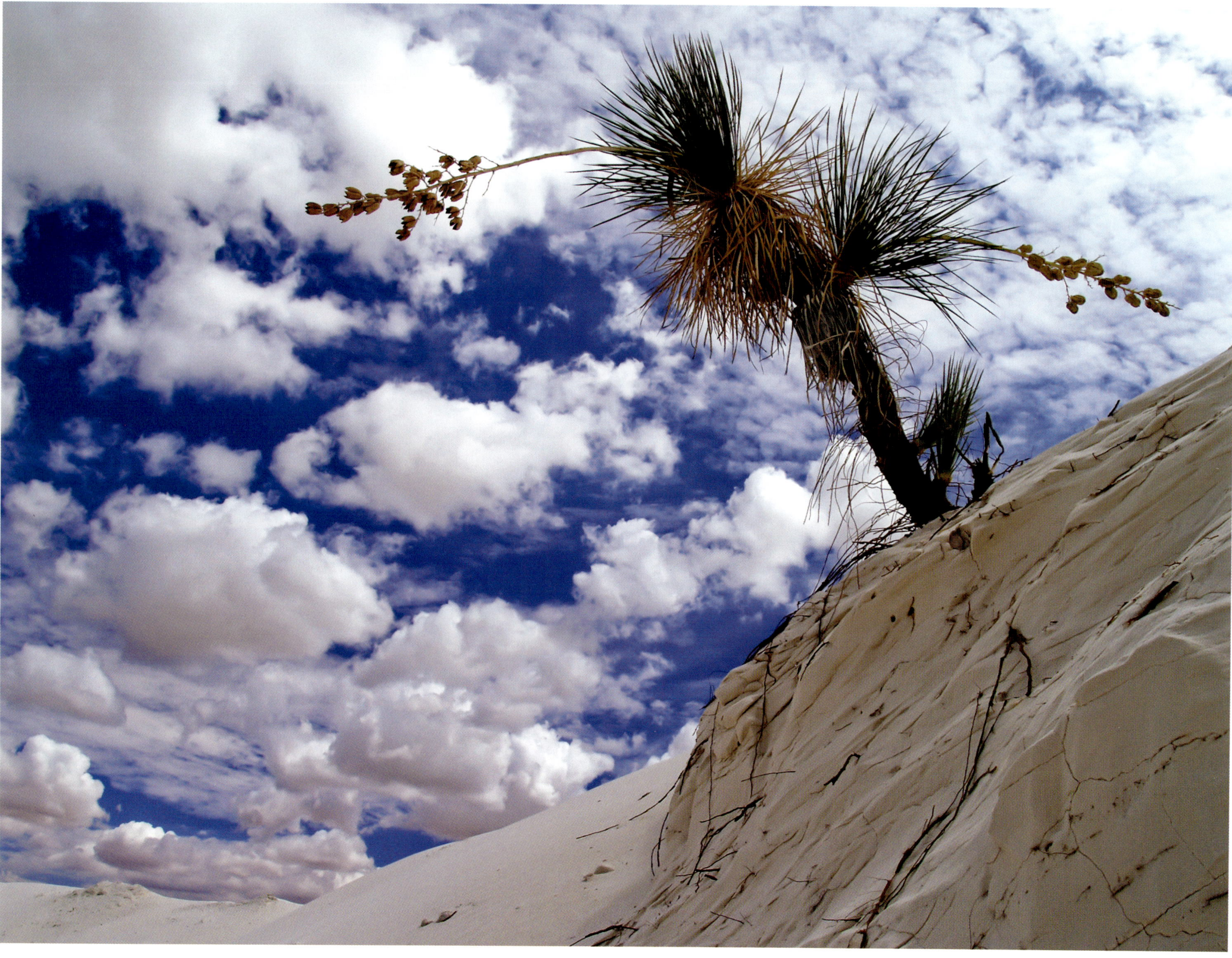

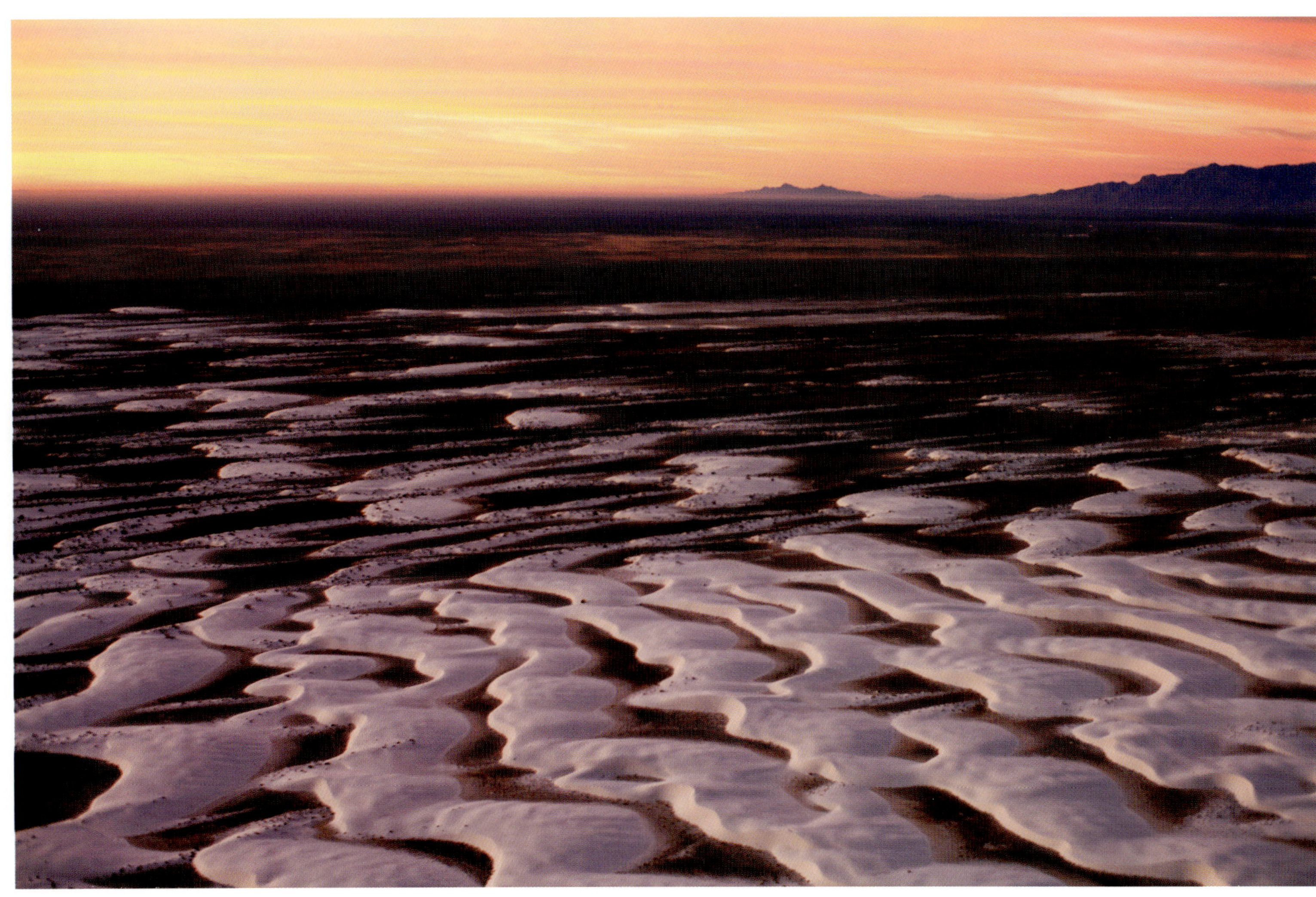

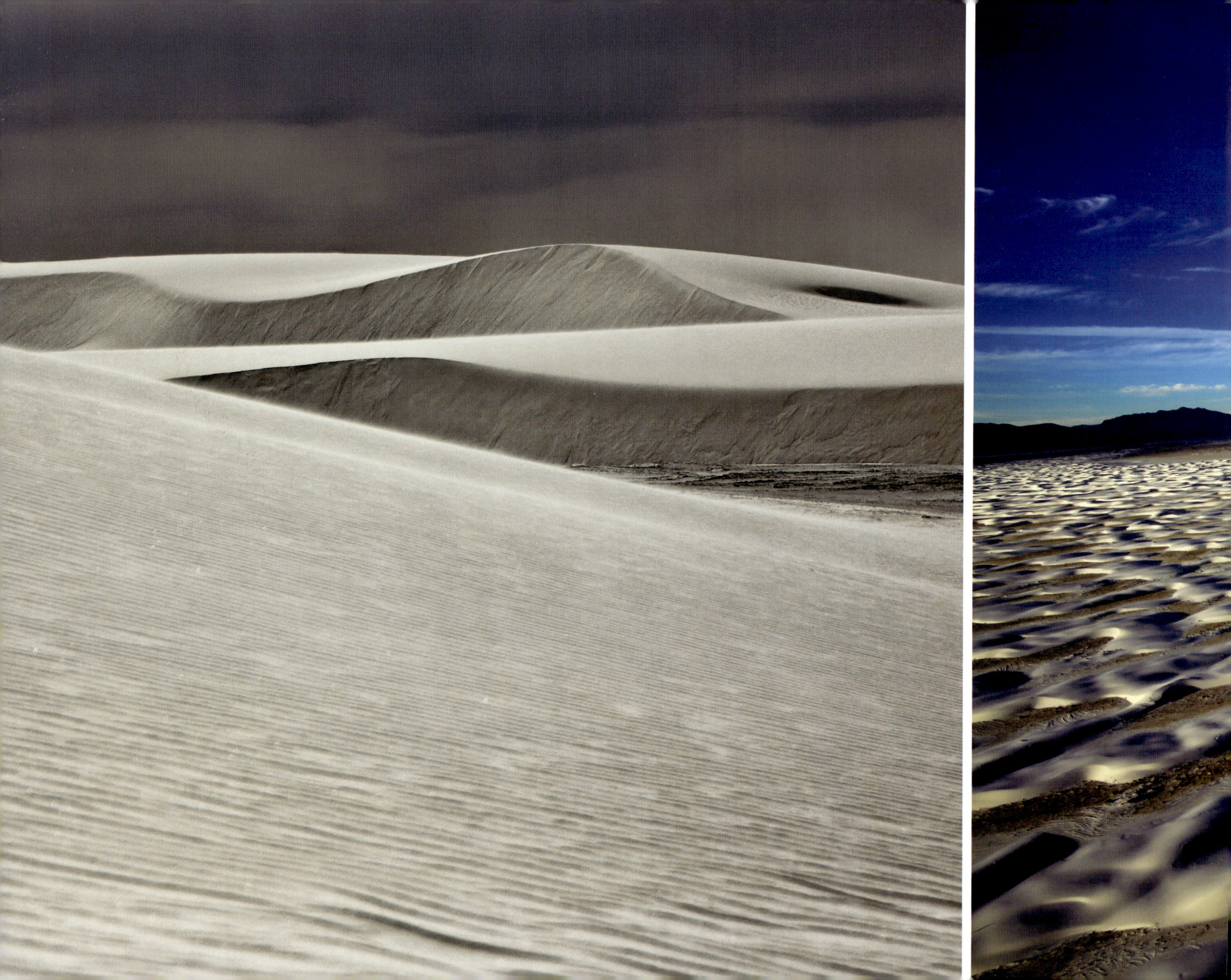

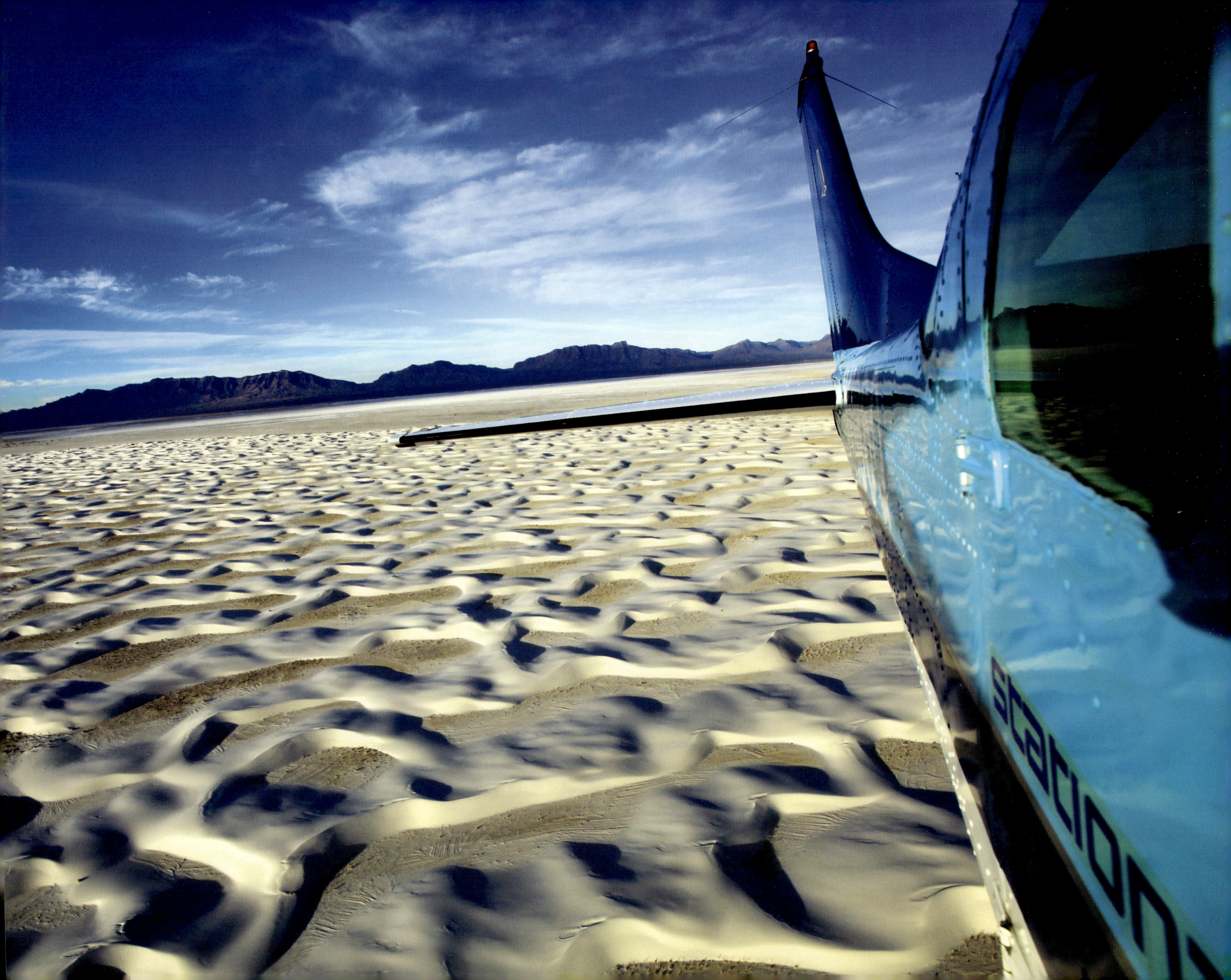
station

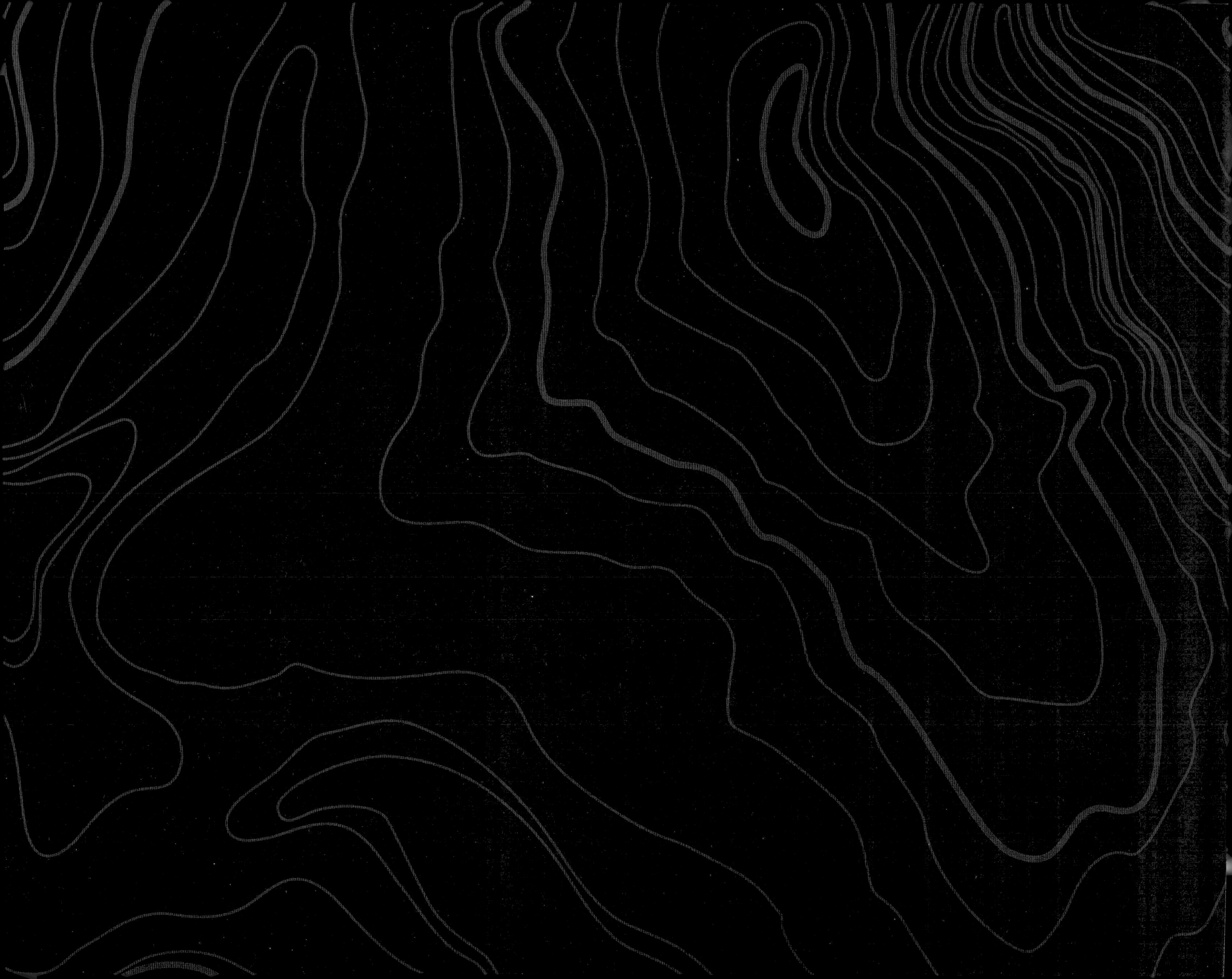

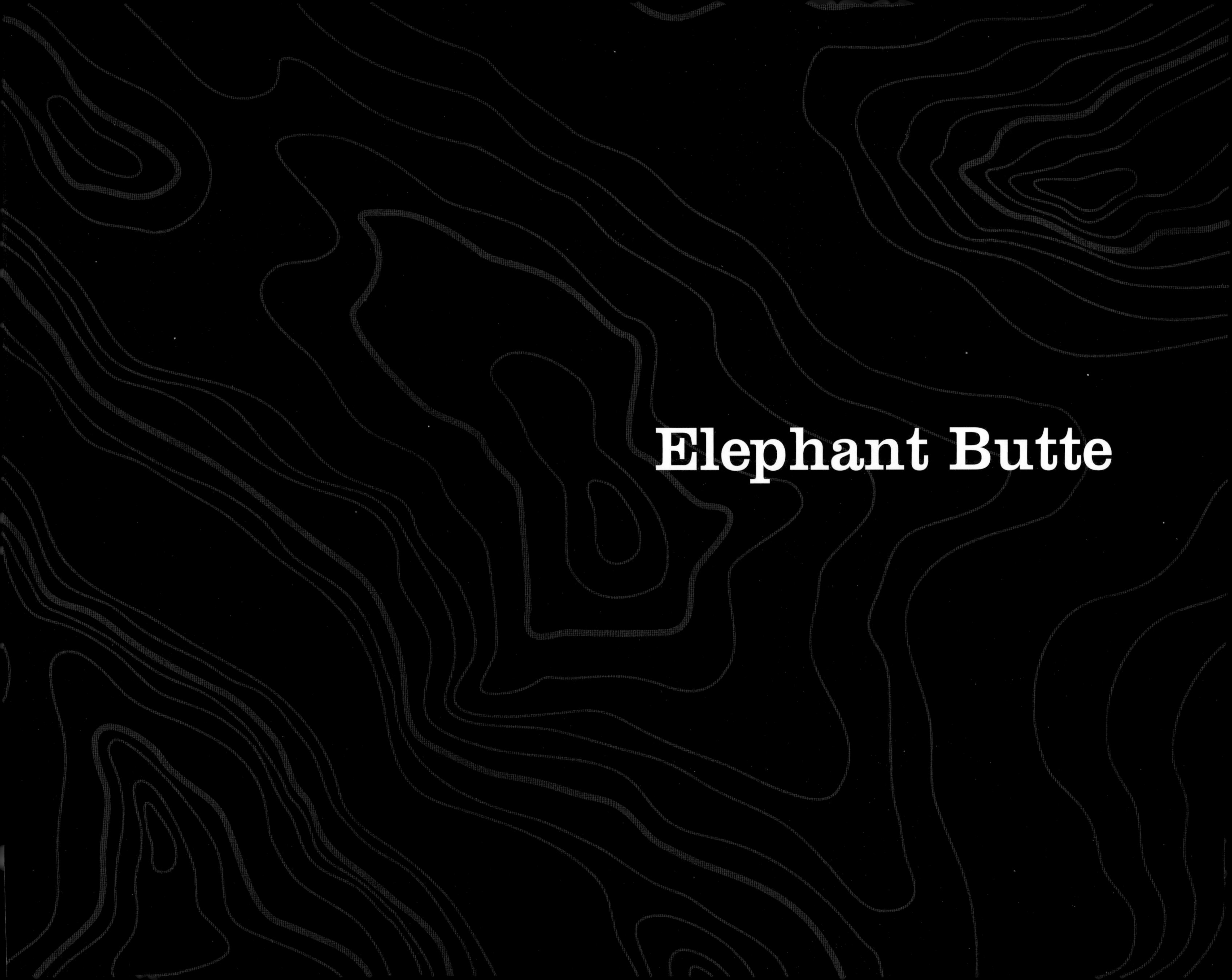
Elephant Butte

Elephant Butte

DISTANCE FROM EL PASO
120 miles north

LATITUDE
33°62’50” N

LONGITUDE
-107°00’94” W

ELEVATION
4,147 feet (1,264 meters)

AREA
36,500 acres
(14,771 hectares)

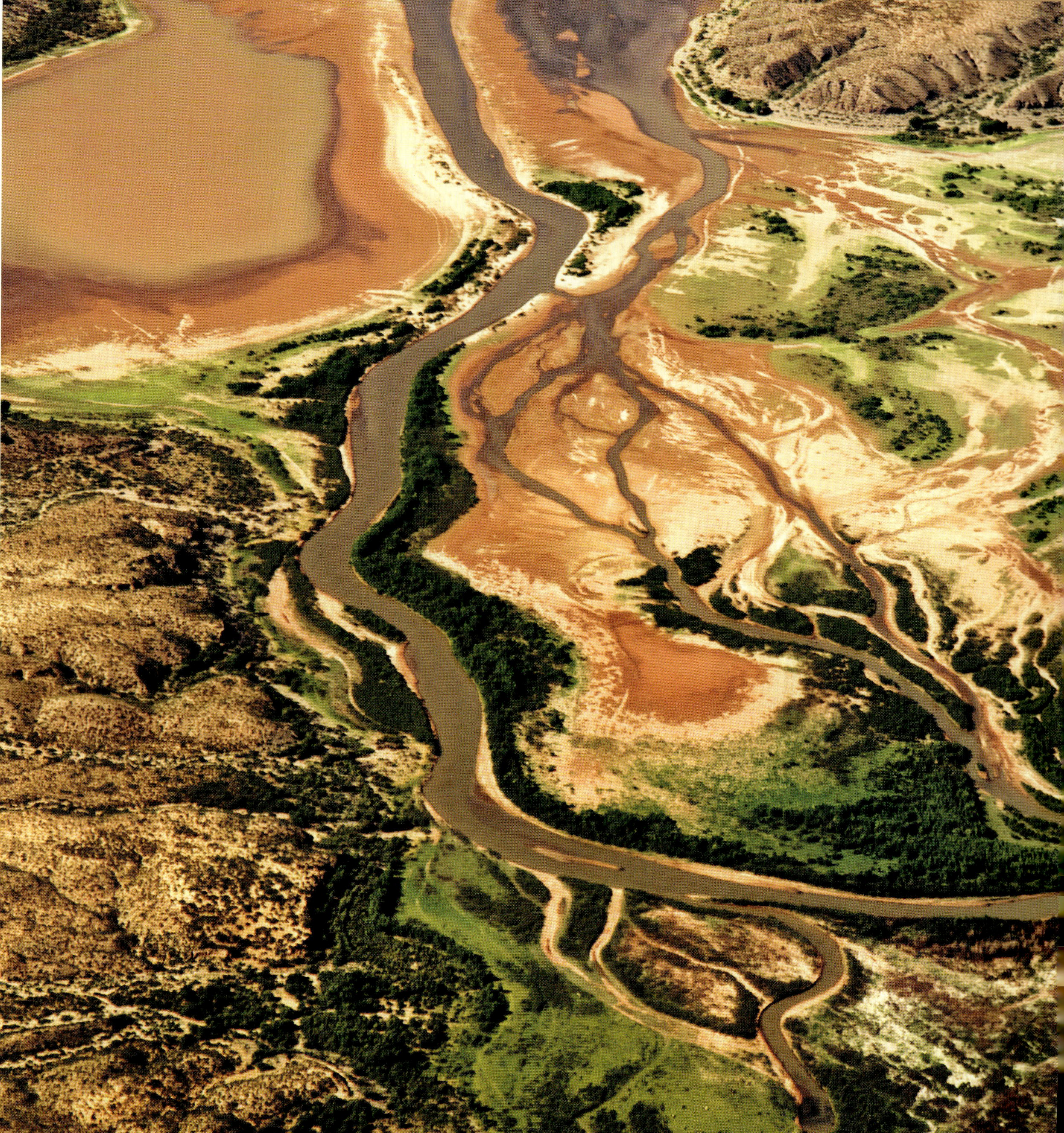

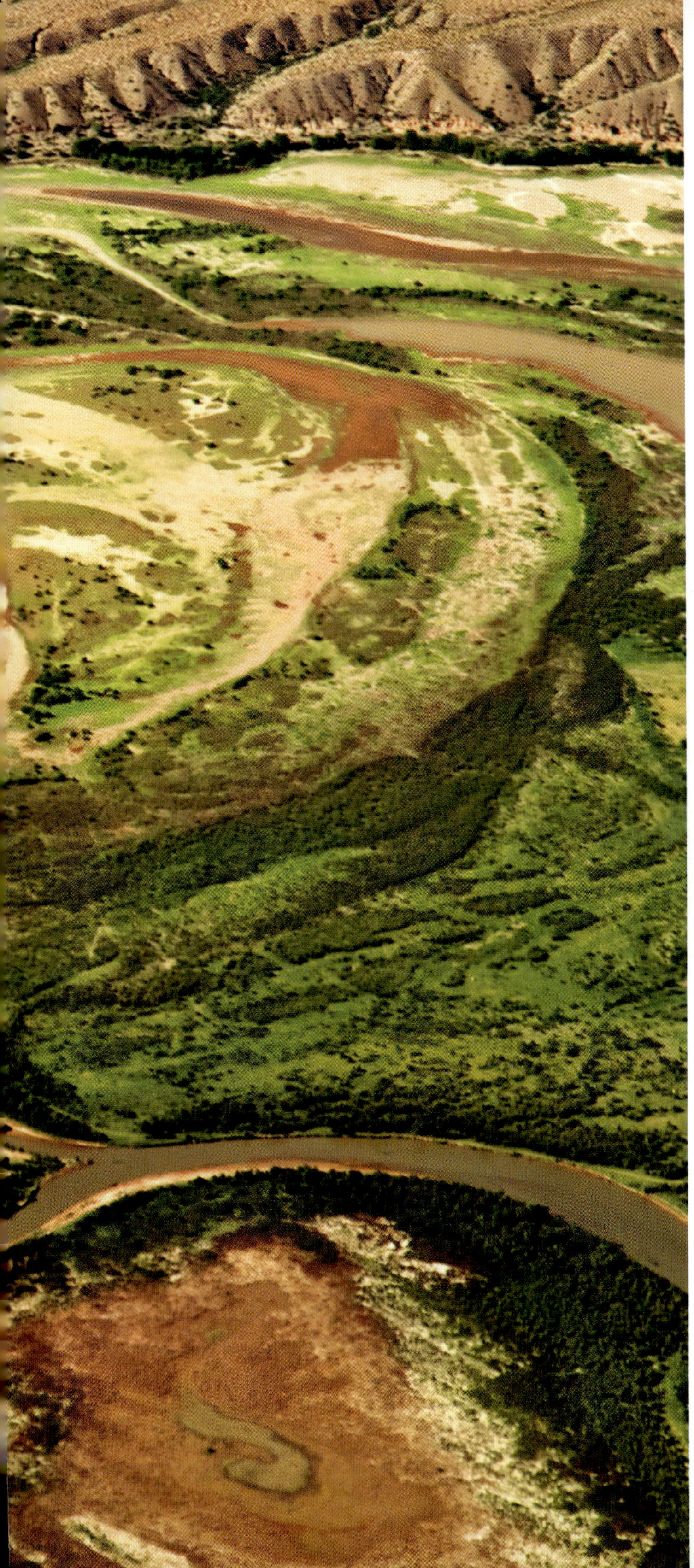

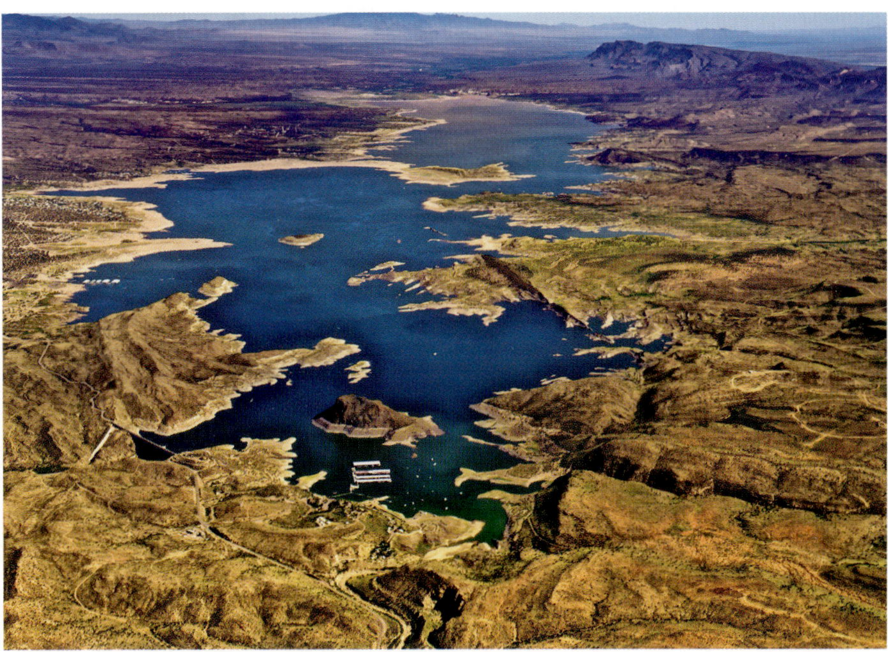

Flying high above Elephant Butte offers a delightful study in contrasts. The lake's stunning cobalt-blue water strikes my eye as if a painter had left masterful strokes on the desert floor below. Draining into the once mighty Rio Grande, the blue water sends out tendrils in brilliant complex shapes, like veins. The colors vary splendidly in pastoral shades of green and yellow where water nurtures the conspicuous vegetation clinging to its banks. Has Van Gogh been here with his artistic touch, I wonder? The answer is clear, as is the evidence of the importance of the Rio Grande.

Over one hundred million years ago, this area was part of a vast shallow ocean. Once the sea receded, the area was the favorite hunting ground of the *Tyrannosaurus rex* dinosaur. Evidence of the rex, one of the largest land-dwelling predators of all time, and other dinosaur species have been discovered in area rock formations. Although fossils of the *Stegomastodon* (a primitive relative of today's elephant) have been discov-

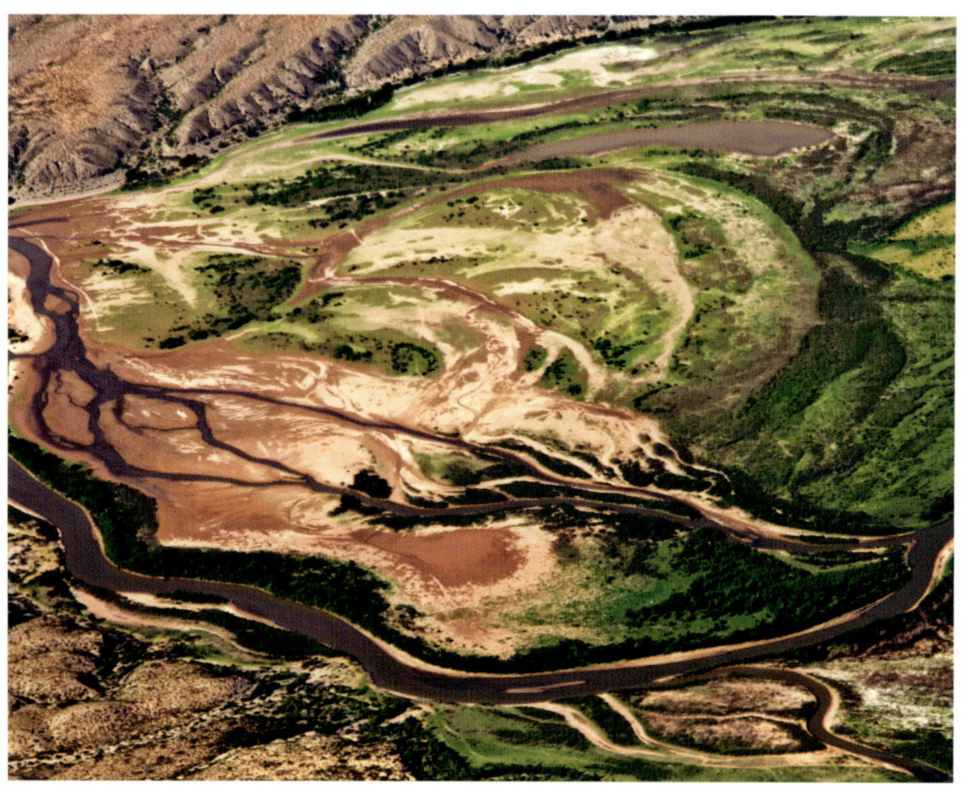

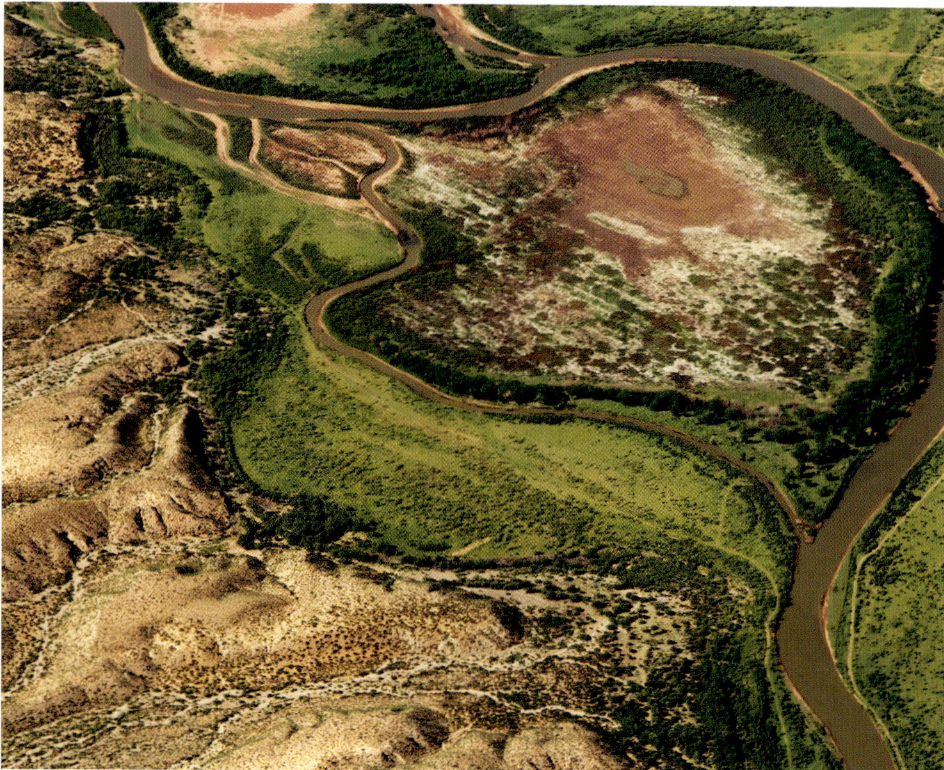

ered near the lake, the area was not named for its former inhabitants, but for an island in the lake—once the core of an ancient volcano—that is shaped like an elephant. The lake itself formed when a dam was constructed across the Rio Grande in 1916. Forty miles long, the lake shoulders more than two hundred miles of shoreline.

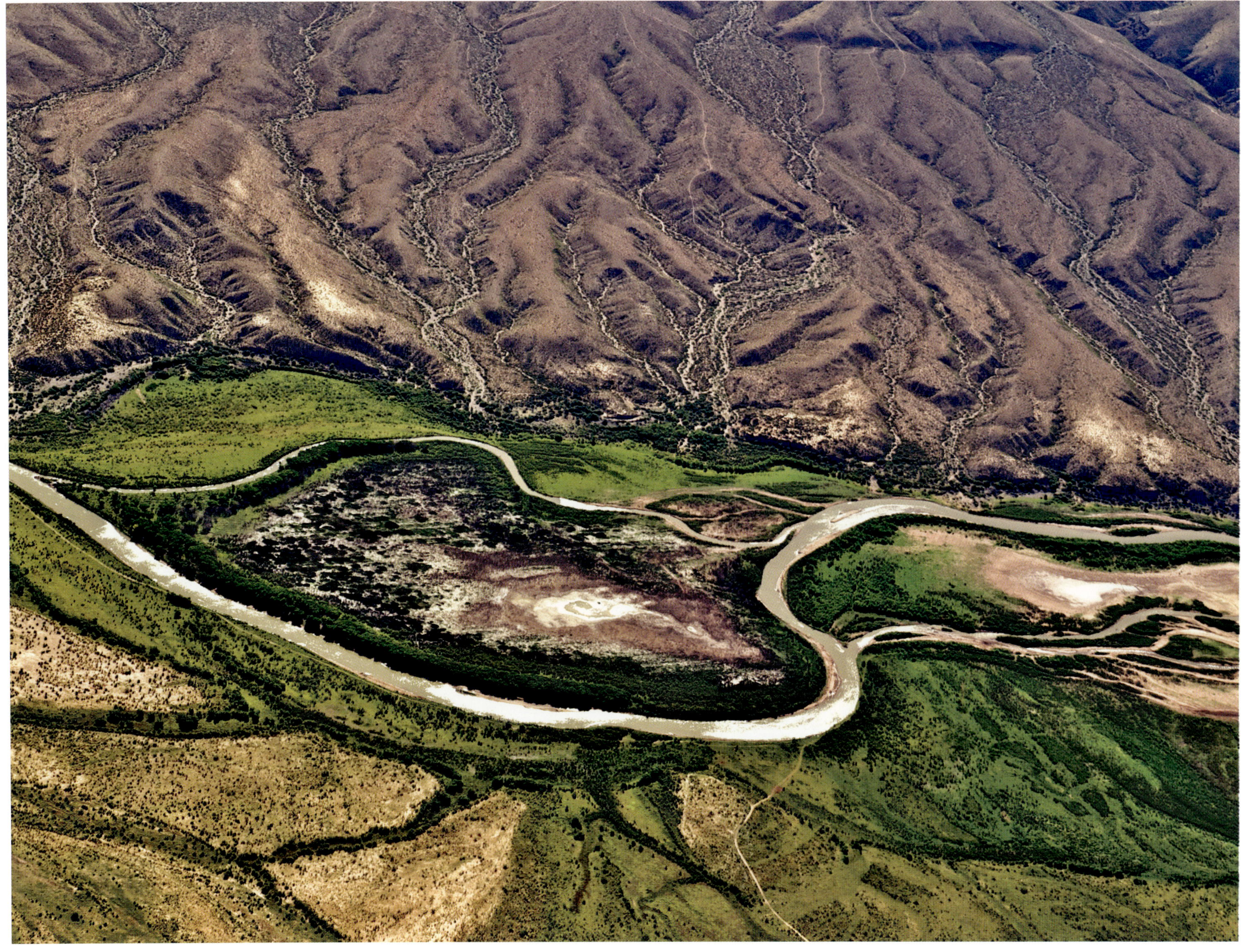

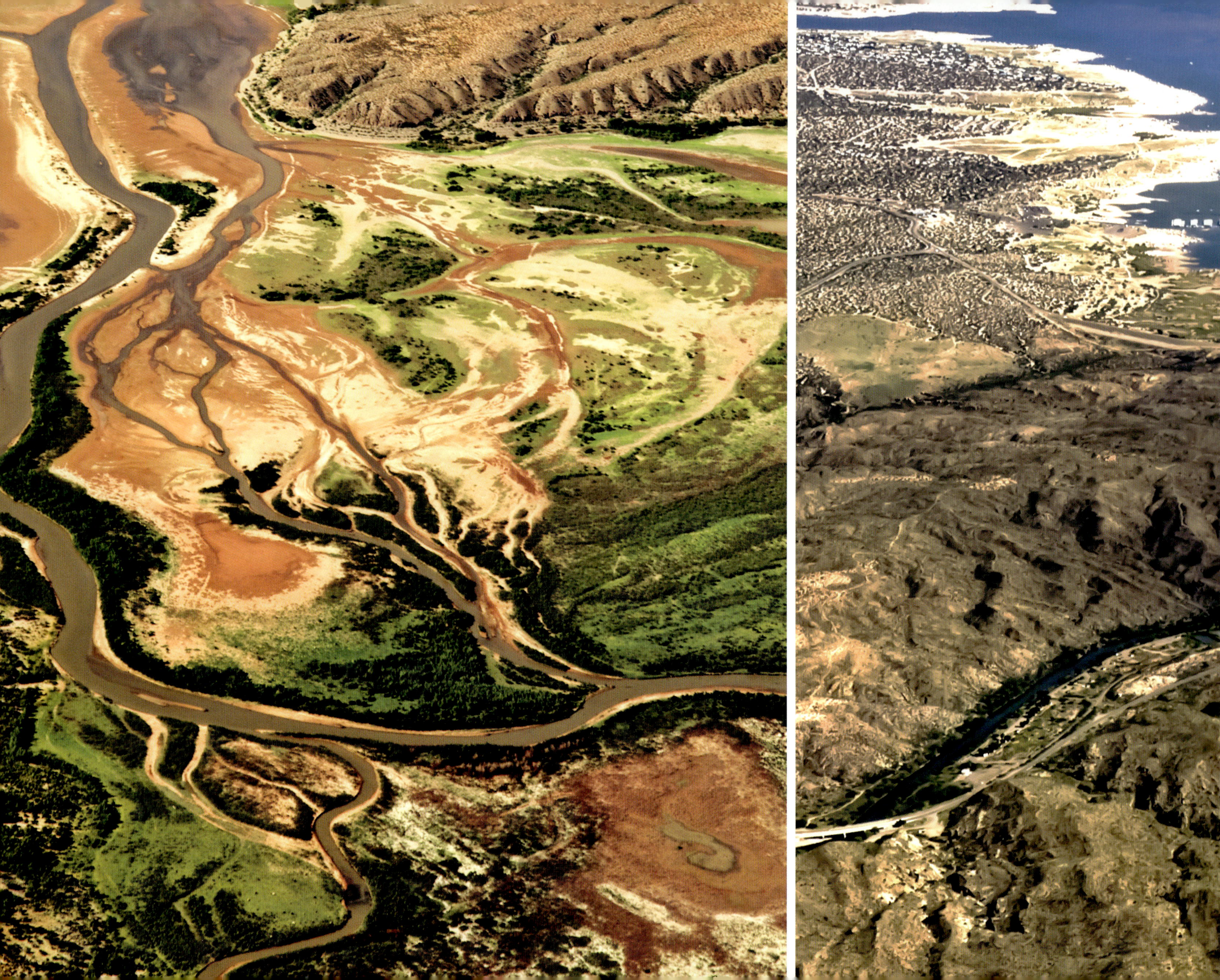

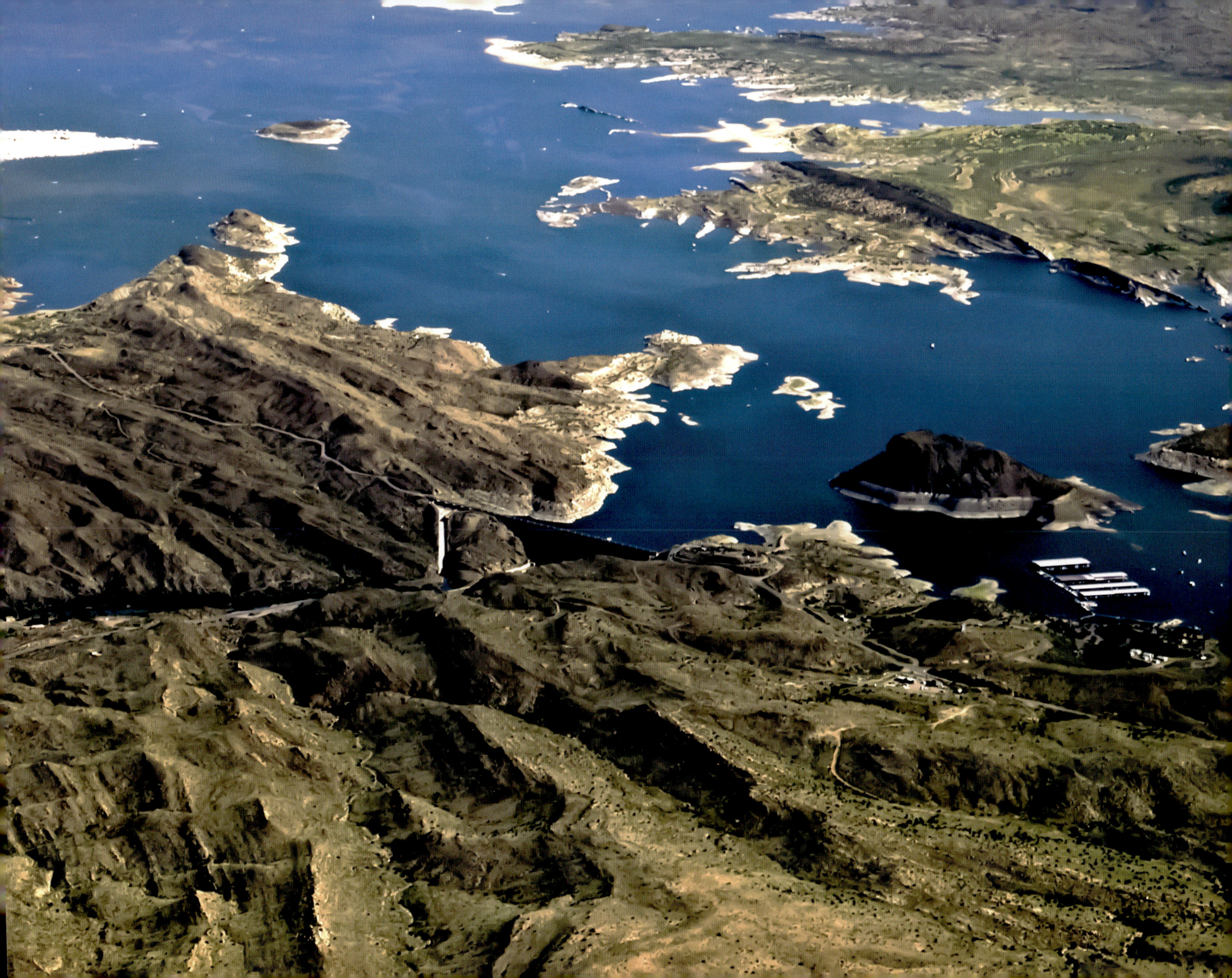

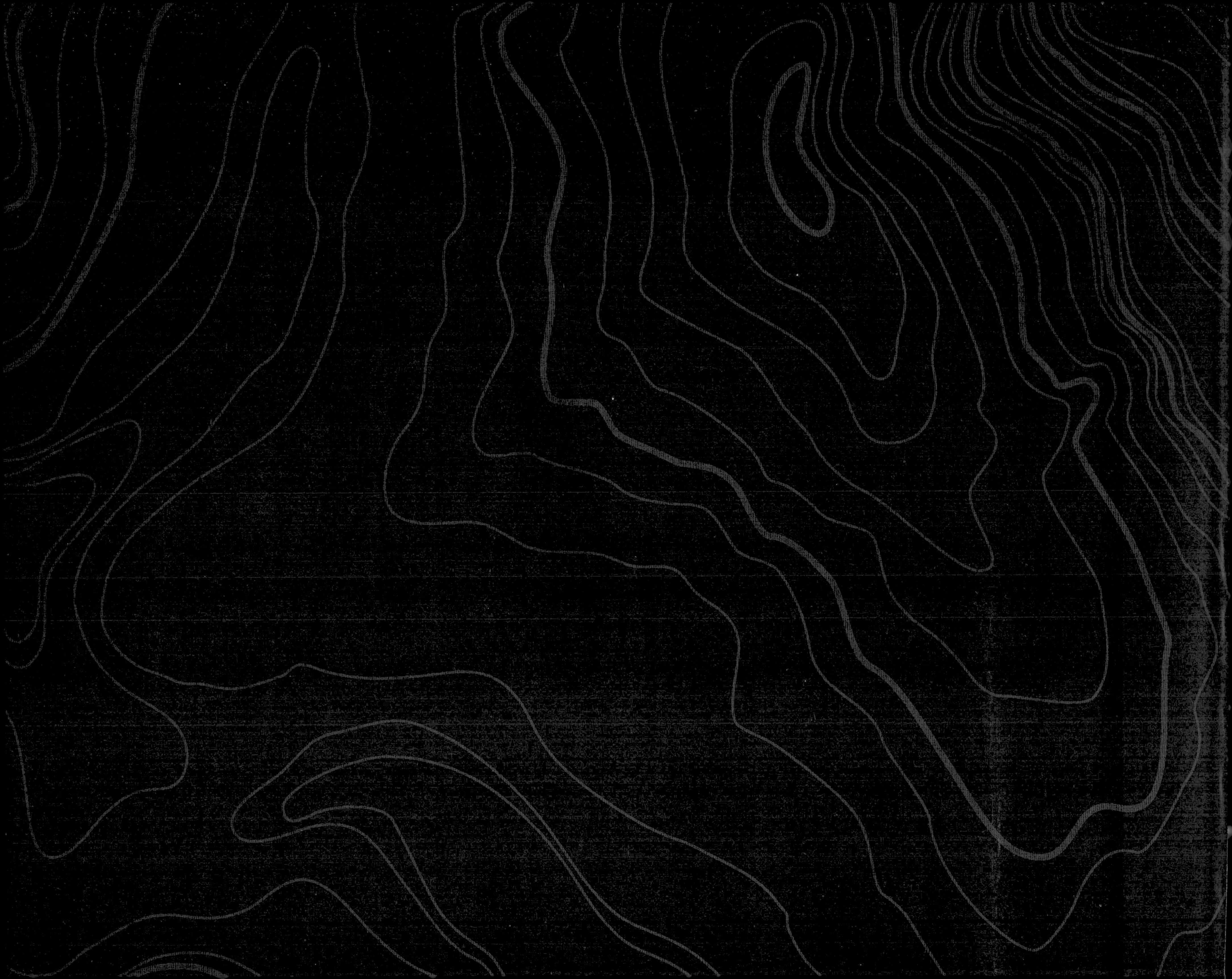

City of Rocks

City of Rocks

DISTANCE FROM EL PASO
120 miles northwest

LATITUDE
32°35'24" N

LONGITUDE
-107°58'33" W

ELEVATION
5,250 feet (1,600 meters)

AREA
1,230 acres
(497.8 hectares)

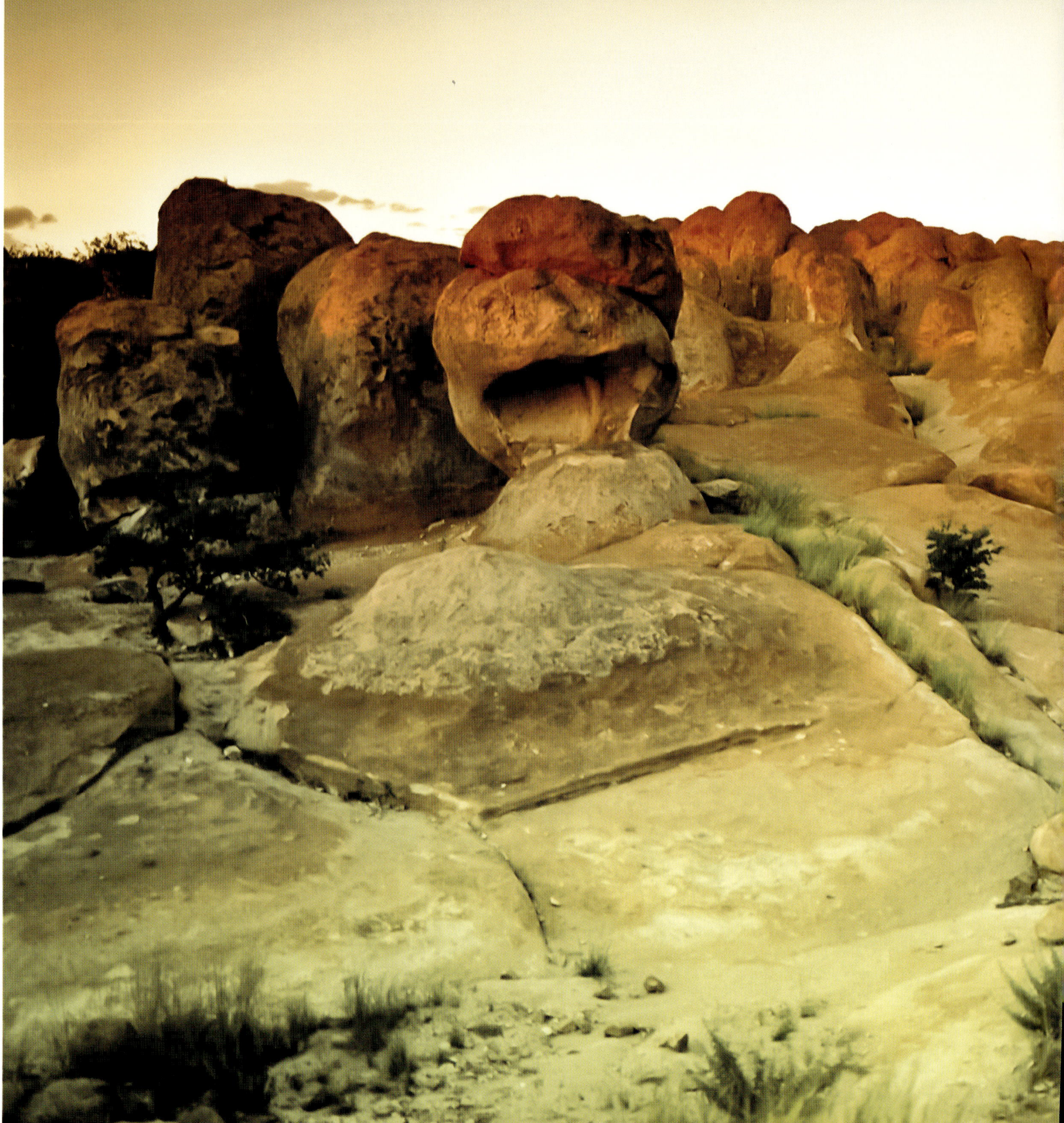

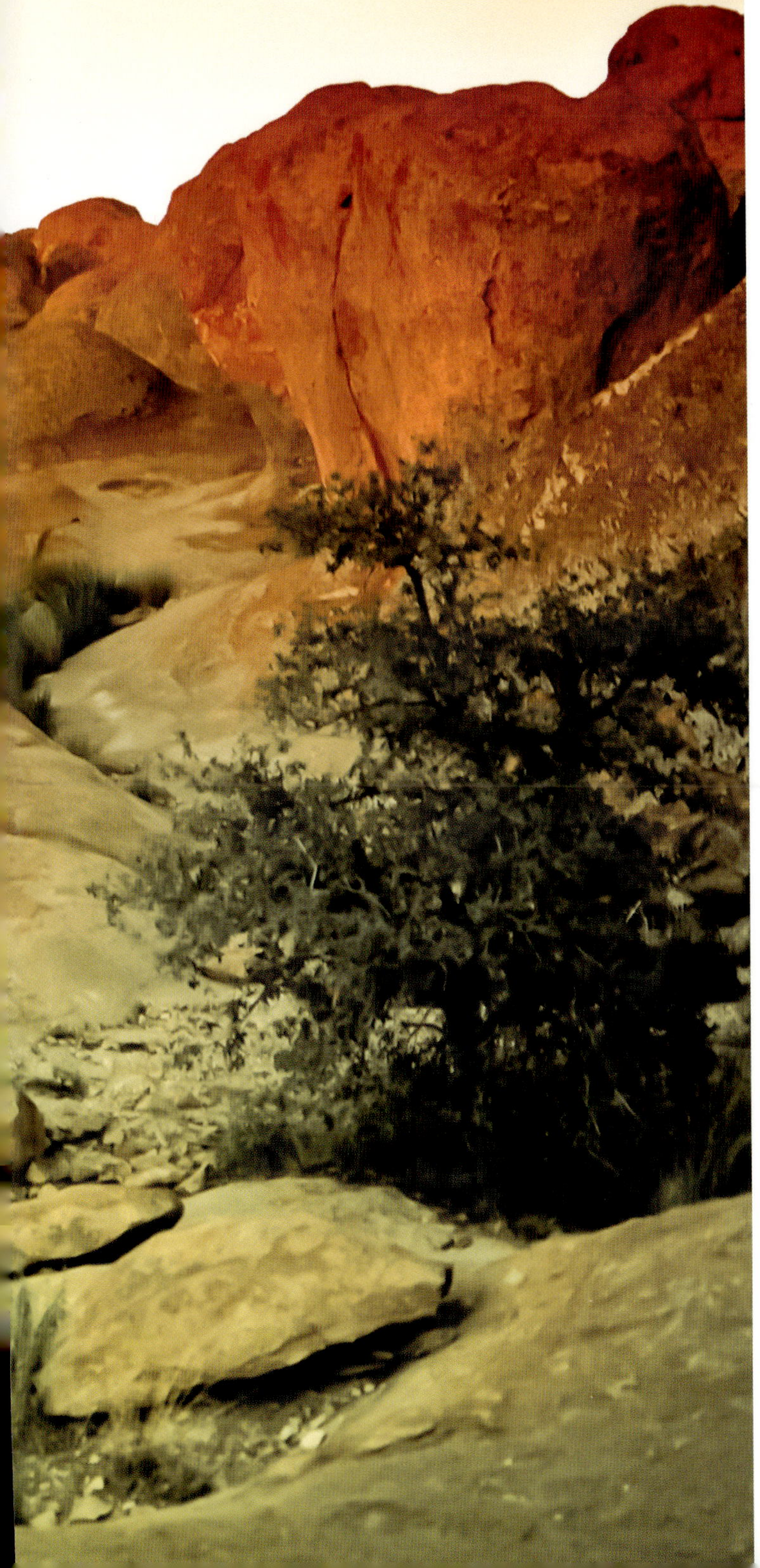

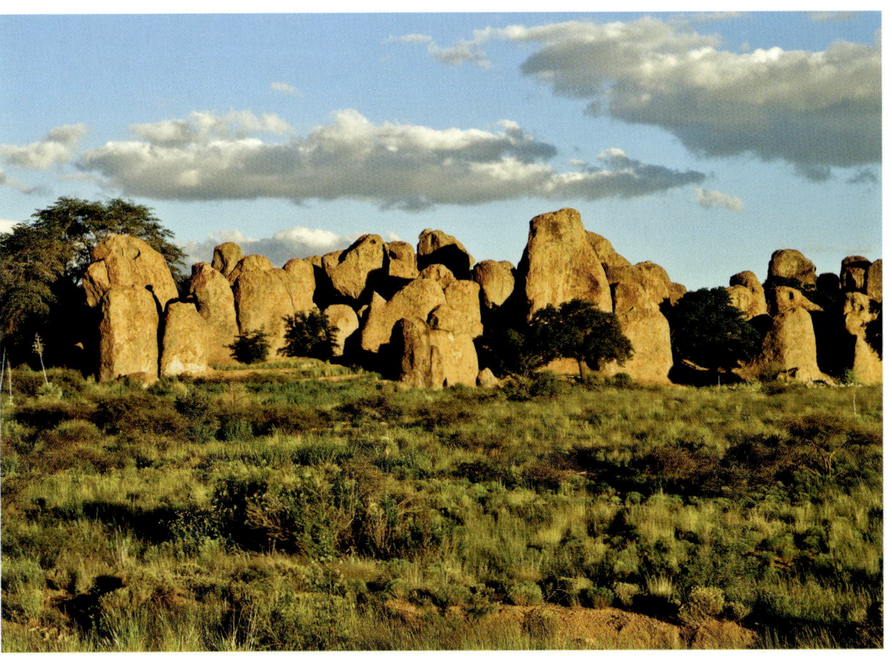

Unexpectedly arising from southern New Mexico's barren landscape is a natural arrangement of larger-than-life rocks reminiscent of urban high-rises created from hot volcanic ash that solidified nearly thirty-five million years ago. These formations have been carved by the elements into gnomish shapes and fanciful columns that can reach forty feet high. Only a handful of places in the world have formations like these.

Popular with many overnight campers, the "city" is webbed with pathways that I am pleased to trundle through, feeling dwarfed along the way, until dusk. It is during the golden hour, when the sun begins to set, that the magic begins. The sun's rays bounce from the ancient volcanic rock giving off an exquisitely rich cornucopia of color—sparkling hues of pink, orange, yellow, and purple—that you can only see in these moments. The "city" comes to life, making this an ideal time to begin clicking the camera's shutter.

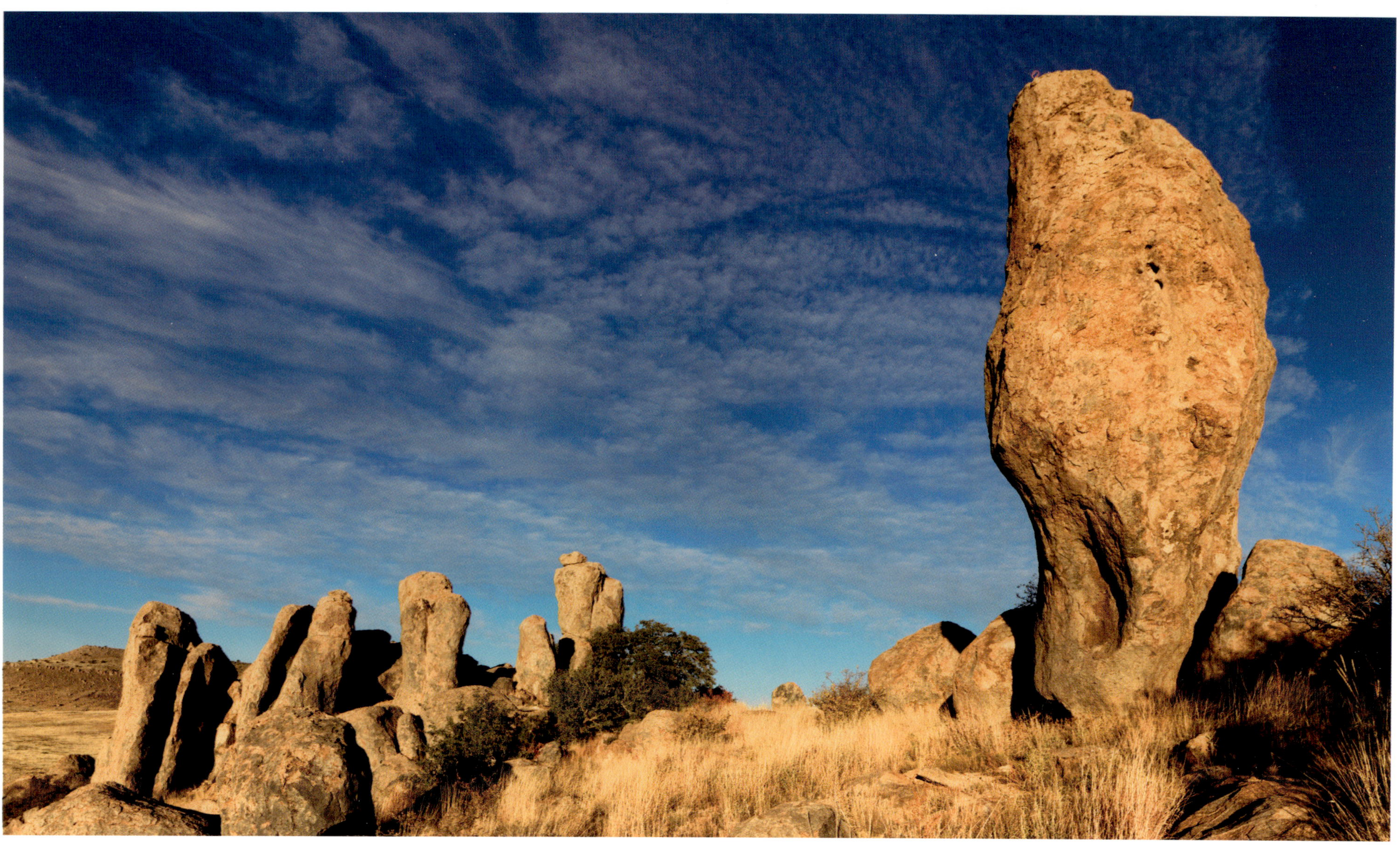

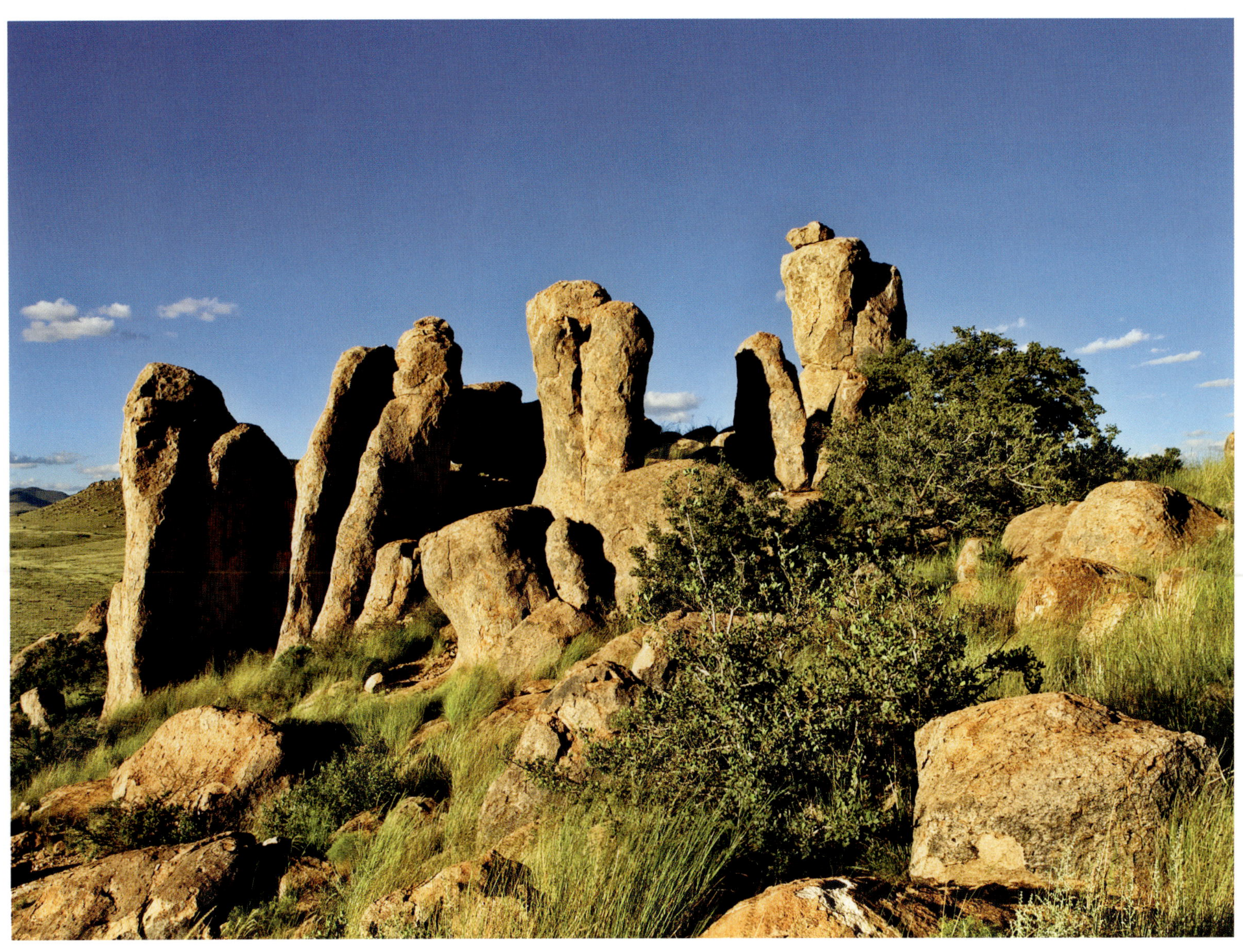

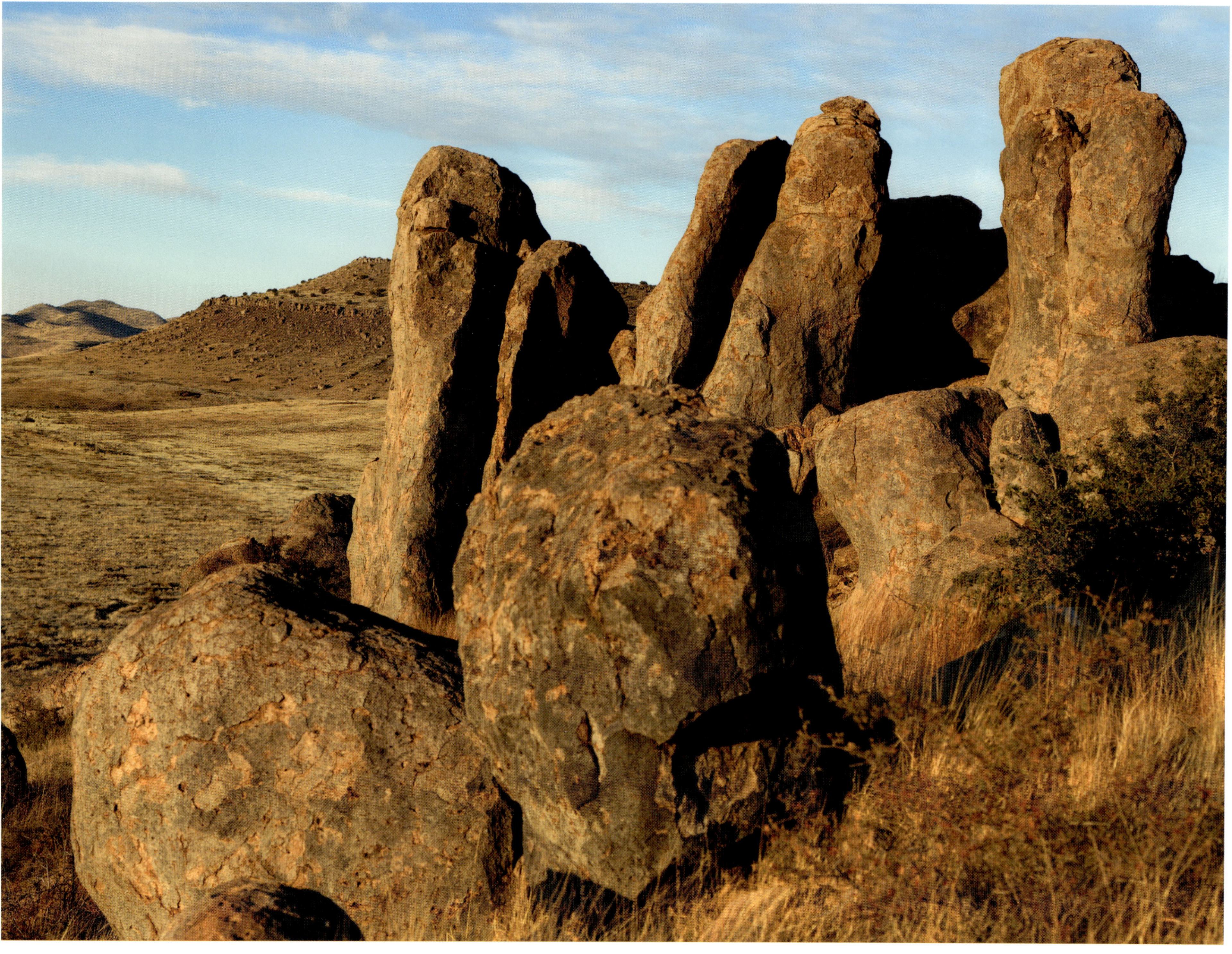

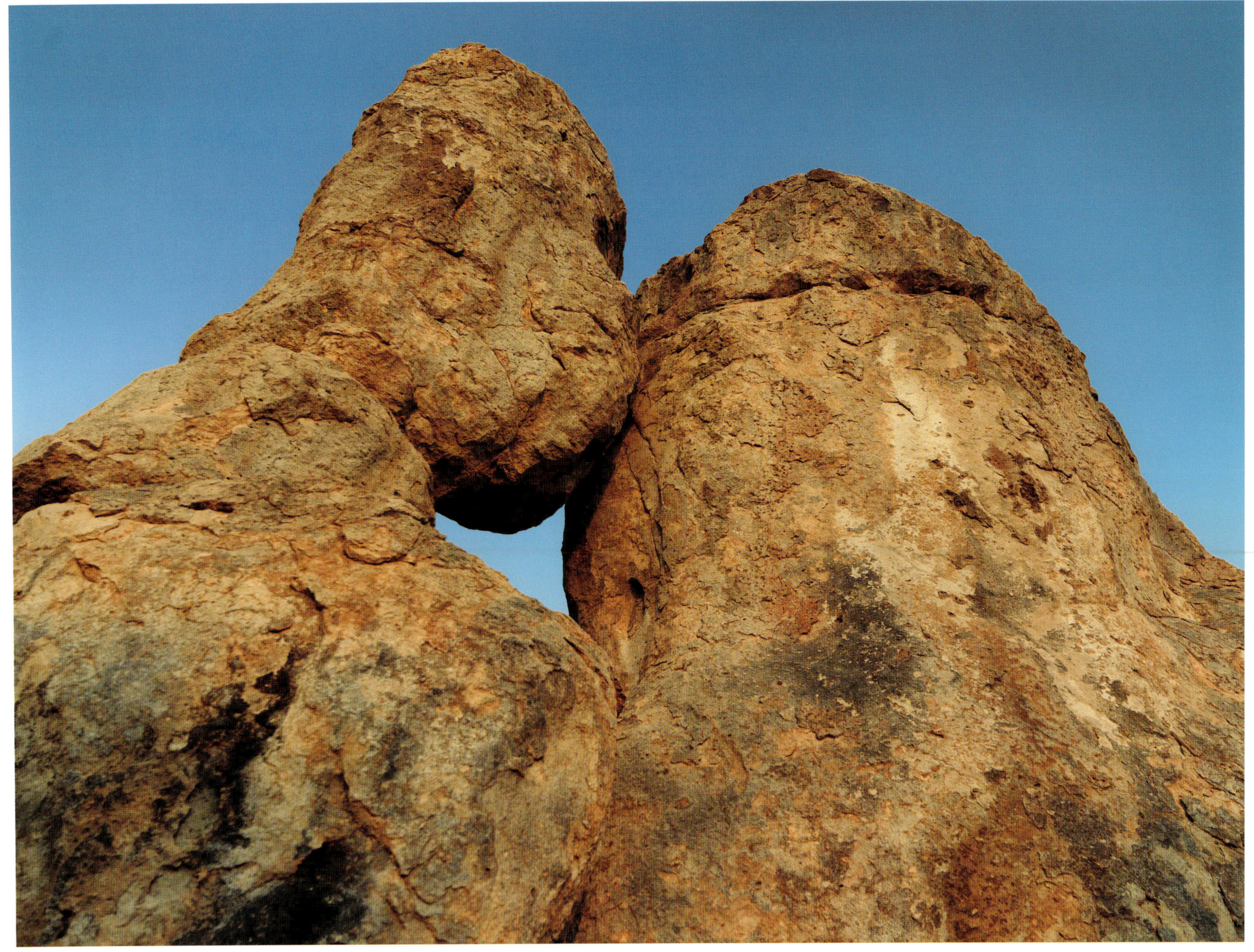

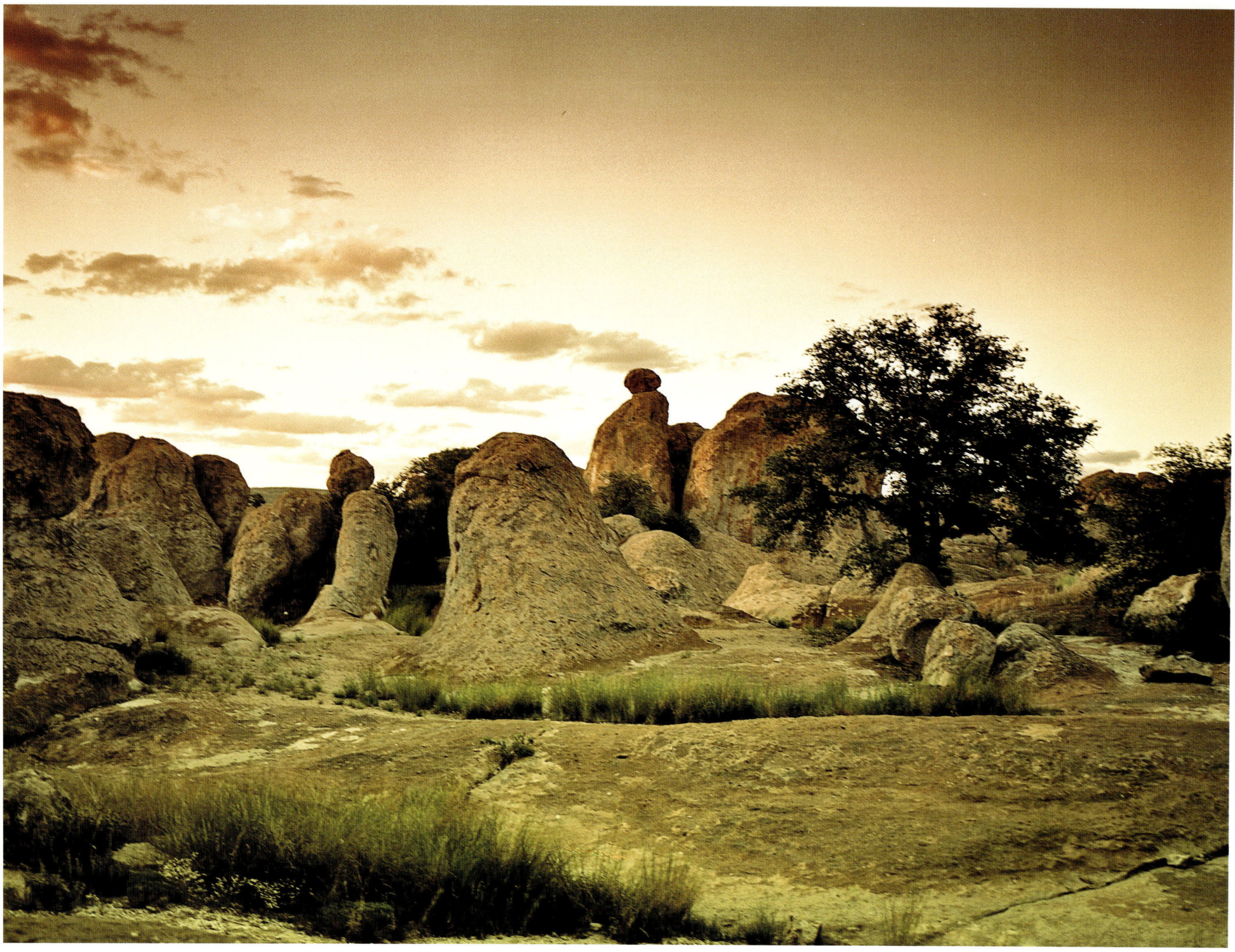

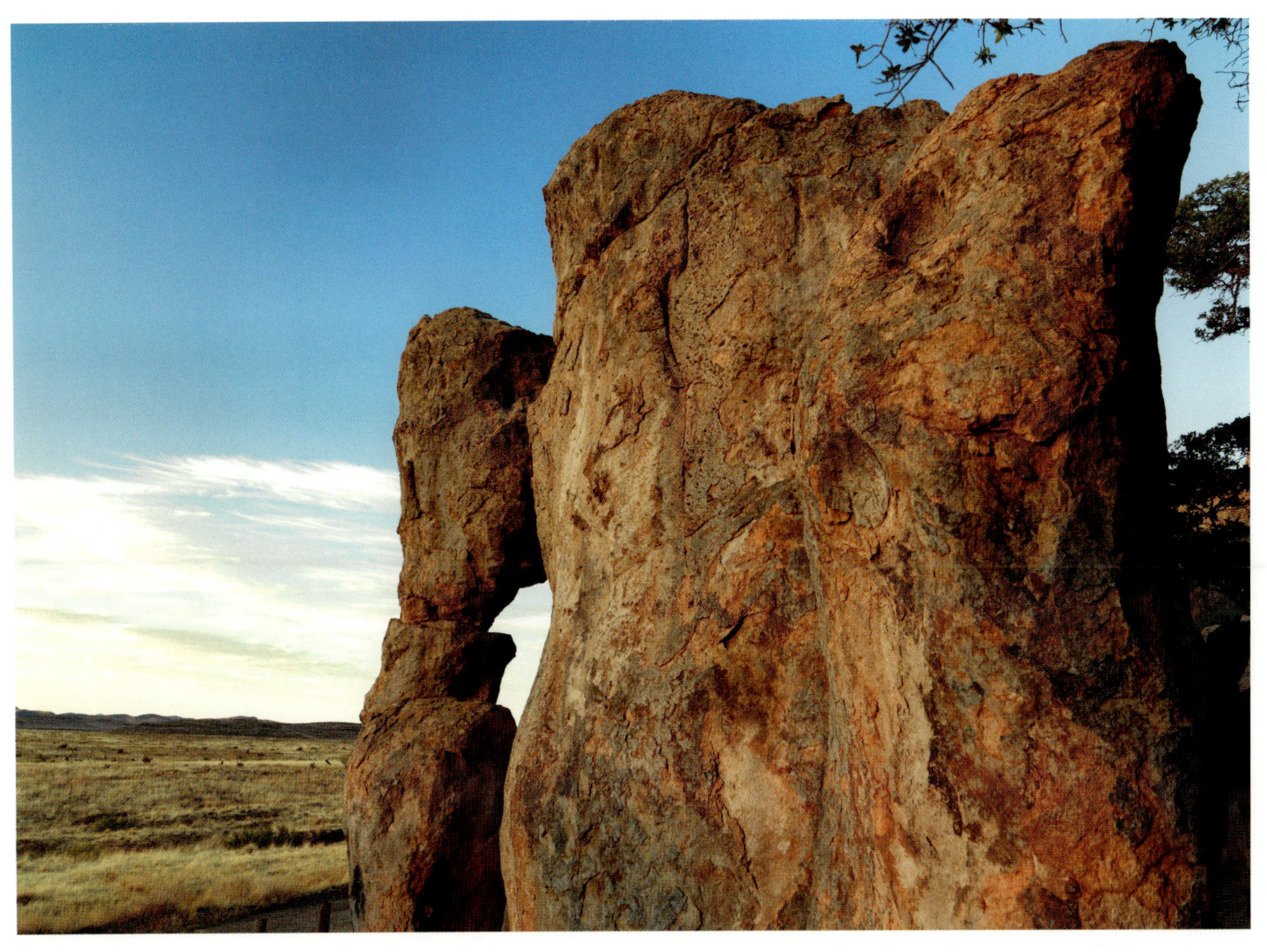

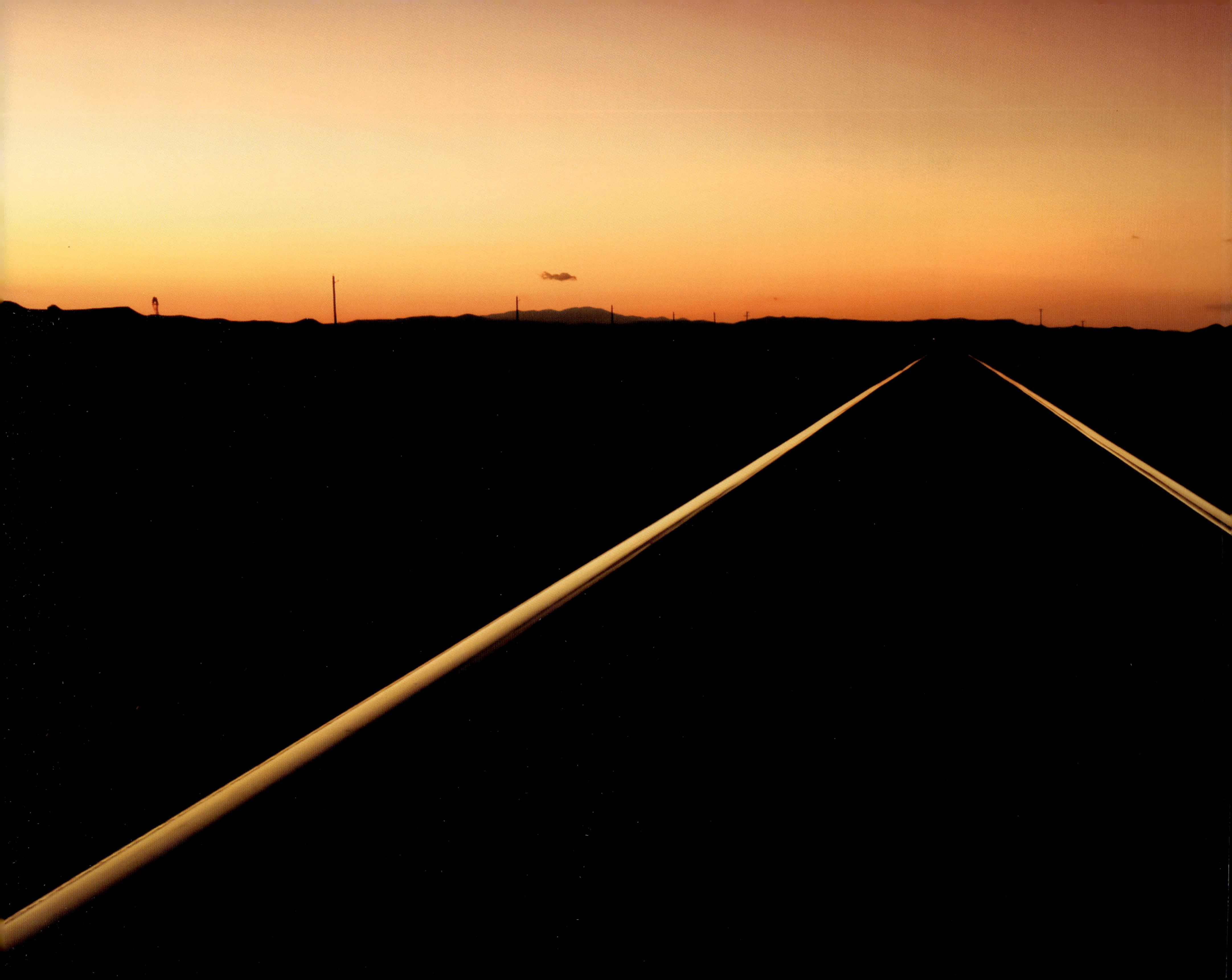

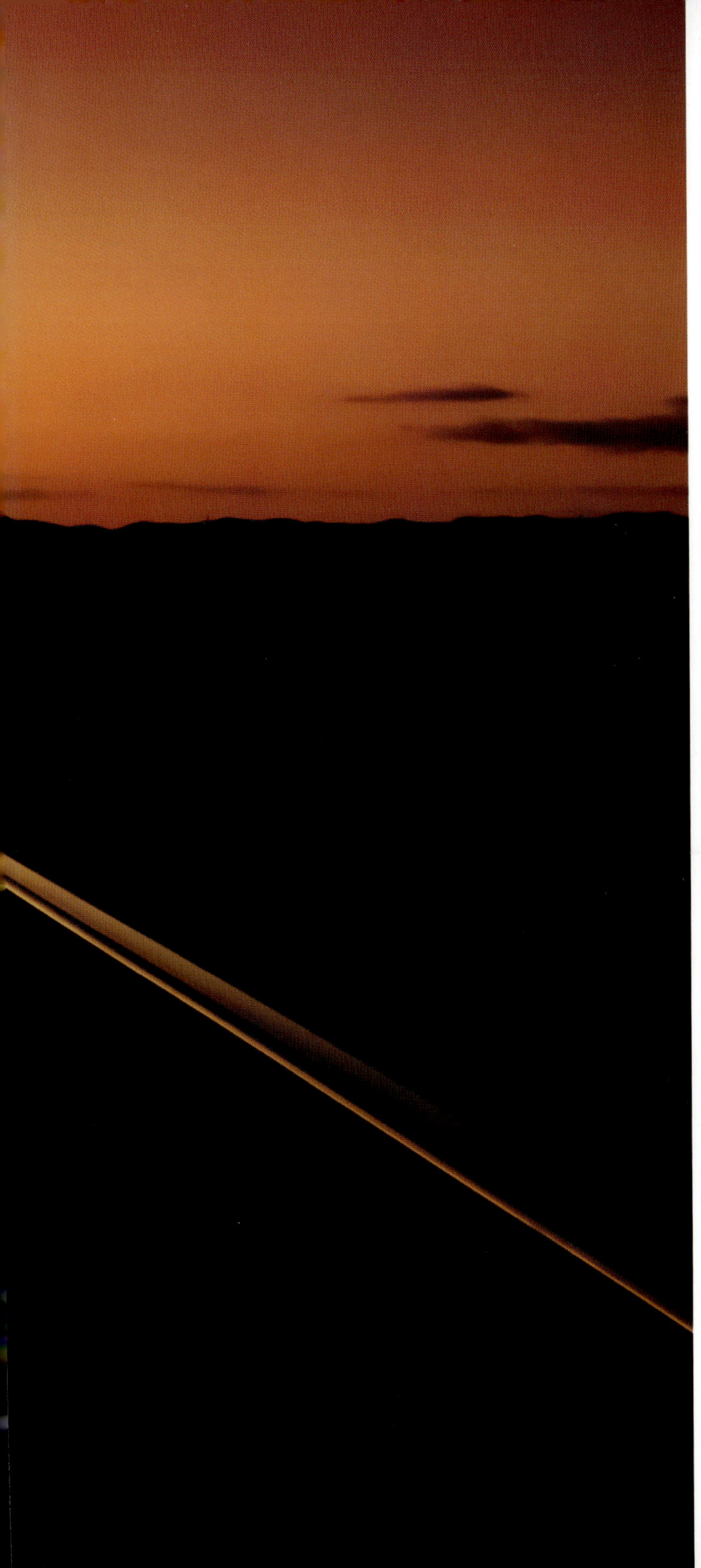

Driving West Texas

Four wheels rotating on the steamy blacktop, moving me forward to what looks like the edge of the earth. Mile after mile, the landscape steadily zooms by, yet the destination ahead remains motionless, in full view. Other than a stray tumbleweed rolling across the pavement on a windy day, or a few passing cars racing by, there is only wide-open space feeding the spirit of freedom I so very much adore. Only in the western United States have I found this, and it is something I look forward to after being confined within urban boundaries. Often, it is the journey that opens my mind to any possibility, permitting me to truly appreciate the destination.

Sincere gratitude to all who assisted with this project
and always encourage me to explore

SUZIE AZAR
KEVIN DUNSHEE
JOHN MOSES
DARAGH MCDONALD
RICHARD G. SCHWARTZ
PRES DEHRKOOP
NORMA GELLER
SALLY GILBERT
HAL MARCUS
PATRICIA MEDICI
ELIZABETH THURMOND-BENGTSON
ERIC SMITH
JILL JUVRUD
KATHERINE BRENNAND
KELLY FOSS

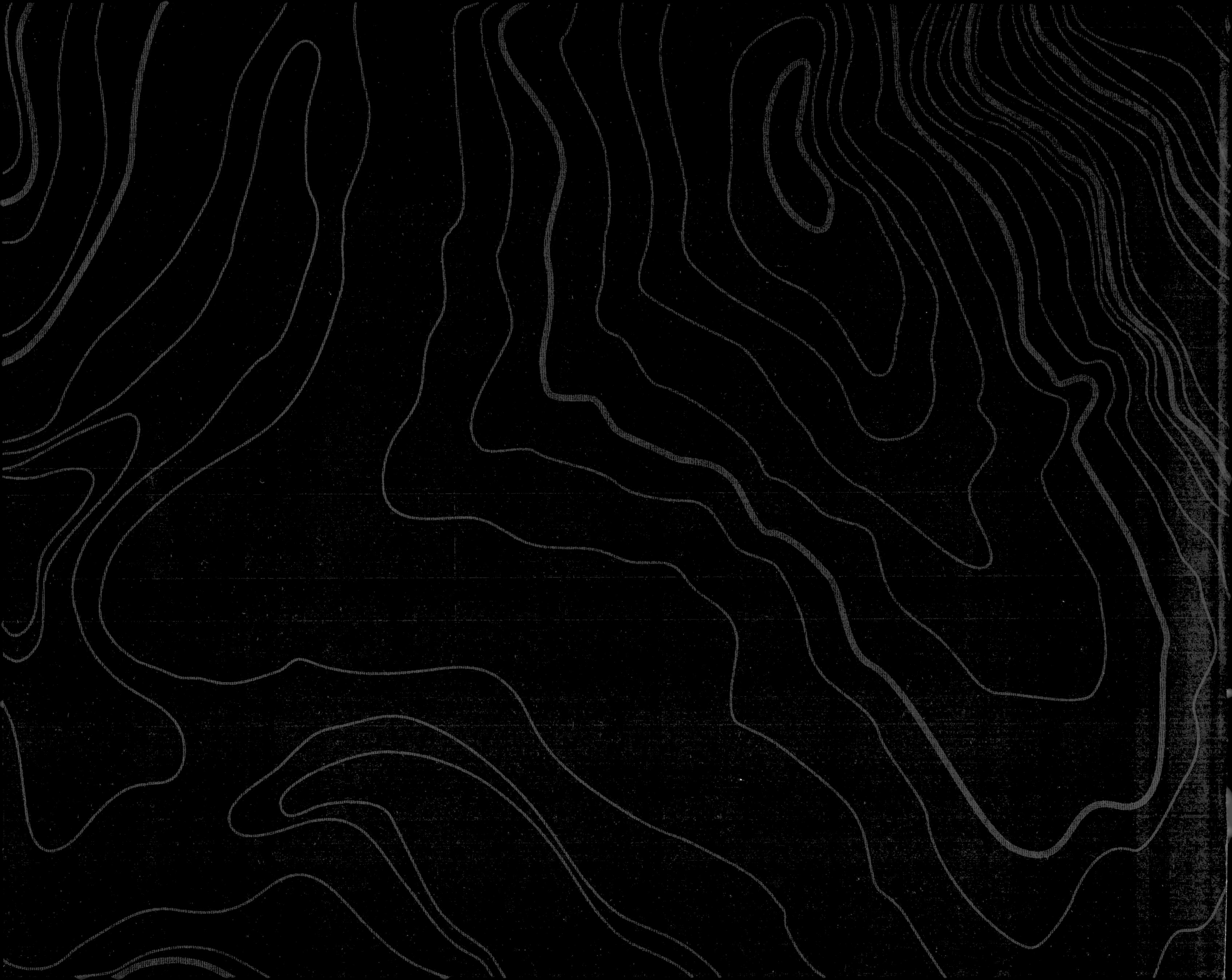